D1712005

Belle Boyd in Camp and Prison

Also by Curtis Carroll Davis

Chronicler of the Cavaliers: A Life of the Virginia Novelist, Dr. William A. Caruthers

The King's Chevalier: A Biography of Lewis Littlepage

Editor, *John Sergeant Wise's "The End of an Era"* (1899)

MISS BELLE BOYD,
"THE REBEL SPY."

This young lady, who has, by her devotion to the Southern cause, called down upon her head the anathemas of the entire Yankee press, was in our city last week. Through the politeness of Mr. Cowel, the artist at Minnis's gallery, we are enabled, in this issue of our paper, to present her picture.

Isabelle ("Belle") Boyd at age eighteen and a half—the earliest known likeness. (Woodcut in Richmond, Va., Southern Illustrated News, October 11, 1862. From the file at the Library of Congress)

Belle Boyd in Camp and Prison

Written by Herself

A New Edition Prepared from New Materials

by

Curtis Carroll Davis

South Brunswick
New York • Thomas Yoseloff • London

Thomas Yoseloff, Publisher
Cranbury, New Jersey

Thomas Yoseloff Ltd
18 Charing Cross Road
London W.C. 2, England

6487
Printed in the United States of America

Preface

Quite 90 per cent of all spy stories belong to the realm of fiction and fantasy. On the other hand the remaining 10 per cent deal with incidents which have won or lost wars.

> Col. Emil Seeliger, in *Spying Still Goes On: Four Spies Speak*, comp. H[einz] Ecke, trans. from the German (New York [1935]), p. vii

This is the beauty of spies : they show you faces long ago dust, alive with passion.

> Andrew Lang, "Some Spies," *Cornhill Magazine*, n.s. III, 526 (Oct., 1897)

The present volume represents the first fully edited publication of the memoirs of a Civil War spy. It would, indeed, be difficult to cite any American spy memoirs that have been presented to the reading public in a suitably authenticated manner. One reason for this, of course, is that it is so difficult to authenticate them. Their authors are customarily vague about dates and places. The events they describe sound dubiously melodramatic. The sum of their accomplishments, even where known to be bona-fide, usually constitutes but a

7

fraction of the total Intelligence effort a nation mounts against its foe. Worst of all, the spy's recital of his activity hovers under a self-disseminated atmosphere of speculation, because what he (or she) affirms must, by and large, be taken at face value : those competent to adjudicate his statements are usually silenced by a security oath imposed by their governments. Hence historians and biographers have picked their way daintily past spy memoirs as unremunerative of their time and labor.

By this decade of the twentieth century, however, the average citizen is at last aware of the damage spies can do — and the triumphs they can register. From the time of Alexander Bryan and Charles Webster in the Revolution to the missions of certain men and women serving the Office of Strategic Services in World War Two spies have had, upon occasion, a crucial effect upon events. It is only a question of time, moreover, before proof of their activity in the Korean, Vietnamese, and "cold" wars will become a matter of record. And the events they influence, take note, are almost invariably political and social, as well as narrowly military. Hence it seems clear that espionage as a field of study ought most properly to be appraised as an aspect of social history.

In the case of Belle Boyd's, one has a spy memoir that may, or may not, set a precedent. It has proved itself out as reliable to a high degree, and that fact makes it all the more interesting reading. But it remains to be seen whether other spy memoirs will tempt other editors to the testing point, and what their verdict may be. If the verdict proves favorable, an increasing effort by scholars to assess the narratives of secret agents will unquestionably result in a slight readjustment, and hence a fuller comprehension, of the over-all view of the 1861–1865 conflict — of any conflict, for that matter.

The eternally intriguing field of The War Between the States has attracted so many investigators in the past quarter century, and notably during the centennial observation of 1961–1965, that anyone editing any of its ana happily confronts a splendor of research riches to draw upon in presenting his contribution. The present editor has drawn heavily upon such scholarship, as a glance at his annotations to the text will reveal. Without trying to prove a point or glorify a heroine, but merely to assess a situation, he has found much to buttress Belle Boyd's statements and more than he needs to supplement them. (There is. a qualification here : Belle's correspondence. When two epistles by her came on the market in the autumn of 1963, Manhattan dealer Charles Hamilton termed the earlier "the first letter of Belle Boyd ever offered at auction, and an autograph of superlative rarity.") The bibliography, accordingly, is restricted to solid efforts only, and only to those mentioning her.

Since our subject proffers her own war story, the Introduction concentrates on fleshing out the hitherto scanty information on her later career, which was, in several ways, remarkable. It is intriguing to note, for example, how the great conflict — as it did to so many thousands of American women — transformed Belle Boyd's life by "emancipating" her person. Not only did it bestir her to the economic enterprise of publishing a book. It was indirectly responsible for putting her on the legitimate stage and then on the speaker's platform. It very likely caused her interest in politics, slight though this was.

In attempting all these things the editor has incurred the customarily wide range of indebtednesses. It is a pleasure to record them herewith.

Acknowledgments

AUSTIN, TEX. : Llerena Friend, Barker Texas History library; Frederick J. Hunter, curator, Hoblitzelle Theatre Arts library; and Ronald A. Seeliger, newspaper librarian, University of Texas Library. BALTIMORE, MD. : Irene J. Heretick. BERKELEY SPRINGS, WEST VA. : Mrs. Mary Hunter Swartz. BROOKLAND-VILLE, MD. : Mrs. Walter H. Buck, of "Buckton." COLUMBIA, S.C. : Mrs. A. C. Watson, custodian, South Carolina Confederate Relic Room. CONCORD, MASS. : Mr. and Mrs. Raymond Emerson. DUBLIN, EIRE : G. Slevin, chief herald, Office of Arms, Dublin Castle. DURHAM, N.C. : Mrs. Virginia R. Gray, manuscript department, Duke University Library. LONDON, ENG. : W. R. Lefanu, librarian, Royal College of Surgeons. LOS ANGELES, CALIF. : Mrs. Anne Ramer Berry, great-granddaughter of BB's favorite slave (Eliza Corsey). MANCHESTER, ENG. : Elizabeth Leach, librarian, Arts Library, Manchester Public Libraries. MARTINSBURG, WEST VA. : Mrs. G. Roderick Cheeseman, of "Boydville." Paul Martin, editor in chief, Martinsburg *Journal*. Judge and Mrs. Gray Silver, Jr., he being a great-nephew of that Zephaniah Silver who served as one of BB's secret couriers. MONTGOMERY, ALA. : Peter A. Brannon, director, Department of Archives and History, State of Alabama. MORGANTOWN, WEST VA. : Charles Shetler, curator,

West Virginia Collection, West Virginia University Library. NEW ORLEANS, LA.: Rev. H. Wayne Marrs, canon pastor, Christ Church Cathedral. NEW YORK CITY: Francis Brown, editor in chief, *New York Times Book Review*. Paul Myers, acting curator, Theatre Collection, New York Public Library. NORFOLK, VA.: Lenoir Chambers. PROVIDENCE, R. I.: Brown University Library, for permission to reproduce a BB letter to Abraham Lincoln. RICHMOND, VA.: Virginius Dabney. SAN MARINO, CALIF.: Huntington Library and Art Gallery, for permission to reproduce BB letters to Ward Lamon. STRASBURG, VA.: James J. Crawford, editor in chief, *Northern Virginia Daily*. SUMMIT POINT, WEST VA.: Mrs. Stuart W. Crim. TOLEDO, O.: Mrs. Irene McCreery, Local History and Genealogy Division, Toledo Public Library. UPPER MONTCLAIR, N. J.: Robert K. Black. UTICA, N. Y.: Alice C. Dodge, librarian, Utica Public Library. WASHINGTON, D. C.: Crosby Noyes Boyd, president, *Evening Star* Company. Walter L. Pforzheimer, Jr. WINCHESTER, VA.: David Rowland, former librarian, Handley Library.

CURTIS CARROLL DAVIS

At "2–A"
Baltimore, Maryland
February, 1967

Contents

Illustrations

INTRODUCTION

The Pet of the Confederacy

I. BELLE IN THE POSTWAR WORLD

A female spy is an engaging creature, but in crinoline she has an especial, a romantic and absurd, charm. Belle Boyd, the most famous woman concerned with official secret activities in the Civil War, not only was enveloped in a cloud of crinoline, she wore it with grace and elegance. . . .

Joseph Hergesheimer, "Belle Boyd, or the Female Spy," *Swords & Roses* (New York and London, 1929), p. 235.

When Sam Hardinge, abruptly and mysteriously released from Fort Delaware, at last arrived in London in late February or early March, 1865, he found that his wife had, in his absence, been alert to defend his good name.

From London, the day after Christmas, Belle had gotten off a four-page diatribe to W. Douglass Wallach, owner and editor of the *Star* in far-away Washington. Written in ink on blue stationery, in her typically difficult script, the epistle had

15

reached New York City in the forenoon of January 14, and thence wended its way southward. What effect it produced is unknown. But it remains the fullest specimen extant of its composer's (unassisted) ability with the pen.

London, Dec. 26th 1864

Douglas Wallach Esq
Editor, "Evening Star"
Sir—

I do not write you *from* any wish of [?]—but to contradict certain portions of an extract, which I find in your paper of the 6th— concerning the capture of my husband S. Wylde Hardinge, which like all other extracts that emminate [*sic*] from your paper is *false* in the extreme. First, allow me to inform you that I am not "lurking about the vicinity in which my husband was captured," & next, that I *am not* "discarded by the rebel sympathizers in Europe"—I associate with none but Southrons & sympathizers with the South, & the story that my husband had "instructed me to have nothing more to do with the rebel cause" is a base fabrication of your own as false as the inflated dispatches which emminate from the "Lincoln man" [?] Mr. Stanton. Such instruction would have been useless. That I am an open & avowed enemy of your Government *all* knew, That every hope—wish & prayer is for the success of our noble cause, That all the service that a woman could render her Country, *I gave to mine*—& even now could my life save my Country from further disaster, could pay the ransom to our craven hearted foe—gladly would I yield it.

& too well is it known how your Northern Journals have slandered, calumniated & heaped upon me all the vilest epithets, that could be thought of, in the hopes to crush me. But you only added laurels to the wreath.

Your *abuse* was *praise,* & too well well known am I for
your villianous [*sic*] concoctions to be credited. Vilify
me as you please, my reputation, my honor, you have
all tried to [ruin?]—but you shall NEVER brand me as
a *traitor.* It was I who "aided the escape of the Capt.
of the Greyhound" On me let the blame fall. My husband is not guilty—of his feelings & sentiments regarding the South & its cause, I have nothing to say. *Politics,*
we never discussed. But were he still in the Federal
Service no better would I like *your Government,* no less
would I strive to aid my own. I owe no allegiance save
to my husband & the South. I am now an Exile from
America by the orders of your Government. My fate I
endeavor to bear patiently trusting to a brighter future,
when the South shall have gained its independence &
Liberty shall once more [rule?], when Batiles [*sic*] &
Dungeon Cells shall no longer hold victims *whose only
crime,* was their *truth* to *Honor & Liberty.*

                                         Belle Boyd
                                         C S A

Despite the dagger-like bravado infusing Belle's words, Sam
Hardinge found his wife languishing in that "distress of mind
and body" which her literary adviser, G. A. Sala, describes in
his Introduction to her book. More specifically, Belle was
languishing in the traditional posture of debtors : her trunk
sequestered by her landlord, pending payment of debts. What,
if anything, an ex-prisoner in an alien land could have done
about this situation is moot. In any event, after contributing
his fragmentary journal to Belle's book, and siring her first-
born child, Sam Hardinge disappears from notice forever.

The baby, Grace, was probably born toward the middle of
1865. To support herself, Belle had been at work on her
memoirs, and had the satisfaction of seeing them in print in
London by late May and in New York by late July of the

same year. She then made the decision, probably at Sala's suggestion, to try for additional income on the stage. She succeeded. Coached by the Virginia-born actress, Avonia Jones, and the English Shakespearean actor, Walter Montgomery, Belle made her début on Friday evening, June 1, 1866, at the Theatre Royal, up at Manchester, as "Pauline," the leading female rôle in Edward Bulwer-Lytton's romantic comedy, *The Lady of Lyons.* She took second billing only to the star, Montgomery, playing the male lead, "Claude Melnotte."

The Manchester *Observer,* on giving the cast of the play in its issue of the same date, proclaimed Miss Belle Boyd's "first appearance on any stage," and then treated her to a separate column of comment in language that would have sparked the imagination of Phineas T. Barnum. The name of this "celebrated Confederate heroine," the paper affirmed, "will doubtless be familiar as 'household words' to our readers. . . ." She had been "impressed like Joan of Arc with a mission to aid by all the enthusiasm of her excitable temperament and Southern fervour the great cause of her dear-loved country. . . ." "Chained and rescued, her post is by the gallant Stonewall Jackson's right arm — his unerring and devoted aid-de-camp." ". . . we find her dashing down the opposing foe, and, like a brilliant meteor flashing through the night, bent on a message of fierce and fiery portent."

After such an inaugural, one might have expected Belle to linger in England. But in May, 1865, President Andrew Johnson had issued a proclamation of amnesty to most former Rebels, and on April 2, 1866, he had announced that the insurrection in all the former Confederate States except Texas was at an end. So later that year the ex-Confederate and her infant daughter made their exiles' return to the United States.

For the next two years, and a little more, Belle Boyd may be said to have become something of a luminary on the American stage.

She secured an experienced manager, John P. Smith (a native of Richmond), who had started his own career by handling "Artemus Ward." It was decided to bill her as "Belle Boyd, of Virginia." They opened at the Grand Opera House, in Saint Louis, on September 2, 1867. This was the property of one of the Midwest's leading impresarios, Ben DeBar, and he gave Belle a full week of starring rôles. Her first appearance on the American stage was, appropriately enough, on horseback. Her entrance preluded a series of Civil War scenes, probably improvised for the occasion. The rest of the engagement, through September 7, saw Belle taking the female lead in *The Lady of Lyons* again; as Juliet in Shakespeare's *Romeo and Juliet;* and in such circuit standbys as *The Hunchback; Love, or, The Countess and the Serf; The Honeymoon; Faint Heart Never Won Fair Lady; The Stranger;* and *The Artful Dodger.*

The over-all result was sufficiently admired to enable Belle's manager to snare for her the best booking of them all.

On January 9, 1868, Belle appeared in New York City. True, it was only a one-nighter, and the surrounding circumstances were fortuitous, but she had the boards of the French Theatre upon which to trod, and she had as her leading man that Bowery favorite, Robert Johnston. Two comedies were offered, *The Honeymoon* and *Faint Heart Never Won Fair Lady.* It would seem that this fair lady never won the heart of New York, but at least she had the satisfaction of appearing there in a starring rôle.

Belle now revisited the scene of some of her worst moments, the nation's capital. If she really had anything to fear from Governmental vengeance — as the Introduction, and last page, of her book assert — she not only concealed the fact quite well but even went on the offensive. Belle made a direct approach to a figure once prominent in the Lincoln Administration and currently a well-known attorney. In the interests of her career the new arrival in Washington got off the following note:

225 Penn Avenue,
March 2nd /68

Col. W. H. Lamon,
    Dear Col,

    I suppose I am not entirely forgotten; & for the sake of "auld acquaintance" with my Father, I take the liberty of asking you to come & see me. I give a Dramatic Reading at Carroll Hall, on Friday next the 6th & trust that you will honor me with your presence [*inked out*] also your friends.

Respectfully
Belle Boyd
of
Va

Whether the Colonel complied is unknown. But the *Daily National Intelligencer,* which on William Winston Seaton's death in 1866 had been taken over by Snow, Coyle & Co., was more than friendly. Large advertisements in the issues for Thursday and Friday, March 5–6, proclaimed the forthcoming appearance of "Belle Boyd, of Virginia"; and in the latter issue the paper went out of its way to assure readers that "her name is familiar to the country at large. . . . We doubt not the entertainment will be a pleasant one, as it is well known that Miss Boyd is a lady of education and gifts."

Though Belle's subject was not reported, on the morning after, March 7, the *Intelligencer* favored her with a follow-up commentary. There "was a fair audience last night. . . . It was a pleasant entertainment. She reads with intelligence and taste, and her efforts on this occasion were received with favor by the refined audience."

Such forays into the theatrical centers, if inconclusive, did Belle's career no harm. She now retreated to the Midwest, and, at Cincinnati, joined the Miles & Bates Stock Company in order to acquire further training. Dropping her "of Virginia" tag, she billed herself as "Nina Benjamin" (commemorating her father and a school chum from Baltimore days). The Cincinnati interlude did not last long before "Nina" moved to Texas. There, at Galveston, she placed herself under the recently formed management of the Greenwall brothers, Morris and Henry, to star in their stock houses in the island city and at Houston. Henry Greenwall was just beginning a career which would soon elevate him into one of the leading managers in the Southwest. Owing mainly to his efforts, the Houston stage—now that the Civil War was only a bitter memory—would take a new lease on life. Toward the close of the year 1868, Belle Boyd journeyed thither.

There she met up with an acquaintance of wartime days in Richmond, the colorful and wide-ranging Colonel Tom Ochiltree. Born in Alabama, Ochiltree had served in the 1st Texas Regiment during the war, and had seen diverse staff and field duties. Toward its close he had fallen prisoner, and upon release had spent several months in Europe. He then returned to Texas, where he became editor of the Houston *Daily Telegraph* in 1866–1867, and a member of the town's first amateur drama group. Belle decided to let the Colonel manage her local stage fortunes.

Things started out well but wound up badly. On the Houston boards Belle starred again in *The Lady of Lyons*. She again played Juliet in *Romeo and Juliet,* and again had the female lead in that standard stock comedy, *The Honeymoon.* The Houston *Times,* though conceding that her name was "all the go now," nevertheless felt she was insufficiently experienced to control a leading part. There was also a falling out among the company, and when one of them, Maud St.

Leon, was dismissed for "conduct unbecoming her position,"
Belle took her side. In addition there was some feeling in town
against Colonel Ochiltree of a political nature, apparently
arising from alleged activities in England, where he had tried
to negotiate a loan for the Confederacy. The over-all result
was an abrupt finale to Belle's appearances.

At the end of the year 1868, Belle and the Colonel bade
adieu to Houston. Ochiltree was a side-splitting raconteur and
a natural politician. He would soon be appointed United
States Marshal for the Eastern District of Texas by his crony,
President Grant. In the 1870's he would serve as Commissioner
of Immigration in Europe for the Lone Star State, and in the
80's would represent it in Congress. This orientation may
explain why he, Belle, one Major Mahone, and a Mr. Deros-
sitte now journeyed up to Austin to the State capitol. There
what Belle labelled the "Black and Tan" legislature was in the
throes of Reconstruction law making, and the visitors attempted
to get a special bill passed, the nature of which remains
unknown. Belle also took the opportunity to give dramatic
readings in Austin.

With the coming of the new year, 1869, Belle engaged
herself as a stock star once again. This time she performed
under the aegis of the influential New Orleans impresario,
David Bidwell, at the Academy of Music in the Crescent City.
She may well have continued indefinitely on the stage had
not marriage intervened.

Belle Boyd's second husband was a native of England
named John Swainston Hammond (*c.* 1829–1886). Said to
have served in the Crimean War, Hammond had emigrated to
America and here enlisted in a company of the 17th Massachusetts Infantry comprised mainly of former Britons. He
fought for a year in the Civil War, rising to the rank of 1st
Lieutenant. (In later years he would flourish the title of

Colonel, probably bestowed as a militia or political accolade.) He was now on the road for various business houses, had been smitten with Belle's stage presence, wooed, and won her. They were married on March 17, 1869, at Christ Church in New Orleans, by its pastor, Rev. Dr. W. T. Leacock. Belle abandoned the theatre.

What happened next she divulged, years later, in the single most revealing public interview she was ever to grant (to a reporter for the New York *World*, February 11, 1889):

> "My health was failing, and I went with my husband to California. Just previous to the birth of my little son my mind gave way and my child was born in the asylum for the insane at Stockton, Cal. My boy was buried there. I was brought to Mount Hope, near Baltimore, and placed under the care of Dr. Stokes. There I made rapid recovery and was soon discharged."

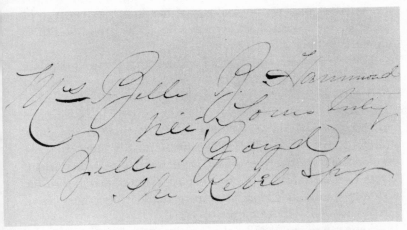

When Belle Boyd came to call . . . she (now Mrs. John S. Hammond) might present such a carte-de-visite **as this. (Courtesy of the Walter Pforzheimer Collection on Intelligence Service)**

They had christened the infant Arthur, and he had probably arrived about January, 1870. Why Belle then chose to travel clear across the country to Mount Hope Retreat (now the Seton Psychiatric Institute, at the Pikesville outskirt of Baltimore) may be explained not only by reason of her girlhood education in this area but also by the fact that Dr. Richard McSherry, the physician who, on March 5, 1870, certified her for commitment, was a native of Martinsburg. Currently Professor of Practice at the University of Maryland medical school, then, as now, located in the heart of Baltimore, he would become the first president of the local Academy of Medicine and one of the State's most influential doctors. Dr. William H. Stokes, a graduate of Yale University School of Medicine, had been Visiting Physician at Mount Hope since 1842, and was a specialist in mental illness. On September 3, 1870, Mrs. Belle Hammond was by him "discharged as recovered."

As the portals of Mount Hope swung shut behind her, she prepared to pick up the threads of her life. For the next 14 years, as the spouse of a travelling man, Belle would find these threads nothing if not ramified.

For several years the family lived in Utica, New York. Here Belle's third child, a daughter, Byrd Swainston, was born on February 26, 1874, at the Butterfield House Hotel. In 1875–1876, the Hammonds were in Chicago. In 1877, they returned to Baltimore. Here, on October 31, 1878, another daughter, Marie Isabelle ("Belle"), came into the world. Here, too, the senior Belle probably renewed acquaintance with her friend from Confederate days, Colonel Harry Gilmor, now one of the Monumental City's more prominent residents as a member of its Board of Police Commissioners.

Some time in 1878, the family transferred north to Philadelphia. Here their last child, John Edmund Swainston Hammond ("Eddie"), was born on August 30, 1881. In

1882, they headed west once more and moved to Chicago, but in autumn of the next year they pulled up stakes for Texas, where they settled down at Dallas. In Dallas, on November 1, 1884, this phase of Belle's life came to an end. She "obtained an absolute divorce from Col. Hammond, and the court gave me our three children."

The cause of the divorce is not known. A Wisconsin magazine article of later years surmised it was Hammond's drinking. At the time the Philadelphia *Press,* in a dispatch from Dallas, claimed Mrs. Hammond had discovered the Colonel already had a wife, had accordingly separated from, and subsequently remarried, him. It also claimed the Colonel then brought suit against *her* "for the most serious of charges." The first situation seems, on its face, implausible; the second is moot. Probably the truth lies in Belle, Jr.'s, statement of later years that her parents gradually found themselves becoming incompatible, and agreed to part. Hammond, his daughter declared, held an admiration for her mother until the day of his death and submitted to the divorce on the technical grounds of "cruelty."

There is no question but that Belle had, by this stage of her career, endured what she told the interviewing reporter were "private sorrows which the world should not demand." They ranged from the vexatious to the searing.

For example, while she was still under treatment at Mount Hope, she was (like Mark Twain) reported dead. Then, by the mid-70's, a corollary situation developed: her name and fame began to attract impersonators. In January, 1876, the Worshipful Master of the Masonic Lodge at Martinsburg agreed to issue the following statement to other Lodges generally:

> We have been informed by the widow of our deceased brother, B. R. Boyd, that there is a certain woman, accompanied by a child, imposing herself on the fraternity

through the South as Belle Boyd, the daughter of the
above named deceased brother, and representing the
child to be her youngest sister, described to us as a
woman of dark complexion, rather stout, with dark hair
and eyes. We wish to warn you against assisting the
above described person, as she is an imposter. The real
Belle Boyd is now married and living in St. Louis, Mo.,
with her husband, and her mother and two brothers
reside in Baltimore. Her only sister is married, and
living in Jefferson County of this State. The real Belle
Boyd has light complexion, light hair and eyes; rather
thin, with roman features.

The Hammonds had scarcely departed their Philadelphia
abode for Chicago when the New York *Herald,* in its issue of
August 28, 1882, in a dispatch from the Quaker City captioned "Alleged Swindling," reported as follows :

For months a female alleged swindler, who has baffled
the combined intellect of the new detective system at
Fifth and Chestnut streets, has been carrying on a
series of "crooked" operations in this city. She has,
however, at last been discovered, though not by any
ingenuity on the part of the police authorities. Some
few months ago an attractive lady visited a grocery
dealer near Twentieth street and Washington avenue. She
ordered goods to the amount of $11, and in payment
therefor tendered a check for $25. The grocery man,
not thinking that such a lady-like person would be
guilty of dishonesty, handed her, after keeping $11 for
the goods, $14. The goods were ordered to be delivered
at the house of one of his best customers, and his
astonishment may well be imagined when, on going
there, the lady of the house refused to take the goods,
as she had not ordered them. It was then that the un-
wary dealer discovered the check to be worthless.

The groceryman himself traced its passer to 1916 N. Twelfth Street, and learned to his further astonishment that the operator was none other than — as one of the papers reprinting the *Herald* story labelled it — "Belle Boyd, the Confederate Spy, in a New Role."

As to whether any arrests were made or other action taken, either by grocerymen or sleuths of "the new detective system," history is silent.

Then there was the episode of Mrs. Murphy, of Waxahachie.

The Hammonds had barely arrived in Dallas ere they learned that Mrs. Murphy was gracing the opera houses of the little towns of Waxahachie and Corsicana as the pulsating embodiment of a certain celebrated female "of Confederate fame." She was also engaged in composing her autobiography. The Austin periodical, *Texas Siftings,* had already stirred the pudding when it proclaimed, on page one of its issue for February 11, 1882:

> Belle Boyd, the Confederate Spy, who died recently at Plymouth, England, is living at Corsicana, Texas, in easy circumstances. She is also living in a garret in Baltimore, where she makes a scanty living by needlework, so the papers say. Belle is beating her Confederate record of being in two places at once.

Belle beat Mrs. Murphy, too. That celebrity promptly "upon my arrival left the state and went, it is reported to Cedar Keys, Fla."

The Hammonds now settled back for a respite. It did not last long.

On October 12, 1884, the Philadelphia *Press,* in a dispatch from Dallas, offered Sunday readers in the City of Brotherly Love a page-one spread on the subject of "Belle Boyd's Pistol."

The Martinsburg *Independent* promptly picked up the story on October 18.

It seems that "a well-placed young man" of Dallas named James Coller had been attentive to Mrs. Hammond's daughter, Maria. He had been so attentive that Maria became pregnant, a condition which left James unperturbed. For this attitude, Maria's mother took two shots at the ravisher. She missed the first time, but the second projectile winged James in the left arm. "Mrs. Hammond, the chief actor in the affair," the *Press* reminded its subscribers, "is a well-known character in the South, and, indeed, throughout the country."

What really happened is anybody's guess. Neither the daily nor weekly Dallas *Herald,* the leading local paper, carried a line on the business, and the Republican sheet, A. B. Norton's *Union Observer,* was likewise silent. The utter versimilitude of the dispatch is, one feels, open to question on at least this ground : daughter "Maria" — more accurately, Marie Isabelle — was six years old !

With another of her offspring, her first-born child, Belle had real trouble. What it was she would not specify; but by at least the late 1880's she was refusing so much as to "speak of my eldest daughter, Grace, by Lieut. Hardinge, as she is dead to the family."

By this time too, however, the skies had partially cleared. Belle's third marriage was proving a happy one. On January 9, 1885, less than six weeks following her divorce from John S. Hammond, she had become the wife of the actor, Nat High.

Nathaniel Rue High, Jr., of Toledo, Ohio — son of a recently deceased Episcopal minister who had been rector of Saint John's Church there — was the juvenile lead in a stock company. In appearance he was the matinée-idol type. It says as much for his emotional make-up as for Belle's physical that, at the time of the nuptials, the bride was forty-one years of age

Belle Boyd in stage costume, reciting "The Perils of a Spy." A rare undated likeness by Morris Photographers, 16 Sixth Street, Pittsburgh, Pa., personally autographed. (Courtesy Confederate Relic Room, Columbia, S.C.)

and the groom only twenty-four. Despite this disparity they lived happily together for 15 years.

With the wife's three minor children to support, however, money was constantly a factor. In order to augment the family income Belle probably had little choice save to return to the stage. But not as an actress, rather as a giver of readings, or what today would be termed a *diseuse*. What she recited, of course, was her wartime activities in espionage.

Belle made her new début at the People's Theatre, a show house of the second class, at Toledo on Sunday evening, February 28, 1886. Her recitation topic was "The Dark Days, or, Memories of the War," and, said she, it "scored an unqualified success." Her appearance had been sponsored, moreover, by local members of the Grand Army of the Republic. As she had explained her situation to a Toledo *Blade* reporter the week before :

> She begs to be remembered, not as Belle Boyd, "the Rebel Spy," but as Belle Boyd who, having learned the true beauty of the stars and stripes, would be willing to take her life in defense of that government she once sought to destroy.

Encouraged by the result at Toledo, the Highs now took to the road in earnest. Nat managed; Belle draped herself in chivalric Confederate costume (as had Pauline Cushman in Federal, on the New York stage in 1864). In due course Byrd and Belle, Jr., got into the act, which often ran two hours. Spying was the favored subject, but the star was not above featuring her own interpretation of such extraneous topics as Pickett's charge at Gettysburg. For the rest of her life Belle Boyd High accumulated an increasingly detailed knowledge of American topography as she peregrinated even more widely than she had on the legitimate stage.

Under G.A.R. auspices the Rebel Spy gave readings throughout the Midwest, penetrating as far as Detroit and Davenport, Iowa. Her first recitation in the South occurred at Norfolk, Virginia, on May 18, 1888. This time the patronage was by the other side: the Pickett-Buchanan Camp, United Confederate Veterans. At the Academy of Music, Belle discoursed upon, and re-enacted, "The Perils of a Spy"; and the next day the Norfolk *Landmark* assured its readers that the audience, though small, had been appreciative.

That same summer the family moved up into its star's one-time combat arena, the Luray and Shenandoah valleys of Virginia. At Front Royal the performance took place in the Presbyterian church. In August the act travelled on to Huntington, West Virginia, where a state Democratic convention was in progress. As with the Texas legislature of 20 years back, the purpose may have been political as well as professional, since on August 18, the Huntington *Advertiser* proclaimed that "Belle Boyd was among the distinguished people on the platform." In November the troupe backtracked to Pennsylvania, settled at Greensburg, and during the winter toured G.A.R. posts in various sections of the Keystone State.

It was in the mid-90's that the Highs penetrated the Deep South. At the Opera House in Atlanta, Georgia, in August, 1895, Belle rated the top of the bill "in her thrilling dramatic narrative: 'NORTH AND SOUTH, or, The Perils of a Spy.'" Probably at this period, March, 1896, there occurred an incident at Montgomery, Alabama (where, so long ago, a vivid young girl had become belle of the ball). Prominent in the proceedings was that distinguished ex-Confederate, Colonel Thomas G. Jones, who had been governor in 1890–1894, and would be appointed a Federal District judge by President

Theodore Roosevelt. As the episode is recounted by the Director of the Department of Archives and History, State of Alabama,

> ... Judge Walter Jones often told the story of his father and three or four old Confederates getting up one morning before breakfast to hurry down to the city jail to bail Belle out. My impression is that they did not know of Belle's arrest the night before. It seems that she refused to take out a license for lecturing. I do not know how the rest of the towns were, but Montgomery had a very strict license against street hawkers and other characters for publicizing their wares. Belle was opposed to paying for the license. I do not think she had any money. If I recall the story, and I have heard it many times, Judge Jones led the movement to get her out of the lock-up and give her a nice breakfast and get her started on to the next place where she had prepared to give a lecture. The veterans here in Montgomery raised a sum of money, and I expect Judge Jones was about as well off as any one at the time, and they made up a sum to send her to the next place and to tide her over until she could recupe her fortunes. So far as your having a citation for the jail episode, you should know enough about us down here to know that such a thing as that would never be allowed to get into the paper.

In 1897–1898, the troupe toured Nat's home state of Ohio extensively.

Throughout these peregrinations Belle never lost track of her favorite maid from the war days, Eliza Corsey. After freedom, Eliza married another ex-slave, young Sam Hopewell, whose barber shop at the corner of Martin and Spring streets, Martinsburg, grew prosperous. Eliza herself, who lived until Christmas Day, 1916, achieving the venerable status of "Aunt" to the community, exhibited skills at midwifery, and for years assisted, in this phase of his practice, the well-known local doctor, James W. McSherry (of the same family as the physician who had tended Eliza's former mistress at Baltimore). From distant parts would arrive gifts for Eliza or her offspring : for her first grandson, a heavy china platter, decorated with the alphabet and a camel crossing a desert; a handsome gray cat, named "Christopher Columbus"; and, not long before the sender's death, a lovely white shawl.

And so, eventually, one June day in 1900, the two of them, Belle and Nat, unaccompanied by any others of the troupe, wound up in the little resort town of Kilbourn (now Wisconsin Dells), some 160 miles northwest of Milwaukee. They put up at the Hile House; and young Johnny Murphy, the hotel's clerk who met them at the station, still remembered, years later, how she looked :

> Perhaps Miss Boyd wasn't beautiful, or as beautiful, physically, as some other women, yet, there was something beautiful about her even then—something a man never forgot. She and her husband appeared in dire straits and she herself appeared ill. Yet, she never flinched. Miss Boyd and Mr. High's clothes were old, out-of-fashion, and threadbare. They did not have much baggage. Yet, Miss Boyd gave a regal impression. . . .

For the last few weeks Belle had been under Doctor's orders —she and Nat had taken a furnished flat at the Central House in Evansville, Wisconsin, for the summer—and was far from her usual buoyant standard. But she was scheduled for recitations before the local G.A.R. post, and she delivered. Two readings were given, at the Methodist church.

She had been thinking about her daughters, Byrd and Belle, Junior, lately, pondering their future. On Sunday, June 10, she scrawled off a two-page letter to the girls in Chicago, in her anxiety neglecting to sign it. Part of it read:

> I feel like a criminal not sending you money. But I have only been able to play one night, and sent you all I had out [of] it over expenses, 2.00. Hope you got it safely. . . . I pray you write me how things are. I will send you some more from here. I wish to God you both were in Evansville. I have been ill in bed three days. I don't know what to say to you except I will be glad to get settled in the flat. . . .
>
> Now write me here. I will be here until Thursday. I have a few more towns I want to play around here and then return to Evansville.

At this point Belle's pencil seems to have faltered. Instead of the usual affectionate ending, she scrawled at the bottom of the second page of note paper: "I am worried to death about you."

The next evening — Monday, June 11, 1900 — a heart attack took her, at her room in the Hile House. She was fifty-six years, one month old and looked nearer forty.

The Women's Relief Corps of Kilbourn, an auxiliary of the G.A.R., chipped in together to provide decent burial raiment. Services were held in the Episcopal church on June 13, and there was a good-sized attendance. Then pallbearers comprised of four veterans of the Union army and two sons of Spanish-American War veterans carried the Rebel Spy out to the handsome municipal cemetery, Spring Grove.

It was not till the following year that the Women's Relief Corps contrived to put up a simple board marker over the grave. It was not till 1919 that a Confederate veteran visiting

The grave of Belle Boyd, at Spring Grove Cemetery, Wisconsin Dells, Wisconsin. Her gravestone, decorated for Memorial Day, 1953, is at lower right, within a trellis arbor erected by the Dells American Legion Post. The Post also donated the permanent flagpole for the Confederate battle flag (here improperly placed to the right of the National Ensign). The Stars and Bars, Stars and Stripes, and the state flag of Virginia were the gift of the Elliott Grays Chapter, United Daughters of the Confederacy, Richmond, Va. (Photo by H. H. Bennett Studio, Wisconsin Dells)

in town from Mississippi — an ex-private from the 3rd Missouri Regiment named Willis A. Everman, who bore no known relationship to Belle — had the feeling that a more suitable tombstone might be in order. He paid for a small granite boulder and, with admirable restraint, had it inscribed:

B E L L E   B O Y D
CONFEDERATE SPY
BORN IN VIRGINIA
DIED IN WISCONSIN
ERECTED BY A COMRADE

II : BELLE'S BOOK

It would fill hundreds of pages to tell only the stories of these clever and daring women [C. V. Baxley, BB, Rose Greenhow]—their underground connections, ruses, courage and biting hatred of Yankees in general and Seward and Stanton in particular.
James G. Randall, *Lincoln the President: Midstream* (New York, 1952), p. 205.

"I think it would be well," wrote she, firmly, "for you & me to come to some definite understanding." Seated at her desk in the Brunswick Hotel, Jermyn Street, London, Belle finished her letter, dated it January 24, 1865, and put it in the mail. Her addressee was Abraham Lincoln.

She had finished her memoirs, Belle warned the American President, and had intended them to be merely personal. But in view of the recent unjustifiable arrest of her husband, S. Wilde Hardinge, she had revised the manuscript to make it "political" as well. Its pages now revealed many "atrocious circumstances respecting your Government" of which Europe did not dream. If, however, her spouse was back by her side by March 25, she would suppress the book. If not, off to the publishers!

As things turned out, Sam Hardinge must have reached her side well before the specified time, since the War Department at Washington had ordered his release from Fort Delaware in a Special Order dated February 3, 1865, and he had sailed from New York City on February 8. Whether the Special Order was issued as the result of this bravura epistle to the President is anybody's guess. Her biographer has demonstrated that the letter could, under ideal circumstances, have reached the seat of government just in time to effect such an end. That it did so is most unlikely, if, indeed, Lincoln ever personally perused it. In any event his assassination in mid-April, the news of which broke in the London papers on April 26, must have struck Belle as an abrogation of the offer she had tendered him. Accordingly she revised, or appended, her final chapter —with its strong implication that the President had been assassinated by influential Federal fanatics like Johnson, Butler, and Lane—and gave the manuscript to the publisher.

Advertised in *The Athenaeum* for April 15 as "Just Ready," as "Now Ready" in *The Times* for May 17 (the date of Sala's introduction), and as "Ready" in *The Athenaeum,* again, on June 3, *Belle Boyd, in Camp and Prison. With an Introduction by a Friend of the South,* selling at 21*s.* the two-volume set, was released by the house of Saunders, Otley & Company, 66 Brook Street (in what is now called the West End of London), probably about the third week in May, 1865. Right at this point Belle's book already carried two handicaps: its publisher, and her editor.

Of these the lesser was the publisher. Saunders, Otley & Company was an established house, not just a printery. It was also in process of issuing, for example, a second printing

of its two-volume edition of Admiral Semmes' *The Cruise of
the Alabama and the Sumter. . . .* Nevertheless the firm was
not in the same class with companies which, some months
earlier, had released two other American books. These titles,
one lauding, the other denigrating, the Southern way of life,
were Rose Greenhow's *My Imprisonment . . .* , carrying the
imprint of Richard Bentley, and actress Fanny Kemble's
Journal of a Residence on a Georgian Plantation, released by
Longmans, Green.

Nor does Belle's firm appear to have advertised its titles
either as frequently or as prominently as some of its competitors. In the pro-Confederate weekly, *The Index,* for
example, which of all outlets one might expect to find
exploited, Saunders, Otley & Company placed but one ad on
behalf of Belle's book, whereas Longmans, Green notices for
The South Vindicated, an English edition of a volume published earlier in the United States by General James Williams
—one of the guests at Belle's wedding—appeared regularly in
The Index from late April or early May almost until the
periodical's demise toward the end of August. Even when
advertised, moreover, Belle's book sometimes found itself in
motley company. Consider these titles, which rubbed shoulders
with it in *The Times* listing of May 17 : third-rate novels like
anon.'s *Butler Burke at Eton,* or Lt.-Col. H. R. Addison's
Behind the Curtain, the Rev. Albert Barnes' ("of America")
Revival Sermons, and the fourth edition of *The Illustrated
Horse Doctor.*

A more perduring handicap to Belle's book than a second-
rate publisher was her choice of literary adviser. George
Augustus Henry Sala (1828–1895) was a native-born Londoner
of Italian descent. His grandfather had emigrated to England
from Rome to become a ballet master and dancing instructor.
His personable mother became a noted singer at Covent

Garden, supporting five children thereby. One of his brothers was an actor in Macready's company.

From such a background Sala, a precocious child reared partly in Paris, absorbed a lively appreciation of the more sensuous aspects of life and living. He had talent as a painter, especially in stage design. From childhood he had been a voracious reader. He was a gourmet. He was one of the founders of that tippling association, the Savage Club, and his membership in the prestigious Reform Club had been sponsored by Thackeray. He had had a play produced and a novel published. His house in Guilford Street was the rendezvous of wits and lordlings, explorers like Richard Burton, and popular authors like George A. Lawrence. But he was too much the toiler to become either boulevardier or bohemian.

Settling on the career of a writer, especially in the field of journalism, Sala drove himself with all the gusto he allotted to concocting a banquet. By the time Belle Boyd met him he had become a regular contributor to Charles Dickens' popular weeklies, *Household Words* and *All the Year Round,* and was widely known for his gossip column, "Echoes of the Week," in the *Illustrated London News.* He had been sent all the way to Russia on assignment. More than just an important journalist, he was now establishing himself as a man of letters. He could write sunnily on any topic under the sun, and for many a long year did just that. Sir Sidney Lee, in his detailed sketch in *The Dictionary of National Biography,* estimates that, for the period 1863–1883, Sala averaged the goodly income of £2,000 annually from his pen alone. His death came from exhaustion through overwork.

But good living did not leave Sala with many shillings at each year's end. (In 1862 he was almost bankrupt, and he would die just short of pauperdom.) Good living depended on good contacts and making good impressions, and on the maintenance of both. English society was riven on the subject of the American Civil War. The subject was, in a word, controversial. Sala had returned in November, 1864, from a year's reporting of the conflict for the London *Daily Telegraph*. He did not get into the Confederacy, and though he had been widely wined and dined by Northern hosts in private, he had also been widely abused by Northern newspapers in public because of his printed criticisms of the Administration. This general background of controversy may explain why the literary adviser to a beguiling Confederate authoress — though he was the grandson of a West Indian slave owner and was himself decidedly pro-Southern — did not see fit to put his name to the English edition of her book, mention it in any of his subsequent autobiographical writings, and in later years deny he had had anything to do with it.

As Sala's biographer, Ralph Straus, puts the case, however, "he was undoubtedly interested in Belle's story, wrote about it just before the publication of the book in his 'Echoes,' and is said to have sung or rather recited to music her favourite song, 'Maryland, my Maryland,' at that time wholly unknown in England, on more than one occasion to gatherings of friends. Undoubtedly he knew both her and her husband, and may have been present at their wedding."

Certainly what Sala had to say about Belle's book in his column (February 25, 1865) reads like a blurb :

> That famous Amazon of Secessia, Belle Boyd, now Mrs. Hardinge—and whose marriage to the gallant but susceptible lieutenant whom she converted, as Omphale converted Hercules, to Southern proclivities was one of the fashionable events of last season—is in London, and proposes, it is said, to publish her memoirs as a Secesh partisan and aide-de-camp to Stonewall Jackson. These memoirs cannot fail to be very interesting. Belle Boyd has been the Flora Macdonald, the Madame

Lavalette, of the South and has suffered captivity, exile, and poverty for the cause which she believes to be the true one. * * *

And of course, in assessing Sala's subsequent silence about Belle's book, one must recall that the appearance of this Southern butterfly on his thronged horizon was not only abrupt but evanescent. His 92 dispatches from the United States to the *Daily Telegraph* had established his reputation as a Special Correspondent of the first rank. In April, he would be off to Algiers on another assignment. He was now readying a second edition of his *Diary in America in the Midst of War*. Before this year of 1865 was out, Sala would have made the journalistic most of his American sojourn by publishing editions of James Russell Lowell's *Biglow Papers,* Oliver Wendell Holmes' *Autocrat,* and the gushings of the popular humorists, "Major Jack Downing," "Orpheus C. Kerr," "Petroleum V. Nasby," and "Artemus Ward."

Out of the blue, and on a platter, comes an identical offer. "Will you take my life?" asks Belle, prettily.

Unfortunately for her, Sala took it.

Many of his colleagues in the London press world held a low opinion of George A. Sala's literary style, despite the unpalatable fact that it exercised a solid attraction for the average reader. Before long a rising California newsman, Bret Harte, would stand alongside his English counterparts in a parody of Belle's and Sala's book — the amusing *Condensed Novels* . . . (1867) — so malicious that each journalist refused to greet the other at a London dinner a few years later. Both Harte and the Fleet Streeters concurred in agreeing that the pen name Sala sometimes employed for his articles described his style succinctly. The pen name was "G.A.S."

The kind of volume Belle Boyd would have produced without George Sala's ministrations will never be known. Her few extant letters suggest that it might have been acceptably plain from the point of view of style and narrative. She was, after all, of superior intelligence and had received, for an American female of her day, a superior education. One thing is certain. Her text would have been less Byzantine, less sicklied o'er with the pale cast of bookishness. A few examples of G.A.S.-eous touches will demonstrate this thesis.

First, there are the outright editorial assists to English readers, such as the footnotes in Chapters 4 and 6. Then there are the learned allusions, *viz.*, Colonel Gardiner (Chapter 4), Nelson's epitaph (Chapter 11), or, and especially, the extract from Vincenzo Monti (Chapter 14), all of which were certainly beyond Belle's ken. Of the numerous literary quotations stippling the text a good dozen are recondite enough to have defied identification. In Chapter 19, again, one seems to detect Sala peeping through, since nothing indicates that Belle had ever been to Italy. And, hovering hazily over all, is the somewhat inflated language. Two examples will suffice. In Chapter 5 we see the two of them having a laugh with one another on this very subject (the metaphor for daybreak). And it seems out of character for a Virginia girl of the period to refer to a slave as a "sable Cassandra" (Chapter 7), unless she were being consciously literary — which, it may be presumed, is exactly what "G.A.S." thought she should be.

At a broader level Belle's book partakes of several characteristics which memoirs by American spies, North or South, were now in process of developing. (For their titles see the Appendix to the present edition.) All of them are also features of the romantic fiction of that sentimental school which was the preferred literary fare for most readers at the time, on either side of the Atlantic.

Every one of these memoirs recounts stories of glamorous adventure, compounded of deeds of derring-do and of stealth. Most of them include dollops of romance, compounded of flirtation, courtship, or marriage. (Belle's book, in the instance of her overseas wedding to Sam Hardinge, offers to American readers not only the sentimental North–South, Blue–Gray alliance but an exotic milieu as well.) All of them, in their cumulative effect, paint their protagonists as figures of heroic stature, or at least of super-normal accomplishment. (Belle and/or her editor do not hesitate to compare her with Joan of Arc and with that romantic stereotype of the spy, Fenimore Cooper's "Harvey Birch.") These gallant knights require, of course, an opponent, *i.e.,* a villain, as a whetstone to bring the cutting edge of their abilities to the fine point. Such a personage is easily come by, since in Civil War memoirs the opposing side is automatically villainous. In Belle's book there is a cavalcade of villains : the Yankee soldier who threatened her mother, reporter Clarke of the *Herald,* detective Cridge, Secretary Stanton, Superintendent Wood, and the Federal sleuths dogging her traces in Canada.

Nearly all of the spy memoirs, again, indulge in direct discourse. In so doing they give evidence of a phenomenon usually associated with a condition of deep hypnosis : total recall. Like the novels of the day, too, these authors often employ dialect. In Belle's book one encounters not only Negro speech but Irish as well (Chapter 22). References to the pleasures of the table also occur. In Belle's book the reader is regaled with a formal mênu (Chapter 9). They are, all of them, grandly vague about dates.

Having affirmed thus much, let it be affirmed also that the spy memoirs, regarded as a literary genre, invite special concessions to credibility. So much that is labelled "romantic" really happened to these people ! Many of them, like Belle, recorded what happened soon after the event, with a resultant verisimilitude. And since these authors were wooing a general audience, who can castigate them for trying to dress up their narrative in an inviting garb ? As narrative Belle's book moves better, with less padding, than Emma Edmonds' *The Female Spy of the Union Army* . . . (Boston, 1864). In style it is less archly genteel, decidedly less peevish, than Rose Greenhow's *My Imprisonment* . . . (London, 1863). It is superior in several ways to the anonymous . . . *The Thrilling Adventures of Pauline Cushman* . . . (Cincinnati, 1864) and Loreta Velaquez's *The Woman in Battle* . . . (Hartford, 1876), both of which would have done credit to any of the dime-novel lists issued by the firm of Beadle & Adams.

All of which ushers in the central query : how authentic is Belle's book?

Anyone who takes the trouble to ponder the annotation to this edition of *Belle Boyd in Camp and Prison* . . . will probably conclude that its contents are entitled to a high degree of credibility.

True, there are frequent misspellings (or misprints) of proper names that one would expect the author should know how to spell, such as the town of Staunton or the family of Nadenboush. But this is a failing — aside from the local pronunciations complicating these instances — which is common to many people who have not, as youngsters, won spelling bees. There are occasional conflicts in chronology. This, too, may evidence a lapse of memory as easily as a flaw in probity. The grossest example — that of Hardinge's journal, in Chapter 25 — may be ascribed to a simple mix-up of his manuscript sheets as they were being readied by or for the printer, since the passage as a whole has internal cohesion. Even such episodes as Belle's eavesdropping on the hapless General Shields (Chapter 5), or the impressive amount of contraband items she managed to conceal upon her person (Chapter 14), strain the credulity only of today's more cynical cast of mind. From North and South alike many parallels to both passages can be cited in the covert operations of the Civil War. The best-known eavesdropping episode — that recorded by General McClellan's chief detective, Allan Pinkerton, when he spied on Mrs. Greenhow — occurred under circumstances far more outlandish. Pinkerton was teetering, shoeless, on the shoulders of two colleagues, peering through a closed window, during a driving snow storm!

Vagueness about dates? This can be as much a badge of integrity as a testimonial to deceit. Ask any law-enforcement official whether it is the criminal or the good citizen who comes up with a precise chronology of past activity!

All of the important episodes in Belle's book, moreover, have been substantiated beyond reasonable doubt: her shooting of the Union trooper, her Front Royal dash between the lines, the details of her two incarcerations, etc., etc. True, the pair of letters sent her by General T. J. Jackson, and so proudly printed in full (Chapters 6 and 11), have never been found. Undoubtedly they ranked among Belle's chief treasures, to be cherished throughout life. Hence it is a fair presumption that they were casualties in the disasters that plagued her manuscripts in later years — two losses by fire, and one by family carelessness. In this connection it may be observed generally that history's residue, whether in the form of paper or stone, carries the iceberg analogy: what is left before our eyes is only about one-ninth of what once was there. In particular it may be observed, in the words of a careful student of Belle Boyd's career, Louis A. Sigaud: "Lack of confirmation that the letters from General Jackson were actually written is not affirmative proof that they were not."

If Belle and "Old Jack" enjoyed something of a father-daughter relationship (had she not dreamed of him, benignly admonishing her, alongside her real sire?), why, then, did the soldier turn her away from his quarters with brusqueness, as the account by his aide-de-camp (page seventy-seven, below) demonstrates that he did? The episode occurred during the latter part of September, 1862.

The answer probably lurks in the nature of some of the Northern newspaper accounts of Belle which strove to saddle her with qualities abhorred by all proper persons of the day : unladylike "sauciness" or "boldness." One such account appeared in the Washington, D.C., *Evening Star* for Monday, August 4, 1862, being an interview somehow contrived during Belle's (first) Old Capitol detention. Toward the close of the article the reporter declared : "She was dressed Saturday in a plain frock, low in the neck, and her arms were bare. Jackson, it appears, is her idol; and she gave vent to romantic desires to occupy his tent and share his dangers. She takes her arrest as a matter of course, and is smart, plucky, and absurd as ever."

Now, Major General Thomas Jonathan Jackson, C.S.A., had a highly developed sense of the worth of what is today termed Military Intelligence. He scanned all the Northern newspapers his staff could assemble in order to profit from the details swarming therein on Federal troop movements, Washington pronouncements, and related topics. He was also, as it happened, immured behind a stone-wall Presbyterianism that made him a textbook example of those "Southern Puritans" of whom there were so many more at the time than one realizes. Jackson's impassive gaze very likely fell upon the *Star* story, or one of similar tenor. If it did, that sly business about Belle's sharing his tent, let alone the bare arms and low bodice, would have been quite enough to lower the General's temperature to the degree recorded by Captain Smith. But Jackson's mind was never a closed one, else his name would not rank among the greatest in the annals of field tactics. He must presently have realized he had been mistaken about this girl. Hence the appearance of his second, and fatherly, epistle to Belle only two months after her fall from grace.

In sum, it seems sufficient to quote the statement of perhaps the most knowledgeable student of this general subject. In

Lee's Lieutenants . . . (I, 378 n.) the late Douglas S. Freeman labels Belle Boyd "one of the most active and most reliable of the many secret women agents of the Confederacy."

What was the press reaction to Belle's book?

On the American side of the Atlantic she had been even less fortunate than at London in her choice of publisher. Blelock & Company, of Beekman Street, New York, seems only to have moved there (from Philadelphia) in this same year of 1865. The firm was essentially a stationer and printery striving to become a publishing house. True, in 1866 Blelock would bring out Thomas C. DeLeon's anthology of Confederate verse, *South Songs,* but by 1870, it would appear, the business expired.

The text of Belle's book was reset by Blelock into one volume. He deleted the frontispiece (of our heroine in riding costume), but for the first time brought G. A. Sala into the picture by proclaiming him on the title page as author of the Introduction. He also misspelled Sala's middle name. In general, however, the edition was accurately copied from the British original, with a few minor chapter adaptations and one major omission: Belle's opinion as to the perpetrators of Abraham Lincoln's murder. No masterpiece of the printer's craft, some copies, at least, of the volume were lined at the spine not with linen but with strippings from magazine pages.

Blelock and Company released *Belle Boyd in Camp and Prison* . . . , with no price quoted, about July 18, 1865.

On neither side of the Atlantic does Belle's book seem to have commanded much reviewing attention. Though it may well have been noticed by several, if not many, Southern newspapers or other periodicals in the United States, only five reviews in all have been uncovered. (As a mere printer, Blelock probably had few distribution facilities.) Three of the reviews were in London, two in New York City. All of them were colored by the periodical's orientation *vis à vis* the Confederacy.

In the British capital all three of the reviews were good-sized, but only one could be termed favorable. No doubt it was a distinction to be noticed by both *The Athenaeum* and *The Spectator*. But George A. Sala, at least, must have winced at the tone of those notices.

"The inquiry which is slowly making progress at Washington may as well be forthwith brought to an end," intoned *The Athenaeum,* because Belle Boyd and her editor have discovered who arranged for President Lincoln's death. It was President Johnson ! "Coming from the lips of a foolish woman, such nonsense should be met with laughter; but it is no matter for mere merriment when Englishmen are found weak enough to believe, and rash enough to publish, irritating and scandalous libels upon the rulers of a great and sensitive people."

The authoress' personal story, continued *The Athenaeum,* reveals her hardness and vanity in such anecdotes as those of her slaying the Federal soldier or cajoling Northern pickets in such a bold manner. True, she shouldn't be blamed for filching pistols from Union officers and smuggling them South, since women ought to be partisans of their husbands and brothers. Nevertheless this particular female has "rendered herself notorious by exploits which will not raise her in the estimation of English gentlewomen." *The Athenaeum's* final verdict: "This is a very dull book."

The notice in *The Spectator* was even lengthier, but just as condemnatory and for much the same reasons. There was a good deal of quotation, including Jackson's letter of May 23, 1862. As with *The Athenaeum,* the reviewer had no special reservations about the accuracy of the narrative. He was merely disgusted with the unladylike qualities and saucy tone which that narrative revealed. The whole thing was the more amusing in view of an opinion given currency by a member of Parliament, John Bright, an admirer of Lincoln, and pro-Northern generally :

> As the mist of prejudice clears away, a number of delusions, which throughout the duration of the American war have been received as recognized truths, will be exposed and laid bare. Foremost among these delusions will be, we think, the belief popular in this country that the champions of the South carried on the war in a spirit of gallantry and chivalry not to be discovered amidst their antagonists. In one of his early speeches on the American question Mr. Bright observed that the *mot d'ordre* had been passed through fashionable society to consider the Southerners as gentlemen, and to all men acquainted with the real facts of the case there was nothing more offensive, in the whole tone adopted by Confederate sympathizers in this country, than the gratuitous assumption that courage, and high breeding, and humanity, and all the other characteristics of gentlemen, were only to be found amidst the slave-owning oligarchy of the South. Happily the Southerners themselves have done their best to dispel this illusion, and few books are likely to disenchant Englishmen more thoroughly with the Confederate cause than the memoirs before us. It is on this account, and this account only, that we commend them to the perusal of the public.

In conclusion *The Spectator* castigated both Belle and her husband for whining about their treatment in prison. If they had conducted themselves on the Continent as they did in America, they wouldn't be here now to publish their opus!

It remained for the Confederate weekly, *The Index* — established by one of Belle's wedding guests, Henry Hotze — to give the only sympathetic appraisal of her book in the United Kingdom. (As with all the notices, this one was unsigned, but may well have been by the Richmond journalist, John R. Thompson, who had run the blockade in 1864 and who was on the staff of the paper till mid-June, 1865.) The reviewer echoed *The Spectator* in affirming that Belle really had little to complain of in her treatment by the Federals. Her suffering was as nothing compared to that endured by Jefferson Davis in his imprisonment or by the victims of such Northern commanders as Butler, M'Neil, Milroy, or Turchin. This volume, said *The Index,*

> belongs to a class of books of which in all probability it is the last. It is not according very high praise to say that it is among the best of its kind that the American war has thrown upon a glutted market. Contrasted with poor Mrs. Greenhow's—*de mortuis nil nisi bonum*—which it most nearly resembles in subject-matter, it lays claim to a large amount of negative excellence. It relates a minor episode, not without dramatic interest, of which a pretty woman is the heroine, in that gigantic national struggle which will long employ the pen of the historian and supply the repertoire of the romancer. It is pleasantly, and upon the whole modestly, written, in a style which, for occasional attempts at being ornate, is nevertheless free from any serious objection.

Belle deserves to be thought well of by the South, the reviewer felt. Her book's chief fault was that of its genre: the danger of the type's becoming too strident an apologia. When the writer is a woman, moreover, a vein of high tragedy is apt to infuse the text, which makes one suspect the breeding of the authoress. In this case she is known as authentic. Her personal situation disarms criticism, and *The Index* wishes her book well if only for its author's pecuniary needs:

There is no greater error than to suppose that every book written with a good Southern intention is therefore a good Southern book, and exempt from Southern criticism. On the contrary, it is a rule that a cause risks more from the incompetency of friends than from the attacks of its enemies. Still, it is in justice due to Miss Belle Boyd to say, that had the Confederate cause never suffered more from unauthorized or awkward advocacy than it is likely to do from her harmless and very readable autobiography, our remarks would have been out of place here.

Across the water the pro-Confederate New York *Daily News*, in an advance blurb for Belle's volume published on July 18, assured readers: "This book contains some spicy chapters, and has been highly praised by the London press." On July 31, 1865, the *News* released its formal review. This was brief but quite favorable:

Belle Boyd has passed from the cloudy regions of romance into the less poetic but more enduring domain of history. That she *deserves* to become historical is conceded. She has shown pluck, wit and talent; she has suffered and struggled; she has fascinated, fought and failed. . . . Her interview with the beast Butler is one of the most spicy records ever penned; short but sharp. Her estimate of Butler's character is in every point correct, and does credit to her penetration. The introduction to the book by Sala is pungent. Altogether, a valuable contribution to our war literature.

A few days later the *Evening Post,* an over-size newspaper, gave Belle the benefit of a solid one-and-a-third columns of small print on page one. True, most of this space was taken up with excerpts, and the verdict was, at best, neutral. Nevertheless its prominence must have caught many a New Yorker's eye.

"She was, as everybody knows," the *Post* began, "notorious as a skilful spy for Stonewall Jackson and other rebel generals, and she closed her career by seducing one Hardinge. . . . The two are now in London, and being in want of money, have printed this book to raise the wind."

General Jackson's letter was given again. Two of the lengthier excerpts pertained to Belle's comments on General Shields and to her shipboard romance with her future husband. The review concluded with the statement that Hardinge should consider himself lucky to have gotten off as well as he did. Whilst for his wife one can't "feel anything but admiration, as a courageous, though vain and addle-pated little woman, for her husband, Hardinge, one can only feel contempt and disgust."

What, in sum, are the virtues of Belle's book? They are two. It is authentic, and it tells a story. Of these qualities the former is by far the more important, for the literature of espionage teems with titles not just shoddy but suspect. The genuine glamor of the subject, plus the tendency of too many of its practitioners to bedizen that glamor with tinsel melodrama, have combined — much more often than not, in the opinion of some students of the subject — to foist upon the public many a performance wherein the element of fiction dominates that of autobiography. And since, by its nature, the genre carries a built-in imperviousness to confirmation, readers are required to take these books on faith. The notes to the present edition demonstrate that Belle's book demands no such faith.

Secondly, the story she tells, despite its interior decoration by a story doctor, boasts that seminal virtue of all successful stories since story telling began: narrative movement. In this sense the Washington *Star* editorialist was correct when he declared, in 1943, that "she wrote 'like a prairie fire'. . . ." For Belle is not out to offer an analysis of an agent operation, or to present a disquisition on selected aspects of Military Intelligence. She is simply telling the story of one agent in that line of work. And since the story invokes those eternal situations of conflict, frustration, accomplishment, defeat, love, and hate, Belle speaks for all humankind. What broader basis for reader identification can there be than this?

Despite its paucity of reviews Belle's book must have done fairly well in sales. Though it is far from equalling the attainments of several other titles in its field (see the Appendix to the present volume), it enjoyed two separate editions, and one of these further enjoyed two separate printings. It is, today, rather a rare book. In Belle's day—specifically, one spring day in 1868—it was circulating well enough to furnish her with a better than modest income. This we know because she wrote to the family friend, Ward Hill Lamon, about her book from the nation's capital. She was now well embarked upon her stage career, and, typically, was short of cash. But unless we are willing to believe that she would distort or falsify her affairs to this prominent and influential Washingtonian, it would seem that *Belle Boyd in Camp and Prison* . . . had proved a good thing for its author.

> 225 Penn Avenue,
> April 7th

Col. Lamon,
　Dear Sir,
　　I wish to leave for New York tomorrow morning to attend to some important business. I have some 7. or 8. thousand dollars coming to me from the sale of my Book, but I cannot get it for a few weeks yet, & it is to ask you to lend me $50 (fifty dollars) that I write.

I will return it by the first of May at the latest. I can give you security for it, if you wish. Did I not *need* it much I'd not ask this favor, but I know that in the past had you come to my Father, he would not have refused you. I am sure you will grant my request. I only want it as a loan for a few weeks, & did I not need it much I would not ask *so* great a favor. Trusting you will grant my request

I am Yours truly

Belle Boyd

[*Postcript*]
Dear Col I beg that you will comply with my request as I am worried quite ill. feeling assured you will not refuse me I am yours truly

B B

Whether the Colonel complied is unknown. In any event his beseecher was presently on her way West once more to a certain amount of fame, if no fortune.

III : THE ENIGMA OF FAME

While this was being done [ousting Union troops from Front Royal, May 23, 1862] I looked for Belle Boyd and found her standing on the pavement in front of a hotel, talking with some few Federal officers (prisoners) and some of her acquaintances in our army. Her cheeks were rosy with excitement and recent exercise and her eyes all aflame. When I rode up to speak to her she received me with surprised cordiality, and as I stooped from my saddle she pinned a crimson rose to my uniform, bidding me remember that it was *blood-red* and that it was her "colors."

Henry Kyd Douglas, I Rode with Stone-wall (Chapel Hill, N. C. [1940]), p. 52

Some say that she was a myth and never existed at all.
    Willis F. Evans, *History of Berkeley Coun-
ty, West Virginia* ([Wheeling], 1928), p. 268

"Who was this Belle Boyd there's so much advertizing about around here?"

The question was asked of a filling-station attendant at Front Royal, Virginia, on Labor Day, 1964. His answer was prompt, and delivered in a conspiratorial whisper : "She wuz th' Suth'run lady that made luv to th' Yune-yun Gin'rul."

Two months later the same query was posed to the proprietress of a restaurant in Front Royal sporting Belle's name. This time the response varied : Belle Boyd was the girl who ran down the street in her underwear to warn General Andrew Jackson.

Aside from the degree of accuracy in these responses, the fact that they were made at all suggests that, well over half a century after her death, Belle's name is still one for social historians to reckon with. It has been so ever since that occasion in 1861 when, just a bit past seventeen, she celebrated Independence Day by promoting the Yankee soldier to glory.

Why Belle Boyd? Though at one time or another she saw service as courier, mail carrier, or smuggler — was, in a word, a spy — the feat which drenched her in publicity, her forewarning of Jackson at Front Royal, was not an act of espionage. It preceded what was merely an engagement (not a battle, let alone a major one). Silhouetted in this particular limelight, therefore, Belle may fairly be called the war's most overrated spy. The most valuable trait of spies, moreover, is unobtrusiveness. Yet Belle Boyd was, within 13 months of the war's advent, notorious as a "secret" agent !

So why not — to select two women whose activity was undoubtedly of more value to their respective sides — Rose Greenhow for the South, and Elizabeth van Lew for the

North? Or, since those ladies were operating at a strategic level, why not—confining the business to field agents, like Belle—Antonia Ford and Loreta Velaquez for the South, or Emma Edmonds and "Miss Major" Pauline Cushman for the North?

One reason, of course, is that two of those cited (Ford and van Lew) neglected to leave behind them that most perduring of monuments, a book. But, then, the rest of them did. Yet today their names are familiar only to Civil War addicts, whereas Belle Boyd's name is known, however distortedly, to the public at large. For example, a feature in the *New York Times Magazine* in 1929 went so far as to assert (echoing Thomas C. DeLeon, who had asserted the same thing in 1890) that, of all American women whose careers were factually based, only "Molly Pitcher" rivals Belle in renown.

As it happens, the only reason "Molly Pitcher" (Mrs. Mary L. H. McCauley, 1754–1832) is remembered today is because —in a single, scintillating thrust toward fame—she is traditionally supposed to have manned her slain husband's field gun in a battle of the Revolution. (The feat was, in fact, performed by an entirely different woman.) And she did not engage in espionage. Hence to compare Belle with her is an imperfect analogy. It would be more suggestive to compare some of the circumstances of Belle's career with those of one whose name, even more than hers, has become synonymous with spying. This is the Dutch woman shot by the French for alleged espionage on behalf of Germany: "Mata Hari" (Margaretha Zelle, 1876–1917).

The similarities in their story range from the trivial to the basic. As youngsters both Belle and Margaretha composed sentimental verses to girl chums. As adolescents both incurred the jealously of girl chums. Both grew into tall adults, with prominent noses (though Margaretha was flat-chested). Both were fine horsewomen (each at least once riding her mount up into a house). Both were attracted by the military uniform. Both became stage stars. Both drew imitators or impersonators. Both were women of commanding personality and decided articulateness.

The last sentence provides a second reason why Belle Boyd is remembered. Hers was a personality people felt. During the war it was newspaper notoriety (or adulation) that established her name. At its close the appearance of her book revived that name. In the postwar years her wide-ranging travels as actress and *diseuse* retained it in dozens of local newspapers. The occasional mishaps already discussed gilded her in the wider limelight of regional publicity, ranging from Pennsylvania to Texas. Two other such episodes — one flattering, one lurid, both newsworthy — did so on a broad scale also.

The first was *Belle Lamar*. This melodrama by the popular Irish-American playwright, Dion Boucicault, ran at Booth's Theater, New York City, in the summer of 1874. A Civil War romance, it is laid in the Valley of Virginia, and features a heroine who gathers information for "Stonewall" Jackson. Belle was not in the play, and no evidence has appeared to suggest that author and subject ever met; but they could well have done so and, in view of George Sala's connections in the English theatre, probably did. For Boucicault was in London during the spring of 1864 revising his Irish comedy, *Arrah-na-Pogue,* at the same time Belle resided there.

The second publicizing incident was Belle Starr. On February 3, 1889, out in the Indian Territory of Arkansas, that notorious gunwoman and consort of criminals took a load of buckshot in the back that summarily shuffled her off this mortal coil. At once the New York *World* ran a prominent, page-two dispatch in its issue of February 6, headlined, "Belle Boyd Was Ambushed." The biographical part of this item effectively ensnarled the careers of the two Belles. Five days later the paper disentangled the mix-up via an interview with the non-outlaw at Greensburg, Pennsylvania, but by that time the original dispatch had been widely disseminated. Until the day of her death, and beyond, shreds of Belle Starr clung to Belle Boyd. For example, the *World*'s statement that the gun-woman possessed "the physical strength and elasticity of an Amazon" found its way, eleven years later, into the obit on Belle in the Kilbourn, Wisconsin, newspaper. And the *World*'s revelation that its Belle had married the Quantrill guerrilla, "Cole" Younger, became embedded, a quarter century later still, in the entry on Belle Boyd in the *National Cyclopaedia of American Biography.*

Even concerning the last seconds of Belle's life there lingers an element of mystery. As Nat High and the housekeeper of the hotel, Mrs. Addie Nease, looked down at her, they knew that the dying woman was concealing a revolver under her pillow. She had shown it to Mrs. Nease the day before, saying, "This is my best protection." After all these years, the Southern Spy still felt cause to dread Yankee vengeance!

When his wife's breathing stopped, High thereupon took the pistol and pocketed it. Tears were in his eyes as he murmured, "My poor Belle! You won't need this any more. Nobody can hurt you now — ever." Had there really been some inexorable Federal Javert dogging this woman's steps?

Here, then, are three distortions of personality. Perhaps it might be better to term them variations on a theme. The theme duly ripened into legend. Three variations among the many that fell into place in that legendry, across the decades, may be selected as typical for mention.

In 1900, the Toledo *Blade,* recounting Belle's career during the course of a lengthy obit, advised its readers, among other details of her wartime service: "She married a major who was killed at Antietam on his wedding day." In 1910, the Baltimore *American,* publicizing the gift to a local G.A.R. post of a watch once belonging to Belle, saw fit to enlighten its subscribers on her background : "She was a Maryland girl. She captured three or four steamboats during the war, landing the federal soldiers aboard them on the James River and turning them over to the Confederacy." In 1954, the Richmond *Times–Dispatch* carried a prominent article about "a newly discovered picture of Belle Boyd," in uniform, which had been presented to the local U.D.C. chapter president by a Wisconsin woman in memory of her late father (who had been smitten with Belle's renown even though he had fought for the Union). The article ran a cut of the photograph, captioned, "La Belle Rebelle in Uniform." There were just two things wrong with this picture : the uniform was Federal, and the girl was Pauline Cushman !

Is it any wonder that, even during her lifetime, Belle Boyd felt constrained to produce certification as to her identity? We have seen the Masonic credential written for her in 1876. In 1895, the prominent military editor, Methodist minister, and commander of the Georgia division of the United Confederate Veterans, ex-Brigadier General Clement A. Evans, issued a similar pronouncement on Belle's behalf at Atlanta. In 1898, the opposing forces duplicated the compliment, in the case of R. B. Hayes Post #92, G.A.R., out of Washington Court House, Ohio.

This reaffirmation of identity dogged Belle's footsteps till she was long past caring. At the time of her very interment Nat High thought it advisable to certify for local authorities the bona-fides of the deceased. There had been several women over the years, the Kilbourn *Mirror-Gazette* reminded its readers, who claimed to be Belle Boyd, "but there seems to be no doubt of the genuineness of this one. Her husband submitted several instances of proof which could hardly be disputed."

Aside from being a celebrity, Belle was also something to look at. Though not a beauty, she had been reared as the healthy, outdoors type, and showed it. By seventeen she was physically mature, with an excellent figure. By the summer of 1862, aged eighteen, her presence was enough to stimulate a conniving letter, from the vicinity of Thornton's Gap, Virginia, to the Secretary of War of the United States. It is difficult to pronounce whether this epistle was motivated out of revenge or out of jealousy. It was, in any event, out of channels, and remains withal an intriguing tribute to one girl's personality.

> Head Quarters 1st Army Corps Va
> July 30, 1862

Dear Sir,

I communicate to you a fact that the celebrated Belle Boyd the "Rebel Spy" now at Front Royal has apparently fallen in love or is anscious [sic] to make a victim of the Medical Director of the 1st Army Corps (Dr Rex) with whom she is in correspondence. Where [sic] that *used* by higher authority at the War Department Jackson and all the Rebel officers with whom she is in direct communication might be trapped. Where a skilful "Detective" placed by the Government easily could these rascals be led into captivity. She believes the Medical Director of the 1st Corps of the Army of Virginia is a wealthy & influential man and will ultimately marry her and then reside in Europe.

I mention these facts that the Government may make what *use* they think proper of them and I *know* that the Medical Director will with General Siegel [sic] coopperate to-gether to use *this woman* for our common cause.

> With Entreaty of high personal
> Regard & Esteem I Remain Respectfully
> Washington Duffee Dr
> I Brigade Surgeon
> II Division Siegels 1st Army Corps
> Va

Secretary Stanton
Washington *D C*

Though the Brigade Surgeon probably did not know it, Belle was in fact arrested that same day, and taken off under guard to Washington City and its Old Capitol prison. When a fellow prisoner, J. O. Kerbey (a Northerner), met her there, he found himself confronted "by the lithe and graceful figure of a neatly-dressed young lady, who had presented herself to my vision so suddenly as to suggest a spirit from the other world." The Union man recalled that Belle — then eighteen and a half years old — "was of light, rather fair complexion, and I think her hair was inclined to be a strawberry blonde. While she was not strictly a handsome woman, there was something in her manner that was very attractive."

By 1876 Belle was still, as seen by her Masonic certifier at Martinsburg, "rather thin, with roman features." In 1885, after two marriages and aged almost forty-one, her appearance caught the fancy of a man seventeen years her junior (and held it till death). A little over a year later a Toledo *Blade* reporter declared that, "for one with such a remarkable career, time has dealt gently with her. She is 5 feet 8 inches in height, has an erect military bearing, is fascinating and beautiful, with a wealth of golden hair."

Exactly three years later — when the Belle Starr episode erupted in February, 1889 — Colonel Tom Ochiltree was interviewed in Manhattan by the *World* on the newly arisen controversy as to his former acquaintance's identity. The Colonel prefaced his observations by recalling how popular she had been in the old Confederacy, especially with Mosby's men, because of her allegiance to the cause. Then he discoursed upon their joint foray into the Texas theatrical world at Houston. True, he hadn't run into her in recent years, but how well he remembered her from those far-off days! The Colonel's eyes glinted with amusement: "I would gamble that I would know her now, because of the peculiarities of her features. She was very bright and handsome, but with strangely protruding teeth and a prominent nose."

By 1894 when Belle, aged fifty, was visiting in Baltimore and preparing to take a pleasure cruise aboard the *Emma Ford* up the Chester River, over on the Eastern Shore of Maryland, a reporter for the Baltimore *American* decided that she was "a matronly looking woman."

Here, then, was an individual of pronounced personality, intriguing to gaze upon, possessed of a glamorous present and a controversial past. It is scarcely surprising that, about such a woman, two schools of opinion should arise. They arose about the same time, and are still in session.

The anti-Belle school has based its animus on several counts. First of all, the girl was over-bold in the manner whereby, during the war, she consorted with common soldiers. She was also, at times, under-dressed. At other times she was wrongly dressed, *viz.*, in men's clothing. As the Winchester *Evening Star* put this proposition, during the course of its obit, she "appeared in the dress of both sexes and was daring to recklessness." The Baltimore *Sun*'s version, as voiced by Belle's friend there from school days, Mrs. John H. Tegmeyer, went like this : "She wore male costume and otherwise acted in a way that evoked criticism." Years earlier the Augusta matron, Mrs. Jefferson Thomas, speaking of a fellow Georgian and family acquaintance, had confided to her diary, September 17, 1864, that "Gen Longstreet who met with her in Richmond thought her masculine in her manners and appearance." (The entire subject of disguise during the Civil War—especially where, as in some instances, it seems to verge upon transvestitism—offers a diverting field of inquiry. In Belle's case the persistence of the condemnation probably stems from two bases : her status as honorary aide-de-camp to Jackson, and her postwar costume appearances in the theater). As if all this were not enough, the hussy had the sauciness to parade the story of herself in print and submit it to the public gaze over her own name. She was not only a divorcée but had indulged in three marriages ! To cap all, she went on the stage.

Small wonder that, from 1861 to today in Belle's "home country," an undercurrent of genteel hostility has run deep. As a Martinsburg matron succinctly summarized the business in the spring of 1965 : "Belle Boyd was more of a camp follower than heroine."

But the pro-Belle school has confronted this attitude with much meaningful activity. Things have been named for her. Areas she frequented have been memorialized.

About 1894, for example, the Belle Boyd Chapter, United Daughters of the Confederacy, was formed in Pocahontas County, West Virginia. Since at least 1928, a Virginia Conservation Commission highway marker has stood sentinel three miles south of Front Royal, close to the entrance of the Skyline Drive, to remind the leisurely tourist of today about Belle's sweaty dash of yesterday across the neighboring slopes to give warning to "Stonewall" Jackson's troopers. In 1952, a motor cruiser to transport other tourists over the Wisconsin River at the Dells was christened, in her name, with James River water. In 1956, the cities of Richmond and Wisconsin Dells announced, with all requisite mayoral Proclamations and *Whereas'es,* that June 1 would henceforth be known as "North-South Understanding Day," in order to pay tribute to her memory. In 1962, the city of Martinsburg issued a gilt coin bearing her profile in classic mode. In 1957 and 1964, at Martinsburg and Dallas, respectively, when houses that had once been home to her were in process of being razed, their demolition became news because — and only because — of her.

For years after her death the grave tucked away in the pine-scented acres of Spring Grove Cemetery, at Kilbourn, was faithfully tended by Northern hands, especially by members of the local American Legion Post (with an occasional assist from the Winnebago Indian Veterans Organization). Then, on Memorial Day, 1952, the South reacted. A delegation from the Richmond, Virginia, chapter of the United Daughters of the Confederacy, specially designated by the Governor of the Commonwealth, John S. Battle, made the journey up to Wisconsin. There they proceeded to flank the grave site with replicas of the two flags its occupant had fought so single-mindedly to glorify : the State colors of Virginia, and the Stars and Bars of the Confederacy. On the grave they placed a floral wreath bursting with her favorite blood-red roses. The following year there came a consignment of Virginia soil, taken from the banks of the James, to cover the grave. In 1954, it was a planting of gray-petalled Confederate violets.

Now, both these schools, pro and anti, were commenting upon an individual variously identified as "the Siren of the Shenandoah" or Mrs. Sam Hardinge, "a Rebel Jean d'Arc" or Mrs. Nat High, "the Secesh Cleopatra" or Mrs. Colonel Hammond, or "Nina Benjamin," or "Belle Lamar," or even Belle Starr. But the schools were also commenting on a phenomenon which was functioning as a reflection for their own ideas, which is to say, a type of the mythic hero (or heroine). Her obit in the Philadelphia *Evening Telegraph* was captioned, "Career of a Semi-myth."

One large value of a myth is what it tells not about itself but about its observers. So far as the records go, Belle Boyd has been most sharply observed during her early years. Two such observations are recorded in the Introduction to her own book (newsman Mahony and English traveller Buxton). In order to slip within the nimbus of the myth's halo, and attempt to discern its propagator more variously still, let us see what sort of person emerges from the scrutiny of other close-range observers during this period of their subject's young flowering. . . .

At the time of Belle's sudden death in 1900, her chum at Mount Washington Female College, Mrs. John Tegmeyer of Baltimore, recalled her as having been a dashing school girl with vivacious manners and (interestingly) having had command of several languages. This opinion substantially coincides with the earliest description of her to appear thus far. It was recorded by a native of her home country, an officer of Company B, 7th Regiment, Virginia Cavalry. Writing to his wife from Winchester on December 12, 1861, Captain John Q. Winfield (presently to be slain in combat) declared:

> I was at a wedding night before last in Martinsburg, and last night attended a reception given to the bridal party. By the way, I escorted Belle Boyd to the party. She is quite a favorite with me, possessing an originality and vivacity, no-care-madcap-devil-of-a-temperament that pleases. Her mother who is much of a lady and had shown me much kindness asked me to take her daughter under my charge.

The descriptions of Belle from 1862 are the most frequent of all. They commence with an entry on May 19, in his diary at Front Royal, by a native of the area whom most of the other natives cordially damned as a turncoat. This was the artist, "Porte Crayon" (David Hunter Strother), at the moment serving as a civilian topographer with the Federal forces but anticipating appointment as an officer on General Banks' staff. Among the people he knew at Front Royal who condescended to speak with him was Miss Boyd. Strother's painterly eye found her "looking well and deporting herself in a very lady-like manner. I daresay she has been much slandered by reports. She sported a bunch of buttons despoiled from General Shields and our officers and seemed ready to increase her trophies."

About two weeks later another Unionist also came upon

Belle in Front Royal. This was Tom Galwey of Cleveland, a short, beardless, sixteen-year-old sergeant with the 8th Ohio Volunteer Infantry. "On Monday, June 1," the young soldier recalled,

> we surprised Colonel O'Connor and his Confederate force at Front Royal, capturing about three hundred prisoners and a considerable amount of ammunition and stores. During our stay here I was introduced to the famous Belle Boyd, a Confederate female spy who had been taken prisoner when we captured the town. She is rather handsome and has some accomplishments although their luster is somewhat heightened by her rather romantic career.

At just about the same time, on the evening of June 3, 1862, the accomplished female spy was formally interviewed by Nathaniel Paige, war correspondent for the New York *Daily Tribune*. At the moment rain was deluging the little town of some five hundred souls, almost isolating Front Royal from the outside world; so Paige got a good interview (subsequently devoured by thousands of readers). To him Belle freely admitted that she had served as a courier for the Confederates, transporting letters and packages into their lines. She had also acted as a provocator, *i.e.*, had tried to wheedle military information out of the occupying Northern troops, served in related capacities, and generally, as the *Tribune* reporter put it, "performing acts of heroic daring worthy of the days of the Revolution. . . ."

Paige in a private letter advised his managing editor in far-off New York, Sydney H. Gay, that at one point this girl had been "closeted four hours" with General Shields, the Union commander. Nevertheless he did not believe she was the "accomplished prostitute" or "camp cyprian" his competitors reporting for the New York *Herald* and the Philadelphia *Inquirer* were labelling her. Paige then launched into his public assessment—which, considering the tense and bitter circumstances, must be called reasonably objective:

> In personal appearance, without being beautiful, she is very attractive. Is quite tall, has a superb figure, an intellectual face, and dresses with much taste. . . .
>
> That she has rendered much service to the Rebel army, I have not the least doubt, and why she should be allowed to go at will through our camps, flirt with our officers, and display their notes and cards to her visitors, I am at a loss to know. She is a native of Virginia, but professes to be an ardent South Carolinian, at heart—wears a gold palmetto tree beneath her beautiful chin, a Rebel soldier's belt around her waist, and a velvet band across her forehead, with the seven stars of the Confederacy shedding their pale light therefrom. It seemed to me, while listening to her narrative, that the only additional ornament she required to render herself perfectly beautiful, was a Yankee halter encircling her neck.
>
> At her special request, I have, upon simply her unsupported testimony, denied, what to her was the most serious charge preferred by the correspondent of *The Philadelphia Inquirer*. To be frank, however, I think she is not what camp gossip charges her with being. She has naturally a large, warm heart and was very kind to the prisoners taken by Jackson in the skirmish at this place. She is an open foe, and therefore entitled to some respect; but if she expects to mingle freely with the soldiers of both armies, and bandy jests and coarse wit with them, and be subject to the ordinary gossip, she is greatly deceived. She says she is related to prominent families in New-York, who will be greatly shocked to learn what has been said about her; but almost in

the same breath expresses the wish that she could draw the rope around the necks of some who are in the Union army.

Toward the middle of the same month (June, 1862) Belle galloped up to "Oakley" — the Front Royal home of an Ashby family connected with that of the famous cavalryman — in order to pay a visit to a Union staff officer who had been carried there following his wounding at the battle of Port Republic. The son of the household, Tom, was fourteen at the time, and didn't fancy any Southern girl taking up with Yankees. When he published *The Valley Campaigns . . .*, his reminiscences of civilian life in northern Virginia during the war, over half a century had elapsed, but the years had done nothing to mellow his opinion of the family visitor :

> When she rode up to my home to see the wounded German officer she was playing the game of flirt and lowering the dignity of her sex. She was a young woman of some personal beauty, vivacious, attractive, and spirited in manner, and a skilled rider of spirited horses. Nor was she wanting in energy, dash, and courage; but she had none of the genius, inspiration, and religious fervor of the true heroine. She loved notoriety and attention, and was as far below the standard of the pure and noble womanhood of the South as was a circus rider. Her own sex in the South repudiated her, and the true manhood of both armies was as suspicious of her character as Frederick the Great was of Madame de Pompadour. So much for Belle Boyd. Her heroism has long faded into the forgetfulness of her generation. She has found no decent place in history.

On Saturday, July 12, 1862, another reporter interviewed Belle. This unidentified correspondent was writing for the

Philadelphia *Inquirer,* but, in view of the tone of his dispatch, must be presumed as not he whom Belle believed had libelled her. During the course of a dispatch covering the topic of "Southern Female Spies" in the lower Valley, the newsman had enlarged upon two of them : Belle, and Mrs. Charles James Faulkner.

Now, Mrs. Faulkner, though born Mary Boyd, daughter of General Elisha Boyd of "Boydville," on the outskirts of Martinsburg, was no kin to her townswoman. But here was a gaping pitfall, and the reporter promptly fell into it. When his dispatch was reprinted three weeks later, moreover, in Frank Leslie's widely circulated *Illustrated Newspaper* at New York City, a third spy was brought onto the carpet, one Belle (*sic*) Jamieson, and Mrs. Faulkner had become "Belle" Faulkner ! The conduct of all three of "these feminine desperadoes," shrilled *Leslie's,* stood in dire contrast to the noble behavior of Northern ladies, for "the fair ones of Secessia have signalized themselves by a reckless disregard for the holiest instincts of their sex characteristic of the criminality of the cause they serve."

This merry-go-round of identities, while perhaps useful from the point of view of espionage, dogged Belle Boyd almost as annoyingly during the war years as would her confusion with Belle Starr 27 years later.

Of these women connivers, the *Inquirer* man averred, the chief was Belle Boyd. "Her acknowledged superiority for machination and intrigue has given her the leadership and control of the female spies in the Valley of Virginia." Whenever he detected Belle practicing her arts upon the young Federal lieutenants and captains, he at once warned them. She was introduced, he had learned, as a "Miss Anderson," or a "Miss Faulkner," etc. By now she had become so well known that only the rawest recruits fell for her line. Nevertheless, she controlled a trained group of helpers — young girls from the age of sixteen on — who discreetly stayed inconspicuous and whose identities were known only to the chieftainess. When their nuggets of information were brought in, Belle and the other ringleaders, all of whom employed false names, would meet to compile the material and then have it spirited across the Union lines. In a description also to be widely perused beyond the boundaries of Virginia, the *Inquirer* correspondent continued :

BELLE has passed the first freshness of youth. She is a sharp-featured black-eyed woman of 25 [*sic*], or care and intrigue have given her that appearance. Last summer, whilst Patterson's army lay at Martinsburg, she wore a revolver in her belt, and was courted and flattered by every lieutenant and captain in the service who ever saw her. There was a DI VERNON dash about her, a smart pertness, a quickness of retort, and utter abandonment of manner and bearing which were attractive from the very romantic unwontedness. . . .

She has undergone all that society, position and education can confer upon a mind suited to the days of CHARLES the Second, or LOUIS the Fourteenth—a mind such as MAZARIN or RICHELIEU would have delighted to employ from its kindred affinities.

The reports that she is personally impure are as unjust as they are undeserved. She has a blind devotion to an idea, and passes far the boundary of her sex's modesty to promote its success. She, with all her faults and false devotion to ideas, which are at the foundation of our political and social disorders, has not yet lost the crowning virtue of woman. Reporters who attack a woman, defenceless within their province, exceed the license which justice and fairness even allot to outlaws.

During the past campaigns in the Valley, this woman has been of immense service to the enemy. She will be now, if she can. She, therefore, should at once be passed beyond our lines, sent to Richmond, and allowed to remain with those with whom she deeply sympathises.

Later the same month (July, 1862), C. W. D. Smitley came to town. It was a bad day for Belle Boyd. This experienced Union scout had been specially detailed to outwit her. The manner of his doing so — as related by the chronicler of his outfit, the 5th West Virginia Cavalry — says almost as much about the relative crudity of Intelligence techniques at the time as it does of Belle's several deficiencies therein :

> Miss Belle Boyd, who later acquired considerable notoriety as a southern spy, was at Front Royal on parole. Being suspected of violating her parole, one of Gen. Schenck's aids requested Smitley to see if he could entrap her. He went to one of the prominent southern citizens of the village under an assumed name, and representing himself to be a paroled confederate officer, secured boarding. The host was exceedingly hospitable and communicative, informing him that Miss Boyd was in town. Smitley affected surprise, and eulogized her valuable services to the southern cause. He soon learned that Miss Boyd was the sensation of the village, that the intensely loyal confederates idolized her, and that she had a large following of Federal officers, who were ready to do her homage.

> Smitley's advent to the inside circles of the village, and his expressed admiration of Miss Boyd's exploits as a spy, were carried to her by his host's daughter, and the same afternoon he received an invitation through the daughter, to take tea with the fair scout, at one of the southern residences. He went, was introduced, and found her to be a lady of culture, a brilliant conversationalist, expert with piano and rather pretty. In the

course of the evening, a number of young ladies called, accompanied by Federal officers, and Miss Boyd appeared to be the centre of attraction. Toward the officers Smitley assumed a lofty, patronizing air, but with the ladies was exceedingly bashful and diffident. When the doxology of the occasion, 'The Bonny Blue Flag,' was being sung and played by Miss Boyd, he stepped forward and sang the bass, with all the feeling and power of his strong voice, though his heart burned within him to sing 'Down with the Traitors and up with the Stars.' This effort settled his social status with the confederates, and thereafter he was one of the 'charmed circle.'

He stayed in the village several days as Lion No. 2, and secured Miss Boyd's confidence to such an extent, that she informed him boastingly of the manner in which she was violating her parole, and urged him not to consider a parole binding to the much hated Yankees. About the third evening of his stay, at an evening party, a federal officer in the secret of Smitley's identity, to whom Miss Boyd turned a cold shoulder, became so incensed at her marked attention to the scout, that he tauntingly told her that Smitley was a Yankee scout. She scornfully resented the accusation against his loyalty, but a night's reflection on the situation brought her early in the morning to Smitley, greatly agitated and shedding tears like a child. Her informant was the staff officer who requested Smitley to entrap her.

And so, on Wednesday, July 30, 1862, Belle was arrested, at Winchester. By way of Martinsburg she was conducted to Washington, where she began her first incarceration in the Old Capitol prison. There on August 4, the *Evening Star* published an interview with her which was at once picked up by the Frederick, Maryland, *Examiner* and undoubtedly by other papers. "Romancers," the *Star*'s reporter advised his readers,

> have given this female undue repute, by describing her as beautiful and educated. She is merely a brusque, talkative woman, perhaps 25 years of age, red haired, with keen, courageous gray eyes. Her teeth are prominent, and she is meager in person. There is a certain dash and *naivete* in her manner and speech that might be called fascinating, but she is by no means possessed of brilliant qualities, either of mind or body. Being insanely devoted to the rebel cause, she resolved to act as a spy within the Union lines, and managed in divers ways to recommend herself to our officers. One of the Generals formerly stationed in the Shenandoah Valley is mentioned rather oddly as associated with her, and Belle boasts of having once wrapped a rebel flag around his head. Our young officers, dazzled, perhaps, took her out riding often, and she was frequently a habitant of our camps in the Shenandoah. From facts gleaned in this way of our movements and projects, she kept up a pretty regular budget of intelligence, and the enemy was advised of our favorite designs. She admitted in prison Saturday that she had informed Jackson of our situation at Front Royal; but this, she said, was done to prevent the effusion of blood.
>
> Passing through her native place, she was groaned at by the citizens on Thursday. The proper people of Martinsburg have steadily disliked her. She passes, indeed, if not for a village courtesan, at least for something not far removed from that relation.

During her first Old Capitol sojourn—most of the month of August, 1862—one gets a triple view of Belle Boyd, twice from fellow prisoners and once from their custodian. Of the prisoners the more important was the political detainee, George Henry Clay Rowe, a Fredericksburg lawyer and newsman.

"I learned from her her own life history," Rowe confided to his diary. "It was quite interesting, but too long to narrate here. Indeed, it was near one o'clock when she finished. She was quite an important character in the prison." Some of Rowe's reasons for thinking so were as follows:

My ideas of a government that could incarcerate such a woman, in such a place, and with such associations, may be imagined, but cannot be described. For be it known, that our floor was the only part of the prison where there was the least show of decency, either in the apartments or the character of those occupying them, and this lady was on one of the lower floors. I felt interested in her case, and went to the head of the stairs where I could see her without being seen. She had been here nearly a month and had become somewhat accustomed to the hardships of her situation which she bore with remarkable fortitude and was now swearing at, deriding, abusing and singing Southern songs to the sentinal [*sic*]. The fellow was forced by his orders from making reply to anything she said, nevertheless she kept up a continual and galling fire on the brute who seemed rejoiced when he was relieved at the expiration of his time. With the new sentinal Miss Boyd's manner changed. He was evidently good natured and she had evidently acquainted herself with his disposition previously. She spoke to him kindly and he replied in an undertone. In a few minutes a side door opened and the head of a young man cautiously peered out. Miss Boyd winked at the sentinal, he smiled, she gave the signal to her lover, for such the young man proved to be! He then advanced to the front of the door, and sang very melodiously, a love song. She replied with another, and quick as lightning, I observed her, whilst the sentinal had his back momentarily turned, pitch her glove to the young man, he dexterously and without detection, caught it. Slipping into his room he drew a billet doux from the glove, read it, and writing an answer which he placed in the little mail bag, he returned to the door and pitched the glove to his lady love without being seen by the sentinal. I am thus particular in these details, because it was a love affair, prosecuted under more difficulties than any I had ever known.

The second prisoner to remember Belle was an Old Capitol regular, Gus Williams, of Vienna, in Fairfax County. While Gus was making himself comfortable one day, he heard a bunch of the boys whooping it up with "Maryland, My Maryland." Whereupon he strolled over, and gave voice to this opinion:

"You boys sing that well, but I've heard 'My Maryland' sung here in the old building in a way that would make you feel like jumping out of the window and swimming across the Potomac. When Belle Boyd was here I was on the same floor. She would sing that song as if her very soul was in every word she uttered. It used to bring a lump up in my throat every time I heard it. It seemed like my heart was ready to jump out—as if I could put my finger down and touch it. I've seen men, when she was singing, walk off to one side and pull out their handkerchiefs and wipe their eyes, for fear some one would see them doing the baby act.
* * *

"And on Sundays, when there was preaching down in the yard, she would be allowed to come down and sit near the preacher. If you could only have seen how the fellows would try to get near her as she passed. And if she gave them a look or a smile, it did them more good than the preaching. You wouldn't hear a cuss word from any of them for a week, even if one of the guards would swear at them or threaten them."

The prison official who likewise remembered Belle was the Provost Marshal of the District of Columbia, young Major William E. Doster. In his reminiscences, *Lincoln and Episodes of the Civil War,* neither the passage of years nor the dignity of his General's rank dimmed the freshness of his recollection of a onetime ward:

Belle Boyd was a lively, spirited young lady, full of caprices and a genuine Rebel. In person she was tall, with light hair and blue eyes. Her features were too irregular to be pretty. It was her dashing manner (fashioned after Lady Gay Spanker), and air of joyous recklessness which made her interesting. At the time of her arrest she was living with her father, a farmer, beyond Winchester, and became known for the influence her coquetry acquired over the Union officers under Banks, and for the information she gave Jackson. . . . She was taken to the room formerly occupied by Mrs. Morris and, as she was at the time the only woman prisoner in Washington, was well pleased with the attention of which she found herself the object.

The first time I called on her, she was reading *Harper's* and eating peaches. She remarked she could afford to remain here, if Stanton could afford to keep her. There was so much company and so little to do. Besides, it was an excellent chance to brush up her literature and get her wedding outfit ready. This defiant indifference soon subsided. Open air and horseback exercise were in her case constitutional necessities. She soon began to languish and begged to be permitted to walk out in the company of an officer. The Secretary [of War], to whom the request was referred, refused to grant the permission. Then she became subdued, always, however, jesting with the surgeon and asking when he intended to give her the medicine he had prescribed—freedom? During the whole stay, she was never, to my knowledge, found in ill-humor, but bravely endured a tedious and companionless imprisonment.

She used to say she was a Rebel to the backbone and, if she had the chance, intended to help the Confederate cause all she could.

Once released from behind bars and, via the exchange vessel, once more on Confederate soil, Belle found the opportunity to pay another visit to her favorite soldier, General Jackson. The time was late September, 1862, in her home country. What ensued was well remembered years later by an eyewitness, Old Jack's aide, Captain James Power Smith (by now a minister of the gospel) :

One day at Bunker Hill, the notable female scout, Belle Boyd, made an appearance on horseback, with the escort of a young Confederate cavalryman. She was well mounted, and quite a soldierly figure, and asked to see General Jackson. But the General was averse, and more than once refused to see the young woman, of whose loyalty he was not altogether assured. She was much disappointed and went away quite angry with the aide who had denied her admission to the general's tent. Some days after this she sent a message that if she ever caught that young man in Martinsburg she would cut his ears off.

Up to this point the eyes gazing upon Belle Boyd have been masculine ones. The year 1862 concludes with an impression by a girl, and one of her own age. This was the former Margaret Bowden, of Norfolk, not long married to Major Joseph van H. Nash, C.S.A., and at the moment (about November 10) residing in the home of a Mrs. Rixey at Culpeper, Virginia. Belle herself was tarrying there, whilst en route from Martinsburg to Charlottesville—see Chapter 11 of her book—in the hope of contriving a visit to General Lee at his temporary headquarters in the Culpeper area. Mrs. Rixey's parlor, that evening, was astir with young Confederate officers and ladies, and a merry party was in progress. When their hostess introduced the two girls, Margaret Nash did not catch the other's name:

> She seemed to be nineteen, or, perhaps, twenty—rather young, I thought, to be traveling alone. True, I was not older, but then I was married, which made all the difference in the world. What made her an object of special interest to every woman present, was that she was exceedingly well dressed. It had been a long, long time since we had seen a new dress! She was a brilliant talker, and soon everybody in the room was attracted to her, especially the men. She talked chiefly to the men—indeed, I am afraid she did not care particularly for the women—and at first we were a little piqued; but when we found that she was devoted to The Cause we were ready to forgive her anything. She soon let us know that she had come directly from Washington, where she had been a prisoner of the United States. She showed us her watch and told us how the prisoners in Washington had made the money up among themselves and presented it to her just before she left. I wish I had listened better to her account of her prison life and her adventures; but I was on the outer rim of the charmed circles. . . .

I got sleepy, slipped quietly out of the room, and went upstairs and to bed. My room-mate undressed and got to bed so quickly that night that I did not wake. The next morning when the maid came in to make the fire, we woke face to face in the same bed, and then she told me that her name was Belle Boyd, and I knew for the first time that my bedfellow was the South's famous female spy. When she got up she took a large bottle of cologne and poured it into the basin in which she was going to bathe. It was the first cologne I had seen for more than a year, and it was the last I saw until I ran the blockade.

May, 1863, in Virginia—in one of the loveliest of its sections—is the scene for a sprightly memory of Belle by the Maryland Confederate cavalryman, Major Harry Gilmor. The temper of that scene is similar to the one limned by Captain J. P. Smith some months earlier. "On my way down the Valley," Gilmor recalled, three years later,

I met at Woodstock my old acquaintance, Miss Belle Boyd, whom I had known since the autumn of '61. Miss Belle begged to accompany me on my expedition. I got off by telling her she must first have General Jenkins's permission. I rose before the sun, and was ready to start, when I discovered she had carried my sabre and pistols to her room, to prevent my slipping off without her, as she was shrewd enough to know I would do. Down came Miss Belle, dressed in her neat-fitting habit, with a pretty little belt round her waist, from which the butts of two small pistols were peeping, cased in patent leather holsters.

She rode with me to the quarters of General Jenkins, to whom I had to report before passing out through his lines. We found him sitting before his tent, and after dispatching my business Miss Belle presented her request. I fixed myself behind her, that I might give a signal to the general not to consent. The fact is, I did not care to be accompanied by a woman on so perilous an enterprise; for, though she was a splendid and reckless rider, of unflinching courage, and her whole soul bound up in the Southern cause, yet she was a little— mark you, only a *little*—headstrong and willful, and I thought it best, both for her sake and mine, that she should not go. I hope Miss Belle will forgive this little ruse.

Just two months later, August 4, 1863, elements of the 1st New York (Lincoln) Cavalry took over Martinsburg so abruptly that many an active Confederate sympathizer was unable to flee South. Among these was Belle Boyd. The Federal officer sent to interrogate her, Captain James H. Stevenson of Philadelphia, had already had a picturesque parley in the field with Major Gilmor. The reactions of these two opponents were substantially the same about their mutual acquaintance :

> She began to tell how irksome it was to be so closely confined, and wanted to know if the *general* wouldn't allow her the liberty of the town (!). I smilingly told her that she was regarded as a very important personage, and capable of doing us too much injury to be allowed to go at large; which seemed to tickle her vanity, and she said, with a curl of her lip :
>
> 'I hope "you all" are not afraid of a poor weak woman ?'
>
> I reminded her of the powerful influence she was said to exert over General Stuart's cavalry, inspiring them to acts which astonished not only the Yankees

When Belle Boyd went riding . . . (Frontispiece to the English edition, Belle Boyd, in Camp and Prison . . . [2 vols., London, 1865]. Her autograph reproduced as Mrs. Sam Hardinge. From the set at the University of North Carolina Library)

but themselves. She laughed heartily at this, and
wanted to know what we had heard of her.

'Well,' said I, 'it is rumored among our men that you
led Stuart's column in his raid around McClellan on
the Peninsula, and also in a similar raid in Maryland.'

This was a 'whopper,' but I wished to gratify her
ruling passion, vanity. She looked very much pleased,
and said : 'You all don't believe that, do you?'

'Well,' said I, 'the men think so, but if you deny it
I will believe you.'

To this she made no reply, but excused herself for a
moment and went up stairs. In a very few moments I
was startled at seeing a tall figure, in the uniform of a
Confederate colonel of cavalry, enter from the rear of
the parlor. It was Miss Boyd, who wished to impress
me with her military appearance. She had a pistol in
her belt, and really looked like a dangerous customer.
I feigned alarm, told her I would surrender, and hoped
she would not shoot me; at which she laughed heartily,
and said that was just the way the Yankees did when
General Stuart met them.

She wore a fine gray cloth jacket, slashed with gold
lace on the breast and sleeves, a pair of white buckskin
gauntlets, a dove-colored soft felt hat, with a long dark
plume, and a gray skirt or riding habit. A fine leather
belt, with a silver-mounted revolver in a patent-leather
case, ornamented her waist, and she carried a fancy
riding whip in her hand. She was tall and of good
figure, and in her uniform looked well.

She wore the rank of a colonel C.S.A., and she told
me she often rode with General Stuart at the head of
his cavalry. She showed me a gold watch, studded with
jewels, presented to her by the officers of Stuart's cavalry, as the inscription fully proved. Altogether she
seemed very proud of her connection with the Con-

federate raiders, and of the services she had rendered
to the Confederacy.

'Now,' said I, 'after seeing and hearing what I have,
you can't blame me if I report to the colonel that you
are altogether too dangerous a person to be at large.'

This seemed to startle her, and she said : 'I hope you
all would not send me to prison?'

'Perhaps not,' said I, 'but we must keep a sharp eye
upon all your movements.'

We had a sentinel at the house, to keep her from
communicating with any of the inhabitants, and to prevent her sending news to the enemy. She had frequently
passed through our lines in disguise, carrying mail to
the south, giving information of our strength and
position. * * *

She had brown hair, hazel eyes, a somewhat long oval
face, with a finely formed but prominent nose, and
rather prominent teeth, which she exposed a good deal
when smiling or talking. Her skin was fair, and her
face sprinkled with small freckles; but she was what
might be called rather good looking, although by no
means a beauty.

Not quite one year later, and how altered is Belle's situation! She languishes in that festering focus of Yankeedom,
Boston, Massachusetts. She is under arrest once more. Her
most recent memory is the frustating one of capture at sea,
and her nearest anticipation is of a forlorn future. Nevertheless, the impression conveyed by an interview in the Boston
Post — reprinted down at Washington on May 25, 1864, by the
Daily National Intelligencer as a page-one story — is scarcely
that of a shattered waif :

She is accompanied by three servants—a white
woman, and black girl, and a black boy. She converses

Belle Boyd—just out of prison? Allegedly taken by Alexander Gardner at Washington City, December 1, 1863, this rare likeness (from the negative) is said to have been made at the order of Secretary of War Stanton, on the occasion of Belle's release from her second incarceration in the Old Capitol-Carroll Prison. She was allegedly escorted to Gardner's studio by Pryce Lewis, a Pinkerton detective assigned to guard duty at the prison. The original of the photograph, presumed lost, was found among Lewis's effects after his suicide in New York City, December 5, 1911. (Courtesy the National Archives)

freely and well, and is evidently a female of intelligence and quick understanding. Her bearing during the passage—in act and speech—is described as strictly becoming and proper in all respects. She entertains and expresses strong admiration of sympathy with the South, but not in offensive terms. She thinks the pending contest between Lee and Grant will terminate the war in favor of the victor. These generals she considers the two ablest officers in the country. During the attack upon the Greyhound Miss Boyd came on deck, took a seat upon a bale of cotton, and quietly sat fanning herself, and watching the explosion of the shells. She is a tall, well-formed female, blonde, and graceful in her manners. There is much curiosity to see her but the Marshal is so choice of his charge that few are gratified. It is thought she will be paroled, and Boston left without a Belle.

So there stands Miss Belle Boyd, glorified against the broad noonday horizon of her career. Something of Joan of Arc, something of Cleopatra, "undeniably," as the Colonel's lady assured Sam Hardinge (Chapter 23), "the pet of the Confederacy."

Considered as a spy, she was too open and amateurish for first-class feats of espionage, yet she engendered confusion amid the foe. Considered as a woman, she was no beauty, yet she proved herself something of a *femme fatale*. Considered as a phenomenon, was she not the personification of pulsing youth swept onwards by breathless idealism for a romanticized cause?

Such an image clings to the memory when more effective ones have faded. The fact that Belle labored for the losing side only adds to the pathos of her story. This pathos increases when we realize—as we watch her, toward the close of her book, embarking at Quebec for the Old World—that she was in fact sailing away into an aftermath. For if the remainder of her life could scarcely be called uninteresting, its supreme hours had tolled. It is as a heroine daring the buffets of storm and stress that one best remembers her.

And if we envisage the name and fame of Belle Boyd as representative of all those who ceaselessly function, who embrace life's circumstances and to a degree shape and color them — if, in a word, we view her as one who *strove* — then we will not only renew our awareness that even the worst of wars can become, to the proper kind of character, a guide line and whetstone, but we will also carry with us a heartening and a sprightly memory.

Belle Boyd in Camp and Prison

BELLE BOYD

IN

CAMP AND PRISON.

WRITTEN BY HERSELF.

WITH AN

INTRODUCTION,

BY GEORGE AUGUSTA SALA.

———

NEW YORK:
BLELOCK & COMPANY,
19 BEEKMAN STREET.
1865.

Contents

CHAPTER V.

CHAPTER VI.

CHAPTER VII.

CHAPTER VIII.

CHAPTER IX.

CHAPTER X.

CHAPTER XI.

CHAPTER XII

CHAPTER XIII.

CHAPTER XIV

CHAPTER XV.

CHAPTER XVI

CHAPTER XXIV.

CHAPTER XXV.

CHAPTER XXVI.

CHAPTER XXVII

CHAPTER XXVIII.

Introduction

BY A FRIEND OF THE SOUTH

"Will you take my life?"

This was the somewhat startling question put to me by Mrs. Hardinge—better known as *Belle Boyd*—on my recent introduction to her in Jermyn Street.

"Madam," said I, "a sprite like you, who has so often run the gauntlet by sea and land, who has had so many hair-breadth escapes by flood and field, must bear a 'charmed life:' I dare not attempt it." Then, placing in my hands a roll of manuscript, she said, "Take this; read it, revise it, rewrite it, publish it, or burn it—do what you will. It is the story of my adventures, misfortunes, imprisonments, and persecutions. I have written all from memory since I have been here in London; and, perhaps, by putting me in the third person, you can make a book that will be not only acceptable to the public and profitable to myself, but one that will do some good to the cause of my poor country, a cause which seems to be so little understood in England."

I took the manuscript, promising to look it over, and return it with an estimate of its merits. I have done so; and hence the publication of *"Belle Boyd, in Camp and Prison."* The work is entirely her own, with the exception of a few suggestions in the shape of footnotes—the simple, unambitious narrative of

99

an enthusiastic and intrepid school-girl, who had not yet seen her seventeenth summer when the cloud of war darkened her land, changing all the music of her young life, her peaceful "home, sweet home," into the bugle blasts of battle, into scenes of death and most tumultuous sorrow.

Believing, with all the people of the South, in the sovereignty of the States, and the absolute political and moral right of secession, our young heroine, like Joan of Arc, inspired and fired by the "tyranny impending," resolved to devote her hands and heart, and life, if need be, to the sacred cause of freedom and independence. How much she has done and suffered in the great struggle which has crimsoned the "Sunny South" with the "blood of the martyrs," we shall leave the reader to gather from the narrative itself.

But, by way of introduction, I have a few incidental facts to relate; and it is proper to add, that I do it entirely on my own responsibility, and without consulting "our heroine" in the matter.

At the time of my presentation to Mrs. Hardinge, above alluded to, I found the lady in very great distress of mind and body. She was sick, without money, and driven almost to distraction by the cruel news that her husband was suffering the "tender mercies" of a Federal prison. Lieutenant Hardinge was in *irons*; and his friends were prohibited from sending him food or clothing! Letters addressed to his young wife, containing remittances, were intercepted; and thus I found her, not quite friendless, in this great wilderness of London, but, what is worse, absolutely destitute of that indispensable and all-prevailing friend — MONEY.

The sight of a pair of flowing eyes, that for thirteen long months had refused to weep in a Northern prison, were enough to call forth the following communication, addressed to the *Morning Herald,* that able and consistent defender of the Southern cause : —

"A WORD TO CONFEDERATE SYMPATHIZERS

"Sir : — Your readers cannot have forgotten the glowing description of the recent romantic wedding of 'Belle Boyd' (*La Belle Rebelle*), so pleasantly celebrated a few months since at 'a fashionable hotel in Jermyn Street.'

"Alas, poor Belle ! Her bridal bliss was 'like the snow-fall on a river.' Her husband of a day is now tasting the sweets of a Yankee prison, and she (who 'was made his wedded wife yestreen') all the bitterness of poverty and exile. After enduring for many a long and weary month the insults, sufferings, and persecutions of the 'Old Capitol Prison,' I heard the afflicted lady say yesterday that she 'had rather be there as she was than here as she is.' And why? Cut off from all pecuniary resources at home, she has had to part with her jewellery piece by piece, including her 'wedding presents,' to pay her weekly bills.

"We can well understand how trouble like that would smite the heart of a high-toned woman, the daughter of affluence and luxury, even more cruelly than the tortures of a Federal prison.

"Without further comment, I will only add that Madame Hardinge (Belle Boyd) has prepared for publication a narrative of her adventures, imprisonment, and sufferings, for which there are no lack of publishers ready to advance a handsome sum; but she has recently received threatening intimations that her husband's life depends upon the suppression of her story !

"The father of 'Belle Boyd,' a most respectable Virginian gentleman, has lately died, at the age of forty-six, from a disease induced by his daughter's sufferings. These are the sad, simple facts of the case, and I commend them to the kind consideration of Confederate sympathizers in England. Surely poverty, in a young and accomplished woman, is not only a sacred claim to the protection of society — it is also the very highest credential of honor."

The above was copied by one of the London morning papers, with the following sympathetic comments : —

"We are in a position to verify all that is here stated, and a great deal more. Probably the history of the world does not contain a parallel case to that of this newly married lady, who has just only emerged from her teens. Her adventures in the midst of the American war surpass any thing to be met with in the pages of fiction. Her great beauty, elegant manners, and personal attractions generally, in conjunction with her romantic history before her marriage, which took place only three months ago at the West End, in the presence of a fashionable assemblage of affectionate and admiring friends, concur to invest her with attributes which render her such a heroine as the world has seldom, if ever, seen in a lady only now in her twentieth year."

Several of the New York journals also copied the above, and one of them, *The World* published the following communication : —

"I would respectfully ask the use of a small space in the columns of *The World* to say a word regarding these statements.

"Within the past few months Mrs. Hardinge's agent in the United States has sent her bills of exchange on London bankers to the amount of eight hundred pounds sterling, or nearly ten thousand dollars in greenbacks. She has never received a sou of this money. Her letters have been opened here and the drafts extracted before going on to her, and this is the reason she is in distress. Too proud to beg, too honorable to borrow, she pawned her jewels and wedding presents, piece by piece, until her situation became known to her friends. Cut off from pecuniary resources, a stranger in a strange land, her husband in a Northern prison, what could she do? 'Surely poverty in a young and accomplished woman is not only a sacred claim to the protection of society, but is also the very highest credential of honor.'

"I received during the week a letter from this poor lady; and she says, 'I think it is so cruel in the Yankees to intercept my letters and stop my money, and I don't know why I am thus persecuted.' It *is* cruel, and it is beneath the dignity of any Government to stoop to such means of revenge. Such things in the dark ages would be called unchivalrous. Good God! can this be the nineteenth century?

"Mr. Hardinge came here, as a peaceable citizen would come, to attend to his private business and return to England. He had no *Confederate duties.* Having nearly completed his labors, he went to Martinsburg to see his wife's mother, and while returning thence, with all the necessary papers and passes in his possession, was arrested this side of Harper's Ferry. Confined in nondescript guard-houses, in jails, and dragged about like a convicted felon, he was finally lodged in the Carroll Prison at Washington, and from thence taken to Fort Delaware. After suffering two months' confinement, he was unconditionally released, and sailed for Europe on the 8th February. She will not be in want or distress when he arrives in London. For what he was arrested and confined is to him yet a mystery.

"The intimation to Mrs. Hardinge that the publication of her work would endanger the life of her husband was not without foundation, as there are officials high in power at Washington of whom she knows more than is generally known, and who will be shown up in their true light and colors in her book. They fear the truth."

It is pleasant to add, that the moment Belle Boyd's necessities became known in London the most generous offers of assistance were literally showered upon her by ladies and gentlemen of the highest and best classes in England. And here I cannot refrain from saying that, after several years of observation and experience, I cannot but regard the real nobility of England as the noblest and most hospitable people in the world. The Southern planters rank—or, alas! did rank—next.

But this is a digression. Let us glance a moment at Belle Boyd in prison, sketched by other hands than her own.

In the month of August, 1862, the editor of the *Iowa Herald*, D. A. Mahony, Esq., a strong Anti-Black Republican, but an able and eloquent supporter of the Constitution and the Union, was taken from his bed, and, without arraignment or trial, and without even being informed of "the things whereof he was accused," hurried away to Washington, and thrust into the "Old Capitol Prison." What he saw and suffered there he has already told the world, in words that ought to burn and brand forever his lawless and infamous persecutors.

The following extracts from Mr. Mahony's journal, published by Carleton, of New York, give us characteristic glimpses of Belle Boyd in prison : —

"Among the prisoners in the Old Capitol when I reached there was the somewhat famous Belle Boyd, to whom has been attributed the defeat of General Banks, in the Shenandoah Valley, by Stonewall Jackson. Belle, as she is familiarly called by all the prisoners, and affectionately so by the Confederates, was arrested and imprisoned as a spy. . . .

"The first intimation some of us newcomers in the Old Capitol had of the fact of there being a lady in that place was the hearing of 'Maryland, my Maryland,' sung the first night of our incarceration, in what we could not be mistaken was a woman's voice. On inquiry, we were informed that it was Belle Boyd. Some of us had never heard of the lady before; and we were all inquiring about her. Who was she? Where was she from? And what did she do? . . .

"Belle was put in solitary confinement, but allowed to have

her room-door open, and to sit outside of it in a hall or stair-landing in the evening. Whenever she availed herself of this privilege, as she frequently did, the greatest curiosity was manifested by the victims of despotism to see her. Her room being on the second story, those who occupied the third story were civilians from Fredericksburg. . . .

"But we must not lose sight of Belle Boyd. I heard her voice, my first night in prison, singing 'Maryland, my Maryland,' the first time I had ever heard the Southern song. The words, stirring enough to Southern hearts, were enunciated by her with such peculiar expression as to touch even the sensibilities which did not sympathize with the cause which inspired the song. It was difficult to listen unmoved to this lady, throwing her whole soul, as it were, into the expression of the sentiments of devotion to the South, defiance to the North, and affectionately confident appeals to Maryland, which form the burden of that celebrated song. The pathos of her voice, her apparently forlorn condition, and, at those times when her soul seemed absorbed in the thoughts she was uttering in song, her melancholy manner, affected all who heard her, not only with compassion for her, but with an interest in her which came near, on several occasions, bringing about a conflict between the prisoners and the guards.

"Fronting on the same hall or stair-landing on which Belle Boyd's room-door opened, were three other rooms, all filled to their capacity with prisoners, mostly Confederate officers. Several of these were personally acquainted with Belle, as she was most of the time, and by nearly every one, called. In the evenings these prisoners were permitted to crowd inside of their room-doors, whence they could see and sometimes exchange a word with Belle. When this liberty was not allowed, she contrived to procure a large marble, around which she would tie a note written on tissue-paper, and, when the guard turned his back to patrol his beat in the hall, she would roll the marble into one of the open doors of the Confederate prisoners' rooms. When the contents were read and noted a missive would be written in reply, and the marble, similarly burdened as it came, would be rolled back to Belle. Thus was a correspondence established and kept up between Belle and her fellow-prisoners, till a more convenient and effective mode was discovered. This occurred soon after some of us were transferred from room No. 13 to No. 10.

"One day Mr. Sheward and I were rummaging in an old, dirty, doorless closet in No. 10, when we discovered an opening in the floor, and, looking down, perceived the light in the room below, which happened to be that occupied by Belle Boyd. Here was a discovery! No sooner was it made, than we set to writing a note, which was tied to a thread and dropped down through the discovered aperture. It happened to be seen by Belle, who soon returned the compliment. Thenceforth a regular mail passed through the floor in No. 10; and though Lieutenant Miller and Superintendent Wood prided themselves on being well informed of every occurrence which took place in prison contrary to the rules, with all their vigilance, aided by the presence, as they admitted, of a detective in every room of the prison, except that of Belle Boyd, they never discovered this through-the-floor mail. It would not be the least interesting chapter in the history of the Old Capitol to give in it these letters of Belle Boyd. But the time is not yet."

These last words of Mahony remind me of the fact that Belle Boyd, the "rebel spy," is in possession of a vast amount of information implicating certain high officials at Washington, both in public and private *scandals,* which she deems it imprudent at present to publish. *"The time is not yet."*

"Belle usually commenced her evening entertainment," writes Mahony, "with 'Maryland.'" Up to this time this patriotic and spirit-stirring song, written by young Randall, of

Baltimore, must be regarded as the "Marseillaise" of the South. And as it is as yet but little known in England, I will here quote it entire —

AS SUNG BY BELLE BOYD IN PRISON.

"The despot's heel is on thy shore,
          Maryland!
His torch is at thy temple door,
          Maryland!
Avenge the patriotic gore
That flecked the streets of Baltimore,
And be the battle queen of yore,
          Maryland! my Maryland!

"Hark to a wandering son's appeal,
          Maryland!
My Mother State, to thee I kneel,
          Maryland!
For life and death, for woe and weal,
Thy peerless chivalry reveal,
And gird thy beauteous limbs with steel,
          Maryland! my Maryland!

"Thou wilt not cower in the dust,
          Maryland!
Thy beaming sword shall never rust,
          Maryland!
Remember Carroll's sacred trust,
Remember Howard's warlike thrust,
And all thy slumberers with the just,
          Maryland! my Maryland!

"Come! 'tis the red dawn of the day,
          Maryland!

Come with thy panoplied array,
     Maryland!
With Ringgold's spirit for the fray,
With Watson's blood at Monterey,
With fearless Lowe, and dashing May,
     Maryland! my Maryland!

"Dear mother! burst the tyrant's chain,
     Maryland!
Virginia should not call in vain,
     Maryland!
She meets her sisters on the plain:
Sic semper, 'tis her proud refrain,
That baffles minions back amain,
     Maryland! my Maryland!

"Come! for thy shield is bright and strong,
     Maryland!
Come! for thy dalliance does thee wrong,
     Maryland!
Come to thine own heroic throng,
That stalks with Liberty along,
And gives a new *Key* to thy song,
     Maryland! my Maryland!

"I see the blush upon thy cheek,
     Maryland!
And thou wert ever bravely meek,
     Maryland!
But, lo! there surges forth a shriek,
From hill to hill, from creek to creek:
Potomac calls to Chesapeake,
     Maryland! my Maryland!

"Thou wilt not yield the Vandal toll,
     Maryland!

Thou wilt not crook to his control,
                    Maryland!
Better the fire upon thee roll,
Better the shot, the blade, the bowl,
Than crucifixion of the soul,
                    Maryland! my Maryland!

"I hear the distant thunder hum,
                    Maryland!
The Old Line's bugle, fife, and drum,
                    Maryland!
She is not dead, nor deaf, nor dumb,
Hurrah! she spurns the Northern scum!
She breathes, she lives; she'll come, she'll come!
                    Maryland! my Maryland!"

"The singing of this song," says Mahony, "often brought
Belle in collision with the guard who passed to and fro in front
of her room-door. It was, of course, provoking; but was such
a place a proper one in which to imprison a female, and
especially one who, whatever may have been her offence, was,
in the estimation of the world, a lady?" . . .

Many a patriotic lady of Baltimore has been arrested by
Federal officers for singing the patriotic song of "Maryland."
But what will the English reader say when he learns the following fact? At one of the most celebrated eating, drinking,
and singing saloons in London, the classical resort of authors,
actors, poets, and wits, for these hundred years at least, the
famous band of boys, who sing better than any choir outside
the Sistine Chapel in Rome, after having got "the words and
air of 'Maryland' by heart," are not allowed to sing it, *for fear
of giving offence!* OFFENCE TO WHOM? It might possibly
"offend" *somebody*, were they to chant the "Marseillaise."
    To return again to our caged bird : —

"Belle was allowed to go in the yard on Sundays, when there was preaching there. On these occasions she wore a small Confederate flag in her bosom. No sooner would her presence be known to the Confederate prisoners, than they manifested towards her every mark of respect, which persons in their situation could bestow. Most of them doffed their hats as she approached them, and she, with a grace and dignity that might be envied by a queen, extended her hand to them, as she moved along to her designated position in a corner near the preacher. We Northern prisoners of state envied the Confederates who enjoyed the acquaintance of Belle Boyd, and who secured for her such glances of sympathy as can only glow from a woman's eyes.

"Belle's situation was a peculiarly trying one. If she kept her room, a solitary prisoner, her health, and probably her mind, would become affected by the confinement and solitude; if she indulged herself by sitting outside her room-door, she became exposed to the gaze of more than a hundred prisoners, nearly all of them strangers to her, and many of them her enemies by the laws of war. Nor was this all. She could not help hearing the comments made on her, and the opinions expressed of her, by passers-by; some of them complimentary and flattering, it is true, but oftentimes couched in expressions which were not what she should hear. The guards, too, were sometimes rude to her, both by word and action. At one time, especially, one of the guards presented his bayoneted musket at her in a threatening manner. She, brave and unterrified, dared the craven-hearted fellow to put his threat into execution. It was well for him that he did not, for he would have been torn into pieces before it could have been known to the prison authorities what had happened.

"Belle was subjected to another worse annoyance and indignity than even this. Her room fronted on A Street, and, as usual with all the prisoners whose rooms had windows opening towards the street, Belle would sit at her window sometimes, and look abroad upon the houses, streets, and people of the city named after Washington. It happened frequently that troops were moving to and fro, and it was on such occasions especially that Belle, prompted by that curiosity which seems to be a law of nature in mankind, would look through her barred window at the soldiers. No sooner would they perceive her, than they indulged in coarse jests, vulgar expressions, and the vilest slang of the brothel, made still more coarse, vulgar, and indecent by the throwing off of the little restraint which civilized society places upon the most abandoned prostitutes and their companions. . . .

"Did the officers of the troops passing by permit the soldiers to thus insult a female, and subject themselves to such scornful and contemptuous reproof? the reader will be apt to inquire. Yes; and participated with the soldiers in uttering the most vulgar language and indecent allusions to the imprisoned woman; and that, too, without having the remotest idea of who she was, or of what she was accused. It was enough for them that she was a defenceless woman, to insult and outrage her by such language as they would not dare to apply in the public streets to an abandoned woman who had her liberty. And these men were going forth to fight the battles of the Union! They had just parted with mothers, wives, and sisters. It would seem that, in doing so, they turned their backs upon the virtues which give beauty to woman and dignity to man. . . .

"At the general exchange of prisoners, which took place in September, Belle Boyd was sent to Richmond. As soon as it became known in the 'Old Capitol' that she was about to leave, there was not one, Federalist or Confederate, prisoner of state, officer of the 'Old Capitol,' as well as prisoner of war, who did not feel that he was about to part with one for whom he had, at least, a great personal regard. With many it was more than mere regard.

"Every inmate of the 'Old Capitol' tried to procure some token of remembrance from Belle, and there was scarcely one who did not bestow on her some mark of regard, esteem, or affection, as their sentiments and feelings influenced them severally, and as the means at their disposal afforded them an opportunity to manifest their sensibility. While every man who had any delicacy of feeling for the apparently forlorn prisoner rejoiced at her release from such a loathsome place, and from being subjected, as she continually was, to insult and contumely, there was not a gentleman in the 'Old Capitol' whose emotions did not overcome him, as he saw her leave the place for home."

Thus kindly and warmly writes the veteran editor of the *Iowa Herald,* one of the victims of Seward's "little bell," for whose improvement and release the "Powers" at Washington, "clothed with a little brief authority," have given no reason or explanation. But was not Mr. Mahony "guilty" of being the Democratic nominee for Congress?

A somewhat more poetic picture of *"La Belle Rebelle"* is given by the accomplished author of "Guy Livingstone," in his "Border and Bastille," written while tasting the sweets of Federal tyranny in that same "Old Capitol" Prison : —

"Through the bars of a second-story window that fronted each turn of my tramp, I saw — this : a slight figure, in the freshest summer-toilette of cool pink muslin; close braids of dark hair shading clear, pale cheeks; eyes that were made to sparkle, though the look in them was very sad; and the languid bowing down of the small head told of something worse than weariness.

"Truly a pretty picture, though framed in such a rude setting; but almost startling, at first, as the apparition of the fair witch in the forest to Christabelle. . . .

"No need to ask what her crime had been : aid and abetment of the South suggested itself before you detected the ensign of the South that the *démoiselle* still wore undauntedly —a pearl *solitaire,* fashioned as a Single Star. I may not deny that my gloomy 'constitutional' seemed thenceforward a shade or two less dreary; but, though community of suffering does much to abridge ceremony, it was some days before I interchanged with the fair captive any sign beyond the mechanical lifting of my cap, when I entered and left her presence, duly acknowledged from above. One evening I chanced to be loitering almost under the window. A low, significant cough made me look up; I saw the flash of a gold bracelet, and the wave of a white hand; and there fell at my feet a fragrant, pearly rosebud, nestling in fresh green leaves. My thanks were, perforce, confined to a gesture and a dozen hurried words; but I would the prison-beauty could believe that fair Jane Beaufort's rose was not more prized than hers, though the first was a lovetoken to a king, the last only a graceful gift to an unlucky stranger. I suppose that most men, whose past is not utterly barren of romance, are weak enough to keep some withered flowers till they have lived memory down; and I pretend not to be wiser than my fellows. Other fragrant messengers followed in their season; but if ever I 'win hame to my ain countrie,' I make mine avow to enshrine that first rose-bud in my *reliquaire* with all honor and solemnity, there to abide till one of us shall be dust."

With this explanatory introduction, I have now only to commend *"La Belle Rebelle"* to the kindly sympathies of her readers—not as an authoress (to this she makes no pretensions); nor as a partisan soldier, although as such she has done good service in the cause; nor even as a freed bird from the "Old Capitol" cage; but simply as a woman—a warm-hearted, impulsive, heroic woman of the South, who, maddened by the wrongs and cruelties inflicted upon her people, and exalted, by the love she bore them, above the common cares and considerations of life, dashed into the field, bearing more than a woman's part in her country's struggle for liberty.

Like the flashing of the plume in the helmet of Navarre, the glancing of the Confederate ensign, when waved by a woman's hand, has never failed to fire the soldier's heart to "lofty deeds and daring high;" and on more than a hundred Southern battle-fields that proud banner, consecrated by prayers and kisses, baptized in tears and blood, has been greeted by the closing eyes of its dying defenders as the oriflamme of victory. Though lost for the moment in clouds and darkness, prophetic Hope, the last solace of the unfortunate, still waits and watches for its reappearance as the harbinger of Southern liberty and independence : —

> "For the battle to the strong
>   Is not given,
> While the Judge of Right and Wrong
>   Sits in heaven !
> And the God of David still
> Guides the pebble with his will.
> There are giants yet to kill,
>   Wrongs unshriven !"

Since the above was written, the Southern people have suffered a heavy calamity in the assassination of the President of the United States. Not that Mr. Lincoln was their friend : on the contrary, every man and woman in the South, and every child born within the last four years, regarded him as the official head and personal embodiment of all their enemies. But, by the removal of the Commander-in-Chief of the great army and navy with which they were contending, a far more vindictive and unrelenting man is invested with the supreme power of the nation. Abraham Lincoln, with all his faults and fanaticism, his angularities of character and vulgarities of manner, had a sunny side to his nature; and there is every reason to believe that, with his idol Union once nominally restored, he would have adopted an indulgent, humane policy towards the brave and vanquished South, believing, with the great poet, that

> "Earthly power doth then show likest God's,
> When mercy seasons justice."

The suspicion which has been officially and wickedly thrown upon an honorable and heroic people, touching "the deep damnation of his taking off," is sufficiently answered by the universal regret expressed throughout the Confederacy at President Lincoln's death, the public denunciation of his murderer, and the horror everywhere felt at the idea of being "ruled with a rod of iron" by such an unprincipled demagogue as Andrew Johnson! It is usual, in cases of murder, to look for the criminal among those who expect to be benefited by the crime. In the death of Lincoln, his immediate successor in office alone receives "the benefit of his dying."

While deploring the event which places the reins of power in the hands of one as unfit to control the destinies of a great nation as was the reckless youth to guide the chariot of the Sun, there can be no injustice in alluding to the fact, that the Northern Powers and the Northern Press have much to answer for on the head of assassination. I have yet to learn that the written programme of Colonel Dahlgren, which designed the burning of Richmond, the ravaging of its women, and the murder of President Davis and all his cabinet, has ever been disavowed or denounced by the Washington Government, or by the newspapers that support it. Philosophy and religion alike teach us that, while *crime* only belongs to the *act*, the *sin* of murder consists in the *intent*. In the light of this judgment, faint in comparison with that "awful light" yet to be thrown, not only upon all human actions, but upon "the very thoughts and intents of the heart," both North and South, friend and foe, rebel and loyalist, the victim and the victor, the living and the dead, must all be tried and sentenced by ONE who "judgeth not as man judgeth."

In the mean time, let us pray, and hope, and labor for liberty, love, and peace.

LONDON, *May* 17*th* 1865.

BELLE BOYD

Chapter I

Home.—Glimpse at Washington City.

My English readers, who love their own hearths and homes
so dearly, will pardon an exile if she commences the narrative
of her adventures with a brief reminiscence of her far-distant
birthplace—

"Loved to the last, whatever intervenes
Between us and our childhood's sympathy,
Which still reverts to what first caught the eye."

There is, perhaps, no tract of country in the world more
lovely than the Valley of the Shenandoah. There is, or rather,
I should say, there was, no prettier or more peaceful little
village than Martinsburg, where I was born in 1844.

All those charms with which the fancy of Goldsmith invested
the Irish hamlet in the days of its prosperity were realized in
my native village. Alas! Martinsburg has met a more cruel
fate than that of "sweet Auburn." The one, at least, still lives
in song, and will continue to be a household word as long as
the English language shall be spoken: the other was destined
to be the first and fairest offering upon the altar of Confederate

117

freedom; but no poet has arisen from her ruins to perpetuate her name.

While America was yet at peace within itself, while the States were yet united, many very beautiful residences were erected in the vicinity of Martinsburg, which may be said to have attained some degree of importance as a town, when the large machinery buildings were raised, at a vast outlay, by the Baltimore and Ohio Railway Company. They were not destined to repay those who designed them.

While they were yet in course of construction, their doom was silently but rapidly approaching. They were destroyed, as the only means of averting their capture by the advancing Yankees, by that undaunted hero, that true apostle of Freedom, "Stonewall" Jackson.

Reader, I must once again revert to my home, which was so soon to be the prey of the spoiler.

Imagine a bright warm sun shining upon a pretty two-storied house, the walls of which are completely hidden by roses and honeysuckle in most luxuriant bloom. At a short distance in front of it flows a broad, clear, rapid stream: around it the silver maples wave their graceful branches in the perfume-laden air of the South.

Even at this distance of time and space, as I write in my dull London lodging, I can hardly restrain my tears when I recall the sweet scene of my early days, such as it was before the unsparing hand of a ruthless enemy had defaced its loveliness. I frequently indulge in a fond soliloquy, and say, or rather think, "Do my English readers ever bestow a thought upon that cruel fate which has overtaken so many of their lineal descendants, whose only crime has been that love of freedom which the Pilgrim Fathers could not leave behind them when they left their island home? Do they bestow any pity, any sympathy, upon us homeless, ruined, exiled Confederates? Do they ever pause to reflect what would be their own feelings if, far and wide throughout their country, the ancestral hall, the farmer's homestead, and the laborer's cot were giving shelter to the licentious soldiers of an invader or crackling in incendiary flames? With what emotions would the citizens of London watch the camp-fires of a besieging army?

> " ' Say with what eye along the distant down
> Would flying burghers mark the blazing town—
> How view the column of ascending flames
> Shake his red shadow o'er the startled Thames.' "

Much has lately been written of the comfort of our Southern homesteads; and now, though so many of them are things of the past, while those that remain are no longer what they were, I may safely say, that not even English homes were more comfortable, in the true sense of the word, than ours; while for hospitality we have never been surpassed.

I passed my childhood as all happy children usually do, petted and caressed by a father and mother, loving and beloved by my brothers and sisters. The peculiarly sad circumstances that attended my father's death will be found recorded at a future page. Where my mother is hiding her head, I know not : doubtless she is equally ignorant of my fate. My brothers and sisters are dispersed God knows where.

But to return to my narrative. I believe I shall not be contradicted in affirming that nowhere could be found more pleasant society than that of Virginia. In this respect the neighborhood of Martinsburg was remarkably fortunate, populated as it was by some of the best and most respectable families of "the Old Dominion"—respectable, I mean, both in reputation and in point of antiquity—descendants of such ancestors as the Fairfaxes and Warringtons, upon whom Mr. Thackeray has lately conferred immortality.

According to the custom of my country, I was sent at twelve

years of age to Mount Washington College, of which Mr.
Staley, of whom I cherish a most grateful recollection, was then
principal. At sixteen my education was supposed to be completed, and I made my *entrée* into the world in Washington
City with all the high hopes and thoughtless joy natural to my
time of life. I did not then dream how soon my youth was to
be "blasted with a curse" — the worst that can befall man or
woman — the curse of civil war.

Washington is so well known to English people that I need
not pause to describe the city, its gayeties and pleasures. In the
winter of 1860–1, when I made my first acquaintance with it,
the season was pre-eminently brilliant. The Senate and Congress halls were nightly dignified by the presence of our ablest
orators and statesmen; the *salons* of the wealthy and the
talented were filled to overflowing; the theatres were crowded
to excess, and for the last time for many years to come the
daughters of the North and the South commingled in sisterly
love and friendship.

I am inclined to think that at the time of which I speak
the City of Washington must have very nearly resembled
that of Paris during those few years which immediately preceded 1789, while the elements of a stupendous revolution
were yet hidden beneath a tranquil and deceitful surface. Like
the Parisians of that memorable epoch, we were wilfully or
fatally blind to the signs of the times; we ate and drank, we
dined and danced, we went in and came out, we married
and were given in marriage, without a thought of the volcano
that was seething beneath our feet.

Who can predict what will be the end and issue of our
revolution, when we consider that the effects of that which
burst forth seventy-five years ago, wrapped all Europe in
flames, and hurled kings from their thrones, are even now but
partially developed? How many thousands of our sons have
fallen in battle, against oppressors who would not confess that

our freedom was beyond their power! How many hapless women and children have perished miserably, or been driven forth to beg their bread in foreign countries, before enemies who with heavy hands have sought to rivet our chains —enemies who could not discern the truth of the Irish orator's memorable axiom, and acknowledge that the genius of liberty is universal and irresistible!

Chapter II

Political Contest.—Commencement of the Great Struggle in
America.—Secession of the Southern States.—We hear of
the Fall of Fort Sumter.—Call for Troops.—The Stars and
Bars.—Volunteers.—Enlistment of my Father.—Patriotism
of the Southern Women.—Harper's Ferry.—Visit to Camp.
—Picnics, Balls, &c., &c.

The gayeties of Washington, to which I alluded in my first
chapter, were soon eclipsed by the clouds that gathered in the
political horizon.

The contest for the Presidentship was over, and the men of
the South could no longer hide it from themselves, that the
issue of the struggle must determine their fate.

The secession of the Southern States, individually or in the
aggregate, was the certain consequence of Mr. Lincoln's
election. His accession to a power supreme and almost unparalleled was an unequivocal declaration, by the merchants
of New England, that they had resolved to exclude the landed
proprietors of the South from all participation in the legisla-
tion of their common country.

I will not attempt to defend the institution of slavery, the
very name of which is abhorred in England; but it will be
admitted that the emancipation of the negro was not the object

of Northern ambition; that is, of the faction which grasps exclusive power in contempt of general rights. Slavery, like all other imperfect forms of society, will have its day; but the time for its final extinction in the Confederate States of America has not yet arrived. Can it be urged that a race which prefers servitude to freedom has reached that adolescent period of existence which fits it for the latter condition? Meanwhile, which stands in the better position, the helot of the South, or the "free" negro of the North—the willing slave of a Confederate master, or the reluctant victim of Federal conscription?

And here I must take leave to ask a question of two great authors, both formerly advocates of an instantaneous abolition of slavery. Is the ghost of Uncle Tom laid? Has the slave dreamed his last dream? Will Mrs. H. B. Stowe and Mr. Longfellow admit that in either instance the hero owes his reputation for martyrdom to a creative genius and to an exquisite fancy? or will they still contend that the negro slave of the Confederate States is, physically and morally, a real object of commiseration?

The first champion of freedom—I speak advisedly, and in defiance of a seeming paradox—was South Carolina. She was a slave-holding State, but she flung down the gauntlet in the name and for the cause of liberty. Her bold example was soon followed; State after State seceded, and the Union was dissolved. It was now that we heard of the fall of Fort Sumter and Mr. Lincoln's demand upon the State of Virginia. He called upon her to furnish her quota of 75,000 recruits, to engage in battle with her sister States. He sowed the dragon's teeth, and he soon reaped the only harvest that could spring from such seed.

Virginia promptly answered to the call, and produced the required soldiers; but they did not rally under the Stars and Stripes. It was to the Stars and Bars, the emblem of the South, that Mr. Lincoln's Virginia soldiers tendered the oath of military allegiance. The flag of the once loved, but now dishonored Union, was lowered, and the colors of the Confederacy were raised in its place.

Since that memorable epoch, those colors have been baptized with the blood of thousands, to whose death, in a cause so righteous, the honor and reverence that wait upon martyrdom have been justly awarded : —

> "Oh, if there be in this earthly sphere
> A boon, an offering, Heaven holds dear,
> It is the libation that Liberty draws
> From the heart that bleeds and breaks in her cause."

The enthusiasm of the enlistment was adequate to the occasion. Old men, with gray hairs and stooping forms, young boys, just able to shoulder a musket, strong and weak, rich and poor, rallied round our new standard, actuated by a stern sense of duty, and eager for death or victory. It was at this exciting crisis that I returned to Martinsburg; and, oh! what a striking contrast my native village presented to the scenes I had just left behind me at Washington! My winter had been cheered by every kind of amusement and every form of pleasure : my summer was about to be darkened by constant anxiety and heart-rending affliction.

My father was one of the first to volunteer. He was offered that grade in the army to which his social position entitled him; but, like many of our Virginian gentlemen, he preferred to enlist in the ranks, thereby leaving the pay and emoluments of an officer's commission to some other, whose means were not so ample, and whose family might be straitened in his absence from home, an absence that must, of course, interfere with his avocation or profession.

The 2nd Virginian was the regiment to which my father

attached himself. It was armed and equipped by means of a subscription raised by myself and other ladies of the Valley. On the colors were inscribed these words, so full of pathos and inspiration : —

"Our God, our country, and our women."

The corps was commanded by Colonel Nadenbush, and belonged to that section of the Southern army afterwards known as "the Stonewall Brigade." "The Stonewall Brigade !" — the very name now bears with it traditions of surpassing glory; and I seize this opportunity of assuring English readers that it is with pride we Confederates acknowledge that our heroes caught their inspiration from the example of their English ancestors. When our descendants shall read the story of General Jackson and his men, they will be insensibly attracted to those earlier pages of history which record the exploits of Wellington's Light Division.

My father's regiment was hardly formed when it was ordered to Harper's Ferry; for the sacred soil of Virginia was threatened with invasion, and it was thought possible to make a stand at this lovely spot, to see which is "worth a voyage across the Atlantic." At the outbreak of the war Harper's Ferry could boast of one of the largest and best arsenals in America, and of a magnificent bridge, which latter, spanning the broad stream of the Potomac, connected Maryland with Virginia. Both arsenal and bridge were blown up in July, 1861, by the Confederate forces, when the Federals, pressing upon them in overwhelming numbers, compelled a retreat.

My home had now become desolate and lonely : the excitement caused by our exertions to equip our father for the field had ceased, and the reaction of feeling had set in. A general sadness and depression prevailed throughout our household. My mother's face began to wear an anxious, careworn expression. Our nights were not passed in sleep, but in thinking painfully of the loved one who was exposed to the dangers and privations of war.

My mother, the daughter of an old officer, was left an orphan when very young; she had married my father just as she entered upon her sixteenth year; and now, almost for the first time, they were parted, under circumstances which made the separation bitter indeed. For myself, I endeavored to while away the long hours of those summer days by the aid of my books, and in making up different kinds of portable provisions for the use of my father, to whom I knew they would, in his novel position, be a luxury.

But, notwithstanding all the restrictions I laid upon myself, and all the self-control I endeavored to exert, I soon found these employments too tame and monotonous to satisfy my temperament, and I made up my mind to pay a visit to the camp, *coûte qui coûte*. I had no difficulty in prevailing upon some of my friends to accompany me in an expedition to headquarters. Like myself, they had friends and relations to whom they felt their occasional presence would be a source of encouragement and solace; and we all knew that such a goodly company as we formed could return safely to Martinsburg at almost any hour of the day or night.

The camp at Harper's Ferry was at this time an animated scene. Officers and men were as gay and joyous as though no bloody strife awaited them. The ladies, married and single, in the society of husbands, brothers, sons, and lovers, cast their cares to the winds, and seemed, one and all, resolved that whatever calamity the future might have in store for them, it should not mar the transient pleasures of the hour. Since then I have had occasion to observe that such a state of feeling is not unnatural or unusual in the minds of men standing, as it were, on the brink of a precipice, or walking, as it were, over the surface of a mine. "Perils commonly ask to be paid in pleasures," and the payment is doubly sweet when it is taken in anticipation of the debt.

I fear that at this time many fond vows were exchanged and many true hearts pledged between the girls of the neighborhood and the occupants of the camp; but it may be pardoned to beauty and innocence if they are not insensible to the virtues of courage and patriotism.

A true woman always loves a real soldier. In the earliest ages poets and philosophers foretold that the Goddess of Love and Beauty would ever move in the same orbit and in close conjunction with the God of Battles, and the experience of ages has confirmed the judgment of antiquity. Alas! the loves of Harper's Ferry were in but too many instances buried in a bloody grave. The soldier who plighted his faith to his lady-love was not tried in a long probation, but canonized by an early death. War will exact its victims of both sexes, and claims the hearts of women no less than the bodies of men.

To return from this digression. Our *insouciance* was not of long duration. The advance of a Federal army was reported; and General Jackson, with a force amounting to five thousand men, marched out to reconnoitre, and, if possible, to check their aggressive movement. Our people encamped at "Falling Waters," a romantic spot, eight miles from Martinsburg and four from Williamsport; for at this point of the river, it was rumored, the Yankees had resolved to force a passage.

It was early in the morning of the 3rd July that we "gude folks" of dear Martinsburg were startled by the roar of artillery and the rattle of musketry; and the intelligence was presently circulated that the Yankees were advancing upon us in force, under the command of Generals Patterson and Cadwallader. It turned out, however, that, at the moment of which I speak, their advanced guard only was in motion; but the skirmish between our people and the enemy was sustained during nearly five hours. On both sides some fell, and besides the casualties of the Federals in killed and wounded, we took about fifty of them prisoners.

About ten o'clock, General Jackson's army, in admirable array, marched through Martinsburg. They were in full retreat, their object being to effect a junction with the main body, under General J. E. Johnston, who had evacuated Harper's Ferry, and was falling back, by way of Charlestown, upon Winchester.

Jackson's retreat was covered by a few horsemen under the gallant Colonel Ashby; and scarcely were these latter disengaged from the streets of the town, when the shrill notes of the fife and the roll of the drum announced the approach of the Federal army, which proved to be twenty-five thousand strong.

It was to us a sad, but an imposing sight. On they came (their colors streaming to the breeze, their bayonets glittering in the sunlight), with all the "pomp and circumstance of glorious war." We could see from afar the dancing plumes of the cavalry—

> "the glittering files,
> O'er whose gay trappings stern Bellona smiles!"

we could before long hear the rumbling of the gun-carriages, and, worse than this, the hellish shouts with which the infuriated and undisciplined soldiers poured into the town.

At the time of their entry, I was in the hospital, with my negro maid and some ladies of my acquaintance, in attendance upon two of our Southern soldiers, who had been stricken down with fever, and were lying side by side. These were the sole tenants of the hospital: all the others had been borne off by the retreating army.

I was standing close by the side of one of these poor men,

who was just then raving in a violent fit of delirium, when I was startled by the sound of heavy footsteps behind me; and turning round, I confronted a captain of Federal infantry, accompanied by two private soldiers. He held in his hand a Federal flag, which he proceeded to wave over the bed of the sick men, at the same time calling them "———— rebels."

I immediately said, with all the scorn I could convey into my looks, "Sir, these men are as helpless as babies, and have, as you may see, no power to reply to your insults."

"And pray," said he, "who may you be, Miss?"

I did not deign to reply; but my negro maid answered him, "A rebel lady."

Hereupon he turned upon his heel and retired, with the courteous remark, that "I was a ———— independent one, at all events."

I hope my readers will pardon my quoting his exact words : without such strict accuracy, I should fail to do justice to his gallantry.

Notwithstanding this interruption to our "woman's mission," the ladies to whom I have before alluded and myself were not discouraged; and, before long, we contrived to get our patients moved to more comfortable quarters. They were taken away on litters; and, while they were in this defenceless condition, a condition which would have awakened the sympathy and secured the protection of a brave enemy, the Federal soldiers crowded round and threatened to bayonet them!

Their gesticulations and language grew so violent; their countenances, inflamed by drink and hatred, were so frightful, that I nerved myself to seek out an officer and appeal to his sense of military honor, even if the voice of mercy were silent in his breast. Let me do him the justice to say, he restrained his turbulent men from further molestation, and I had the unspeakable satisfaction of conveying my sick men to a place of safety. The satisfaction was immeasurable; for I never for one moment forgot that insults such as I had just seen offered to defenceless men might at any moment be heaped upon my own father.

Chapter III

The morning of the 4th of July dawned brightly.

I need hardly say, for it is well known, that the anniversary
of the Declaration of Independence has, in each succeeding
year from that of its birth, been hailed with triumphant
acclamations by a nation still too young to moderate its transports and lend its ear to the voice of reason rather than to the
impulse of passion.

The Yankees were in undisputed possession of Martinsburg;
the village was at their mercy, and consequently entitled to
their forbearance; and it would at least have been more dignified in them had they been content to enjoy their almost
bloodless conquest with moderation; but, whatever might have
been the intentions of the officers, they had not the inclination,
or they lacked the authority, to control the turbulence of
their men.

The severance of the North from the South had now become
in feeling so complete, that we Martinsburg girls saw the
Union flag streaming from the windows of the houses with
emotions akin to those with which the ladies of England would

131

gaze upon the tricolor of France or the eagle of Russia floating above the keep of Windsor Castle. Those hateful strains of "Yankee Doodle" resounded in every street, with an accompaniment of cheers, shouts, and imprecations.

Whiskey now began to flow freely; for, amid the motley crowd of Americans, Dutchmen, and other nations, the Irish element predominated. The sprigs of shillelahs were soon at work, and the "sons of Erin" proved that they could use their sticks with no less effect in an American town than at an Irish fair. They set at defiance the authority of those among their officers who vainly interposed to quell the tumult and restrain the lawless violence that was offered to defenceless citizens and women.

The doors of our houses were dashed in; our rooms were forcibly entered by soldiers who might literally be termed "mad drunk," for I can think of no other expression so applicable to their condition. Glass and fragile property of all kinds was wantonly destroyed. They found our homes scenes of comfort, in some cases even of luxury; they left them mere wrecks, utterly despoiled and mutilated. Shots were fired through the windows; chairs and tables were hurled into the street.

In some instances a trembling lady would make a timid appeal to that honor which should be the attribute of every soldier, or, with streaming eyes and passionate accents, plead for some cherished object—the portrait, probably, of a dead father, or the miniature her lover placed in her hand when he left her to fight for his freedom and hers—upon which many a secret kiss had been pressed, many a silent tear had fallen, before which many an earnest prayer had been breathed.

To such applications the reply was invariably a volley of blasphemous curses and horrid imprecations. Words from which the mind recoils with horror, which no man with one spark of feeling would utter in the presence even of the most abandoned woman, were shouted in the ears of innocent, shrinking girls; and the soldiers of the Union showed a malignant, a fiendish delight in destroying the effigies of enemies whom they had not yet dared to meet upon equal terms in an open field of battle.

Surely it is not strange that cruelties such as I have attempted to describe have exasperated our women no less than our men, and inspired them with sterner feelings than those which inflame the bosoms of ladies who know nothing of invasion but its name, who have never at their own firesides shuddered at the oaths and threats of a robber disguised in the garb of a soldier.

Shall I be ashamed to confess that I recall without one shadow of remorse the act by which I saved my mother from insult, perhaps from death — that the blood I then shed has left no stain on my soul, imposed no burden upon my conscience?

The encounter to which I refer was brought about as follows : — A party of soldiers, conspicuous, even on that day, for violence, broke into our house and commenced their depredations; this occupation, however, they presently discontinued, for the purpose of hunting for "rebel flags," with which they had been informed my room was decorated. Fortunately for us, although without my orders, my negro maid promptly rushed up-stairs, tore down the obnoxious emblem, and before our enemies could get possession of it, burned it.

They had brought with them a large Federal flag, which they were now preparing to hoist over our roof in token of our submission to their authority; but to this my mother would not consent. Stepping forward with a firm step, she said, very quietly, but resolutely, "Men, every member of my household will die before that flag shall be raised over us."

Upon this, one of the soldiers, thrusting himself forward, addressed my mother and myself in language as offensive as it is possible to conceive. I could stand it no longer; my indignation was roused beyond control; my blood was literally boiling in my veins; I drew out my pistol* and shot him. He was carried away mortally wounded, and soon after expired.

Our persecutors now left the house, and we were in hopes we had got rid of them, when one of the servants, rushing in, cried out —

"Oh, missus, missus, dere gwine to burn de house down; dere pilin' de stuff ag'in it! Oh, if massa were back!"

The prospect of being burned alive naturally terrified us, and, as a last resource, I contrived to get a message conveyed to the Federal officer in command. He exerted himself with effect, and had the incendiaries arrested before they could execute their horrible purpose.

In the mean time it had been reported at head-quarters that I had shot a Yankee soldier, and great was the indignation at first felt and expressed against me. Soon, however, the commanding officer, with several of his staff, called at our house to investigate the affair. He examined the witnesses, and inquired into all the circumstances with strict impartiality, and finally said I had "done perfectly right." He immediately sent for a guard to head-quarters, where the *élite* of the army was stationed, and a tolerable state of discipline preserved.

Sentries were now placed around the house, and Federal officers called every day to inquire if we had any complaint to make of their behavior. It was in this way that I became acquainted with so many of them; an acquaintance "the rebel spy" did not fail to turn to account on more than one occasion.

When the news reached the Confederate camp at Darksville, seven miles from Martinsburg, on the Valley Road, that I had shot a Yankee soldier in self-defence, together with the false report that for so doing I had been thrown into the town jail,

---

* All our male relatives being with the army, we ladies were obliged to go armed in order to protect ourselves as best we might from insult and outrage.

the soldiers with one accord volunteered to storm the prison and rescue me, or die to a man in the attempt. It is with pride and gratitude that I record this proof of their esteem and respect for what I had done. It is with no less pleasure I reflect that their devotion was not put to the test, and that no blood was shed on my account.

And now, for seven consecutive days, General Jo. Johnston sent in a flag of truce offering battle to General Patterson : this challenge Patterson persistently declined. I am not so ignorant of warfare as not to know that *strategic* reasons justify the most daring general in refusing battle whenever and wherever he pleases.

"If thou art a great soldier, come and fight." "If thou art a great soldier, make me come and fight."

But, though the Federal commander had a perfect right to choose his own battle-field, he had, in my opinion, no right to couple his refusal of the challenge with a threat that, as soon as Johnston should think fit to make an aggressive movement, he would at once shell Martinsburg, which sheltered the non-combatants, the women and the children, the sick and the infirm.

Meanwhile, my residence within the Federal lines, and my acquaintance with so many of the officers, the origin of which I have already mentioned, enabled me to gain much important information as to the position and designs of the enemy. Whatever I heard I regularly and carefully committed to paper, and whenever an opportunity offered I sent my secret dispatch by a trusty messenger to General J. E. B. Stuart, or some brave officer in command of the Confederate troops. Through accident or by treachery one of these missives fell into the Yankees' hands. It was not written in cipher, and, moreover, my handwriting was identified. I was immediately summoned to appear before some colonel, whose name I have forgotten; but I remember it was Captain Gwyne who escorted me to head-quarters. There I was alternately threatened and reprimanded, and finally the following "Article of War" was read to me in a most emphatic manner, and with the caution that it would be carried out in the spirit and the letter : —

" ARTICLE OF WAR.

"Whoever shall give food, ammunition, information to, or aid* and abet the enemies of the United States Government in any manner whatever, shall suffer death, or whatever penalty the honorable members of the court-martial shall see fit to inflict."

I was not frightened, for I felt within me the spirit of the Douglas, from whom I am descended. I listened quietly to the recital of the doom which was to be my reward for adhering to the traditions of my youth and the cause of my country, made a low bow, and, with a sarcastic "Thank you, gentlemen of the Jury," I departed; not in peace, however, for my little "rebel" heart was on fire, and I indulged in thoughts and plans of vengeance.

From this hour I was a "suspect," and all the mischief done to the Federal cause was laid to my charge; and it is with unfeigned joy and true pride I confess that the suspicions of the enemy were far from being unfounded.

On one occasion a friend of mine, Miss Sophia B——, of Martinsburg, a lovely girl, slipped away with a *lettre de cachet,* walked seven miles to the camp of Stonewall Jackson, and handed him important information, which was productive of much good. She, like myself, had brothers enrolled in that band of heroes.

---

* I had been confiscating and concealing their pistols and swords on every possible occasion, and many an officer, looking about everywhere for his missing weapons, little dreamed who it was that had taken them, or that they had been smuggled away to the Confederate camp, and were actually in the hands of their enemies, to be used against themselves.

Chapter IV

Battle of Manassas.—Establishment of a Hospital at Front Royal (Virginia).—A Runaway Excursion.—Capture of Federal Officers.

Throughout the North the utmost confidence was felt that the subjugation of the rebels would be rapid and complete. "Ninety days!" "On, on to Richmond!" was the cry; but the shout was changed to a wail, on Manassas plains, where the first great battle of the war was fought.

The action was precipitated by Patterson's attempt to prevent Johnston from effecting a junction with Beauregard at Manassas. In this he failed, and the result of the movements and counter-movements was the battle of "Bull Run."* This great Confederate victory has become an historical fact; I shall therefore pass it by in silence, and proceed to the narrative of my own personal adventures.

* Here it was that the Stonewall Brigade acquired its name. The fire was very hot, and the —th South Carolina Regiment of Infantry, thrown into confusion, wavered, and was upon the point of breaking.
"Steady, men, steady," shouted Colonel Bartow, in a loud voice. "Look at General Jackson's brigade; they stand firm and immovable as a stone wall. The —th, animated by the voice and gesture of their gallant commander, and by the example of Jackson's men, rallied; and Colonel Bartow, taking advantage of the enthusiasm he had kindled, led his regiment at once to the charge, when he fell covered with wounds and honor.

At the time in question I was at Front Royal (Virginia), on a visit to my uncle and aunt, Mr. and Mrs. S——. I wish it were in my power to give my readers some faint idea of this picturesque village, which nestles in the bosom of the surrounding mountains, and reminds one of a young bird in its nest. A rivulet, which sometimes steals round the obstacles to its course, sometimes bounds over them with headlong leap, at last finds its way to the valley beneath, and glides by the village in peace and beauty.

The scene is far beyond my powers of description. It is worthy of the pencil of Salvator Rosa, or the pen of the author of "Gertrude of Wyoming," and I only wish the great landscape-painter had been given to our age and had wandered to the hills and valleys of Virginia.

To this romantic retreat my uncle and aunt had fled, as deer fly for safety to the hills. They had resided in Washington, but their Southern sympathies were too strong and too openly expressed to allow of their remaining unmolested in the Northern capital. They left a magnificent house, replete with handsome furniture, a prey to the Yankees, who converted it into barracks.

Orders now came from the battle-field of Bull Run to the effect that the General in command had fixed upon Front Royal for the site of an extensive hospital, for the wounded Confederate soldiers. Every one in the village and the neighborhood showed the greatest alacrity — I should say, enthusiasm — in preparing, in the shortest possible time, all that our suffering heroes could require. I bore my part, and, before long, was duly installed one of the "matrons."

My office was a very laborious one, and my duties were painful in the extreme; but then, as always, I allowed but one thought to keep possession of my mind — the thought that I was doing all a woman could do in her country's cause. The motto of my father's regiment was engraven on my heart, and

I trust that I have always shown by my actions that I understand its significance.

After six or eight weeks spent in incessant nursing, I was forced to return to my home at Martinsburg, in order to recruit my health, which had suffered severely; and I leave my readers to imagine with what joy I heard my dear mother's praises of actions which she, in her fond affection, styled heroic.

In October my mother and myself resolved upon a short visit to my father at Manassas. We stayed at a large house, situated in the very centre of the camp. This tenement was then the temporary abode of several other ladies, wives and daughters of officers.

During this period I had frequently the honor of acting the part of courier between General Beauregard, General Jackson, and their subordinates.

This was a happy time, but it did not last long; and, after a few weeks spent as above described, my mother and I returned to Martinsburg. The winter passed very quietly, and brought me but a single adventure worth recording.

I was riding out one evening with two young officers,* one a cousin and the other a friend, when my horse, a young and high-spirited creature, took fright, and ran away with me. Notwithstanding all my efforts, I failed to stop him until he had carried me within the Federal lines, a goal to which my companions could not venture to follow me.

I felt rather uncomfortable, not knowing exactly how to act; but I soon made up my mind that, for this once, at all events, valor would be the better part of discretion, if not prudence itself; so, riding straight up to the officer in command of the picket, I said—

"I beg your pardon—you must know that I have been

---

* My English readers may deem it strange that a young girl should ride alone with young gentlemen, but the practice is not in America considered a breach of decorum.

taking a ride with some of my friends; my horse ran away with me, and has carried me within your lines. I am your captive, but I beg you will permit me to return."

"We are exceedingly proud of our beautiful captive," replied one of the officers, with a bow, "but of course we cannot think of detaining you." Then, after a moment's pause, he added —

"May we have the honor of escorting you beyond our lines and restoring you to the custody of your friends? I suppose there is no fear of those cowardly rebels taking us prisoners?"

"I had scarcely hoped," I replied, "for such an honor. I thought you would probably have given me a pass; but since you are so kind as to offer your services in person, I cannot do otherwise than accept them. Have no fear, gentlemen, of the 'cowardly rebels.'"

They little thought how those words, "cowardly rebels," rankled in my heart.

Off we started; and imagine their blank looks when, soon after they had escorted me beyond their lines, my Confederate friends, who had been anxiously waiting for me, rode out from their ambush and joined the party. All four looked surprised and embarrassed. I broke the general silence, by saying, with a laugh, to the Confederates, "Here are two prisoners that I have brought you."

Then turning to the Federal officers, I said —

"Here are two of the 'cowardly rebels' whom you hoped there was no danger of meeting!"

They looked doubtfully and inquiringly at me, and, after a short pause, exclaimed almost simultaneously —

"And who, pray, is the lady?"

"Belle Boyd, at your service," I replied.

"Good God! the rebel spy!"

"So be it, since your journals have honored me with that title."

After this short colloquy we escorted them, without any

attempt at resistance on their part, to head-quarters, and related all the circumstances of the adventure to the officer in command, who ordered them to be detained.

The Yankees reproached us bitterly with our treachery; but when it is considered that their release followed their capture within an hour, that they had in the first instance stigmatized the rebels, when none were near, as cowards, that they had immediately afterwards yielded without a blow to an equal number of these self-same cowards, I think my readers will admit their spirit of bravado well merited a slight humiliation. Let us hope they have profited by the lesson. I consoled myself that "all was fair in love and war."

Although Bull Run had been fought, and I had witnessed the outrages of July 4th at Martinsburg, we had hardly yet realized the horrors of war, or, to speak more correctly, we did not allow ourselves to believe in their continuance. We hoped that enough had been done to pave the way for reconciliation. Winter set in and closed the campaign, and, with a cessation of active hostilities, our apprehensions for the future were forgotten in our enjoyment of the present.

It was only when spring returned, and brought with it no sign of a dove from the ark, that we realized how far the waters of the deluge were from subsiding. Balls and sleighs, mirth and laughter, vanished with the last snows of winter; and it was with sad and sickening hearts we saw Colonel Ashby and his cavalry evacuate the town.

But a very few years since, Henry, afterwards Colonel Ashby, was one of those young men whose characters have been so often imagined by writers of romance, but are so rarely met with in real life. He united in himself all those qualifications which justly recommend their possessor to the love of the one sex and to the esteem of the other. At once tender and respectful, manly and accomplished, animated and handsome, he won without an effort the hearts of women. Brave and good-humored, he combined simplicity with talents of the highest order. He entertained a strict sense of honor, and never forgot what was due to himself; and he was ever wont to forget an injury, and even to pardon an insult, upon the first overture of the offender.

Endowed with such qualities, it is not surprising he was a universal favorite; and, indeed, it was commonly said the spirit of Admirable Crichton had revisited the world in the person of Henry Ashby.

Such a man was sure to be among the first to draw his sword in the cause of independence.

At an early period of the war he was appointed to the command of a regiment of cavalry, in which capacity he displayed an unusual degree of vigilance and alacrity in the arduous service of outpost duty.

On one occasion his regiment was drawn up at some distance from a railroad which passed directly across his front. On the farther side was broken ground, well calculated to conceal a large body of men. Colonel Ashby, therefore, ordered out a small party to reconnoitre, putting them under command of his younger brother, between whom and himself there subsisted an affection warm, genuine, almost romantic.

Unfortunately "Dick Ashby's" impetuosity overlaid his judgment, and, exceeding the instructions he had received from his brother, he passed some distance beyond the railway, and suddenly found himself in presence of a large body of the enemy.

He retreated in admirable order; but the Yankees pressed hard upon him, and he and his little band were overtaken upon the railroad.

Here a fatal accident befell poor Dick Ashby. His horse stumbled and fell at one of the cuts.* In this defenceless con-

---

* These cuts are large drains, or rather tunnels, cut transversely through the lines of American railways, at short intervals. They serve to carry off

dition he was set upon without mercy, without even quarter being offered, by five Yankees at once.

In spite of these odds, and the disadvantage at which he was taken, he sold his life so dearly that his five assailants were all killed or wounded. By this time Colonel Ashby, leading on his regiment at a gallop, had reached the scene of action, and, the contest being now pretty equal, the Federals soon fled, and were pursued as far as the nature of the ground would permit. The victors then returned to the railway, and hastily dug a shallow grave, into which all that remained of Dick Ashby was consigned.

Colonel Ashby dismounted, and, kneeling by the mutilated body, gently disengaged the sword from his dead brother's hand; then breaking it into pieces, he cast them into the grave, and on that solemn spot vowed to avenge his brother's murder and to consecrate the remainder of his life to the service of his country.

This vow he faithfully kept. His character underwent a change as instantaneous and enduring as that of Colonel Gardiner. All his gayety and high spirits forsook him. In society he was rarely heard to speak, never seen to smile, and, after a brief but glorious career, he fell in an unequal and desperate struggle, cheering on his men with his dying breath.

> "The bravest are the tenderest :
> The gentle are the daring."

I shall conclude this chapter with another short episode, which proves how suddenly national disorders discover the hidden force of individual character.

Miss D., at the outbreak of the war, was a lovely, fragile-

such a rush of water as would otherwise inundate the line after a heavy fall of rain or the overflow of a river. They are of course covered, and the trains pass over them.

looking girl of nineteen, remarkable for the sweetness of her temper and the gentleness of her disposition.

A few days before the battle of Bull Run, a country market-cart stopped in the Confederate lines, at the door of General Bonham's tent. A peasant-girl alighted from the cart and begged for an immediate interview with the General.

It was granted.

"General Bonham, I believe?" said the young lady, in tones which betrayed her superiority to the disguise she had assumed. Then, tearing down her long, black hair, she took from its folds a note, small, damp, and crumpled; but it was by acting upon this informal dispatch that General Beauregard won the victory of Bull Run.

Miss D. had passed through the whole of the Federal army. I dare not now publish her name; but, if ever these pages meet her eye, she will not fail to recognize her own portrait, nor will she be displeased to find that her exiled countrywoman cherishes the remembrance of her intrepidity and devotion.

Chapter V

Advance of the Federal Army.—I leave Home with my Father.—
Battle of Kearnstown.—I am Arrested and carried Prisoner
to Baltimore.—Released and sent to Martinsburg.—I
attempt to go South to Richmond—Shields's Army at
Front Royal.—Incidents, &c., &c.

With the first genial days of spring, the Federal troops broke
up their winter-quarters, and advanced again upon the devastated village of Martinsburg, which had been held during the
winter by the Confederates. Martinsburg, situated as it was on
the border of the State, was incessantly a bone of contention,
and its capture and recapture were of frequent recurrence.

My father, who had been at home on sick-leave for several
weeks, was now able to resume his military duties, and he
decided upon removing me farther south, as our home was in
constant peril, and I had gained a notoriety which would
hardly recommend me to the favorable notice of the Federals
in the event of their shortly reoccupying Martinsburg, which
seemed only too probable.

Accordingly, I was again sent to Front Royal, there to
remain until our home should once more be secure.

A few days after my arrival at Front Royal a battle was
fought close by, at Kearnstown. The Confederates, vastly over-

matched in numbers, were forced to retreat, and Front Royal became the prize of the conquerors. Thus, to use a homely adage, "out of the frying-pan into the fire" had been my fate.

Upon the approach of the enemy, my uncle and aunt, taking with them one daughter, quitted home with the intention of reaching Richmond, leaving their other daughter, Alice S——, a beautiful girl about my own age, our grand-mamma, Mrs. Glynn and myself, to take charge of the house and servants, and act in all contingencies to the best of our ability.

When I found that the Confederate forces were retreating so far down the Valley, and reflected that my father was with them, I became very anxious to return to my mother; and, as no tie of duty bound me to Front Royal, I resolved upon the attempt at all hazards.

I started in company with my maid, and had got safely without adventure of any kind as far as Winchester, when some unknown enemy or some malicious neutral denounced me to the authorities as a Confederate spy.

Before, however, this act of hostility or malice had been perpetrated, I had taken the precaution of procuring a pass from General Shields; and I fondly hoped that this would, under all circumstances, secure me from molestation and arrest; for I was not aware that, while I was in the very act of receiving my bill of "moral health," an order was being issued by the Provost Marshal which forbade me to leave the town.

When the hour which I had fixed for my departure arrived, I stepped into the railway-cars, and was congratulating myself with the thought that I should ere long be at home once more, and in the society of those I loved, when a Federal officer, Captain Bannon, appeared. He was in charge of some Confederate prisoners, who, under his command, were *en route* to the Baltimore prison.

I was more surprised than pleased when, handing over the prisoners to a subordinate, he walked straight up to me, and said : —

"Is this Miss Belle Boyd?"

"Yes."

"I am the Assistant-Provost, and I regret to say, orders have been issued for your detention, and it is my duty to inform you that you cannot proceed until your case has been investigated; so you will, if you please, get out, as the train is on the point of starting."

"Sir," I replied, presenting him General Shields's pass, "here is a pass which I beg you will examine. You will find that it authorizes my maid and myself to pass on any road to Martinsburg."

He reflected for some time, and at last said : —

"Well, I scarcely know how to act in your case. Orders have been issued for your arrest, and yet you have a pass from the General allowing you to return home. However, I shall take the responsibility upon my shoulders, convey you with the other prisoners to Baltimore, and hand you over to General Dix."

I played my *rôle* of submission as gracefully as I could; for where resistance is impossible, it is still left to the vanquished to yield with dignity.

The train by which we travelled was the first that had been run through from Wheeling to Baltimore since the damage done to the permanent way by the Confederates had been repaired.

We had not proceeded far when I observed an old friend of mine, Mr. M., of Baltimore, a gentleman whose sympathies were strongly enlisted on the side of the South. At my request, he took a seat beside me, and, after we had conversed for some time upon different topics, he told me, in a whisper, that he had a small Confederate flag concealed about his person.

"Manage to give it me," I said; "I am already a prisoner; besides, free or in chains, I shall always glory in the possession of the emblem."

Mr. M. watched his opportunity, and, when all eyes were turned from us, he stealthily and quickly drew the little flag from his bosom, and placed it in my hand.

We had eluded the vigilance of the officer under whose surveillance I was travelling; and I leave my readers to imagine his surprise when I drew it forth from my pocket, and, with a laugh, waved it over our heads with a gesture of triumph. It was a daring action, but my captivity had, I think, superadded the courage of despair to the hardihood I had already acquired in my country's service.

The first emotions of the Federal officer and his men were those of indignation; but better feelings succeeded, and they allowed it was an excellent joke, that a convoy of Confederate prisoners should be brought in under a Confederate flag, and that flag raised by a lady.

Upon our arrival at Baltimore, I was taken to the Eutaw House, one of the largest and best hotels in the city, where, I must in justice say, I was treated with all possible courtesy and consideration, and permission to see my friends was at once and spontaneously granted.

As soon as it was known that I was in Baltimore, a prisoner and alone, I was visited, not merely by my personal friends, but by those who knew me by reputation only; for Baltimore is Confederate to its heart's core.

I remained a prisoner in the Eutaw House about a week; at the expiration of which time, General Dix, the officer in command, having heard nothing against me, decided to send me home. I arrived safely at Martinsburg, which is now occupied in force by the Federal troops.

Here I was placed under a strict surveillance, and forbidden to leave the town. I was incessantly watched and persecuted;

and at last the restrictions imposed upon me became so irksome
and vexatious, that my mother resolved to intercede with
Major Walker, the Provost-Marshal, on my behalf. The result
of this intercession was, that he granted us both a pass, by
way of Winchester, to Front Royal, with a view to my being
sent on to join my relations at Richmond.

Upon arriving at Winchester, we had much difficulty in
getting permission to proceed; for General Shields had just
occupied Front Royal, and had prohibited all intercourse
between that place and Winchester. However, Lieutenant-
Colonel Fillebrowne, of the Tenth Maine Regiment, who was
acting as Provost-Marshal, at length relented, and allowed us
to go on our way.

It was almost twilight when we arrived at the Shenandoah River. We found that the bridges had been destroyed,
and no means of transport left but a ferry-boat, which the
Yankees monopolized for their own exclusive purposes.

Here we should have been subjected to much inconvenience
and delay, had it not been for the courtesy and kindness of
Captain Everhart, through whose intervention we were
enabled to cross at once.

It was quite dark when we reached the village, and, to our
great surprise, we found the family domiciled in a little cottage
in the court-yard, the residence having been appropriated by
General Shields and his staff.

However, we were glad enough to find ourselves at our
journey's end, and to sit down to a comfortable dinner, for
which fatigue and a long fast had sharpened our appetite. As
soon as we had satisfied our hunger, I sent in my card to
General Shields, who promptly returned my missive in person.
He was an Irishman, and endowed with all those graces of
manner for which the better class of his countrymen are justly
famous; nor was he devoid of the humor for which they are no
less notorious.

To my application for leave to pass *instanter* through his lines, *en route* for Richmond, he replied, that old Jackson's army was so demoralized that he dared not trust me to their tender mercies; but that they would be annihilated within a few days, and, after such a desirable consummation, I might wander whither I would.

This, of course, was mere badinage on his part; but I am convinced he felt confident of immediate and complete success, or he would not have allowed some expressions to escape him which I turned to account. In short, he was completely off his guard, and forgot that a woman can sometimes listen and remember.

General Shields, introduced me to the officers of his staff, two of whom were young Irishmen; and to one of these, Captain K., I am indebted for some very remarkable effusions, some withered flowers, and last, not least, for a great deal of very important information, which was carefully transmitted to my countrymen. I must avow the flowers and the poetry were comparatively valueless in my eyes; but let Captain K. be consoled : these were days of war, not of love, and there are still other ladies in the world besides the "rebel spy."

The night before the departure of General Shields, who was about, as he informed us, to "whip" Jackson, a council of war was held in what had formerly been my aunt's drawing-room. Immediately above this was a bed-chamber, containing a closet, through the floor of which I observed a hole had been bored, whether with a view to espionage or not I have never been able to ascertain. It occurred to me, however, that I might turn the discovery to account; and as soon as the council of war had assembled, I stole softly up stairs, and lying down on the floor of the closet, applied my ear to the hole, and found, to my great joy, I could distinctly hear the conversation that was passing below.

The council prolonged their discussion for some hours; but

I remained motionless and silent until the proceedings were brought to a conclusion, at one o'clock in the morning. As soon as the coast was clear I crossed the court-yard, and made the best of my way to my own room, and took down in cipher everything I had heard which seemed to me of any importance.

I felt convinced that to rouse a servant, or make any disturbance at that hour, would excite the suspicions of the Federals by whom I was surrounded; accordingly I went straight to the stables myself, saddled my horse, and galloped away in the direction of the mountains.

Fortunately I had about me some passes which I had from time to time procured for Confederate soldiers returning south, and which, owing to various circumstances, had never been put in requisition. They now, however, proved invaluable; for I was twice brought to a stand-still by the challenge of the Federal sentries, and who would inevitably have put a period to my adventurous career had they not been beguiled by my false passport. Once clear of the chain of sentries, I dashed on unquestioned across fields and along roads, through fens and marshes, until, after a scamper of about fifteen miles, I found myself at the door of Mr. M.'s house. All was still and quiet : not a light was to be seen. I did not lose a moment in springing from my horse; and, running up the steps, I knocked at the door with such vehemence that the house re-echoed with the sound.

It was not until I had repeated my summons, at intervals of a few seconds, for some time, that I heard the response, "Who is there?" given in a sharp voice from a window above.

"It is I."

"But who are you? What is your name?"

"Belle Boyd. I have important intelligence to communicate to Colonel Ashby : is he here?"

"No; but wait a minute : I will come down."

The door was opened, and Mrs. M. drew me in, and exclaimed in a tone of astonishment —

"My dear, where did you come from? And how on earth did you get here?"

"Oh, I forced the sentries," I replied, "and here I am; but I have no time to tell you the how, and the why, and the wherefore. I must see Colonel Ashby without the loss of a minute : tell me where he is to be found."

Upon hearing that his party was a quarter of a mile farther up the wood, I turned to depart in search of them, and was in the very act of remounting when a door on my right was thrown open, and revealed Colonel Ashby himself, who could not conceal his surprise at seeing me standing before him.

"Good God! Miss Belle, is this you? Where did you come from? Have you dropped from the clouds? Or am I dreaming?"

I first convinced him he was wide awake, and that my presence was substantial and of the earth — not a visionary emanation from the world of spirits — then, without further circumlocution, I proceeded to narrate all I had overheard in the closet, of which I have before made mention. I gave him the cipher, and started on my return.

I arrived safely at my aunt's house, after a two hours' ride, in the course of which I "ran the blockade" of a sleeping sentry, who awoke to the sound of my horse's hoofs just in time to see me disappear round an abrupt turning, which shielded me from the bullet he was about to send after me. Upon getting home, I unsaddled my horse and "turned in" — if I may be permitted the expression, which is certainly expressive rather than refined — just as Aurora, springing from the rosy bed of Tithonus, began her pursuit of the flying hour; in plain English, just as day began to break.

A few days afterwards General Shields marched south, laying a trap, as he supposed, to catch "poor old Jackson and

his demoralized army," leaving behind him, to occupy Front
Royal, one squadron of cavalry, one field battery, and the 1st
Maryland Regiment of Infantry, under command of Colonel
Kenly; Major Tyndale, of Philadelphia, being appointed
Provost-Marshal.

My mother returned home, and it was arranged that I
should remain with my grandmother until an opportunity of
travelling south in safety should present itself. Within a few
days after my mother's departure, my Cousin Alice and I
applied to Major Tyndale for a pass to Winchester. He at
first declined to comply with our request, but afterwards
relented, and promised to let us have the necessary passport
on the following day. Accordingly, next morning, May 21st,
my cousin, one of the servants, and myself were up betimes,
and equipped for the journey, the carriage was at the door,
but no passes made their appearance; and when we sent to
inquire for the Major, we were informed he had gone "out
on a scout," and would probably not be back until late at
night. We were, of course, in great perplexity, when, to our
relief, Lieutenant H., belonging to the squadron of cavalry
stationed in the village, made his appearance and asked what
was the matter.

I explained our case, and said —

"Now, Lieutenant H., I know you have permission to go
to Winchester, and you profess to be a great friend of mine :
prove it by assisting me out of this dilemma, and pass us
through the pickets."

This I knew he could easily manage, as they were furnished
from his own troop.

After a few moments' hesitation, Lieutenant H. consented,
little thinking of the consequences that were to ensue. He
mounted the box, my cousin, myself, and the servant got
inside, and off we set. Shortly before we got to Winchester,
Lieutenant H. got down from his seat with the intention of

walking the rest of the way, as he had some business at the camp, which was close to the town.

Finding we could not return the same day, we agreed to remain all night with some friends.

Early the next morning a gentleman of high social position came to the house at which we were staying, and handed me two packages of letters, with these words : —

"Miss Boyd, will you take these letters and send them through the lines to the Confederate army ? This package," he added, pointing to one of them, "is of great importance : the other is trifling in comparison. This also," he went on to say, pointing to what appeared to be a little note, "is a very important paper : try to send it carefully and safely to Jackson, or some other responsible Confederate officer. Do you understand ?"

"I do, and will obey your orders promptly and implicitly," I replied.

As soon as the gentleman had left me I concealed the most important documents about the person of my negro servant, as I knew that "intelligent contrabands" — *i.e.,* ladies and gentlemen of color — were "non-suspects," and had *carte blanche* to do what they pleased, and to go where they liked, without hindrance or molestation on the part of the Yankee authorities. The less important package I placed in a little basket, and unguardedly wrote upon the back of it the words, "Kindness of Lieutenant H."

The small note upon which so much stress had been laid I resolved to carry with my own hands; and, knowing Colonel Fillebrowne was never displeased by a little flattery and a few delicate attentions, I went to the florist and chose a very handsome bouquet, which I sent to him with my compliments, and with a request that he would be so kind as to permit me to return to Front Royal.*

* My readers must bear in mind that, in time of war, it is almost

The Colonel's answer was in accordance with the politeness of his nature. He thanked the "dear lady for so sweet a compliment," and enclosed the much-coveted pass. Lieutenant H., having finished his business at the camp, rejoined our party, and we all set out on our return. Nothing happened until we reached the picket-lines, when two repulsive-looking fellows, who proved to be detectives, rode up, one on each side of the carriage.

"We have orders to arrest you," said one of them, looking in at the window, and addressing himself to me.

"For what?" I asked.

"Upon suspicion of having letters," he replied; and then turning to the coachman, he ordered him to drive back forthwith to Colonel Beale's headquarters. Upon arriving there we were desired to get out and walk into the office.

My cousin trembled like a poor bird caught in a snare; and, to tell the truth, I felt very much discomposed myself, although I did not for a moment lose my presence of mind, upon the preservation of which I well knew our only hopes rested. The negress, almost paralyzed by fear, followed my cousin and myself, and it was in this order we were ushered into the awful presence of our inquisitor and judge.

The first question asked was, had I any letters. I knew that if I said No, our persons would be immediately searched, and my falsehood detected: I therefore drew out from the bottom

impossible to travel the slightest distance without a pass signed by some official. On one occasion, when a picket was stationed between our farm-yard and the dairy, the dairymaid was not allowed to milk the cows without a pass signed by the officer of the day. This was a decided nuisance, and I hit upon the following plan to get rid of it. I wrote the following pass and got it duly signed: "These cows have permission to pass to and from the yard and dairy for the purpose of being milked twice a day, until further orders." This pass I pasted between the horns of one of the cows; and I was gratified to find that it had the desired effect, for they were not again stopped on their harmless errand; and whenever my pass came off the head of the cow I took care to replace it by another in the same style.

of the basket the package I had placed there, and which, it will be remembered, was of minor importance, and handed it, with a bow, to the Colonel.

"What!" exclaimed he, in an angry tone—"what is this? 'Kindness of Lieutenant H.!' What does this mean? Is this all you have?"

"Look for yourself," I replied, turning the basket upside down, and emptying its contents upon the floor.

"As to this scribbling on the letter," I continued, "it means nothing; it was a thoughtless act of mine. I assure you Lieutenant H. knew nothing about the letter, or that it was in my possession."

The Lieutenant turned very pale, for it suddenly occurred to him that he had in his pocket a little package which I had asked him to carry for me.

He immediately drew it out and threw it upon the table, when, to his consternation, and to the surprise of the Colonel, it was found to be inscribed with the very identical words —"Kindness of Lieutenant H."—which had already excited the suspicions of the Federal commander.

This made matters worse; and when the package, upon being opened, disclosed a copy of that decidedly rebel newspaper, *The Maryland News-sheet,* the Colonel entertained no further doubt of Lieutenant H.'s complicity and guilt.

It was in vain I asserted his innocence, and repeated again and again that it was impossible he could know that a folded packet contained an obnoxious journal, and that it was highly improbable, to say the least of it, he could be an accomplice in my possession of the letter.

"What is that you have in your hand?" was the only reply to my remonstrances and expostulations on behalf of the unfortunate officer I had so unintentionally betrayed.

"What—this little scrap of paper? You can have it if you wish: it is nothing. Here it is;" and I approached nearer to him, with the seeming intention of placing it in his hand; but I had taken the resolution of following the example set by Harvey Birch, in Cooper's well-known novel of "The Spy," in the event of my being positively commanded to "stand and deliver."

Fortunately, however, for me, the Colonel's wrath was diverted from the guilty to the guiltless: he was so incensed with Lieutenant H., that he forgot the very existence of Belle Boyd, and the precious note was left in my possession.

We were then and there dismissed, Colonel Beale contenting himself with giving a hurried order to the effect that I was to be closely watched. He then proceeded to the investigation of Lieutenant H.'s case. Bare suspicion was the worst that could be urged against him, yet, upon this doubtful evidence, or rather in the absence of any thing like evidence, a court-martial, composed of officers of the Federal army, dismissed him from the service.

Some time after the adventure I have just related the secret of our arrest transpired.

A servant had observed the gentleman to whom I have alluded give me the letter in my friend's house at Winchester. He gave information, and the result was, a telegram was sent to Major Tyndale, who was already incensed against me for having slipped through the pickets and got to Winchester without his pass. He communicated at once with Colonel Beale, and our arrest followed as I have described.

Had it not been for the curious manner in which Lieutenant H. was involved in the affair, and in which that unoffending officer was so unjustly treated, very much to my regret, I should not have escaped so easily.

Chapter VI

Among the Federals who then occupied Front Royal was
one Mr. Clark, a reporter to the *New York Herald,* and,
although an Irishman, by no means a gentleman.

He was domiciled at head-quarters, which were established,
as I have before mentioned, at my aunt's residence; and thus
it was that I saw him daily, for we could not possibly get
into the street without crossing the court-yard and passing
through the hall-way.

This Mr. Clark endeavored upon several occasions to
intrude his society upon me; and, although I told him plainly
his advances were extremely distasteful, he persevered so far
that I was forced more than once to bolt the door of the room
in which my cousin and myself were seated, in his face.

These rebuffs he never forgave, and from an intrusive friend
he became an inveterate enemy. It is to him I am indebted
for the first violent, undisguised abuse with which my name
was coupled in any Federal journal; but I must do the editors
of the Yankee newspapers the justice to admit they were not

slow to follow the example set them by Mr. Clark. They
seemed to think that to insult an innocent young girl was to
prove their manhood and evince their patriotism. I think my
English readers will neither admire their taste nor applaud
their spirit.

On the evening of the 23rd May I was sitting at the window
of our room, reading to my grandmother and cousin, when
one of the servants rushed in, and shouted, or rather shrieked —

"Oh, Miss Belle, I t'inks de revels am a-comin', for de
Yankees are a-makin' orful fuss in de street."

I immediately sprang from my seat and went to the door,
and I then found that the servant's report was true. The
streets were thronged with Yankee soldiers, hurrying about in
every direction in the greatest confusion.

I asked a Federal officer, who just then happened to be
passing by, what was the matter. He answered that the Confederates were approaching the town in force, under Generals
Jackson and Ewell, that they had surprised and captured the
outside pickets, and had actually advanced within a mile of
the town without the attack being even suspected.

"Now," he added, "we are endeavoring to get the ordnance
and the quartermaster's stores out of their reach."

"But what will you do," I asked, "with the stores in the large
dépôt?"

"Burn them, of course!"

"But suppose the rebels come upon you too quickly?"

"Then we will fight as long as we can by any possibility
show a front, and in the event of defeat make good our retreat
upon Winchester, burning the bridges as soon as we cross them,
and finally effect a junction with General Banks's force."

I parted with the Federal officer, and returning to the house,
I began to walk quietly up-stairs, when suddenly I heard the
report of a rifle, and almost at the same moment I encountered

Mr. Clark, who, in his rapid descent from his room, very nearly knocked me down.

"Great heavens! what is the matter?" he ejaculated, as soon as he had regained his breath, which the concussion and fright had deprived him of.

"Nothing to speak of," said I; "only the rebels are coming, and you had best prepare yourself for a visit to Libby Prison."

He answered not a word, but rushed back to his room and commenced compressing into as small a compass as possible all the manuscripts upon which he so much plumed himself, and upon which he relied for fame and credit with the illustrious journal to which he was contributor. It was his intention to collect and secure these inestimable treasures, and then to skedaddle.*

I immediately went for my opera-glasses, and, on my way to the balcony in front of the house, from which position I intended to reconnoitre, I was obliged to pass Mr. Clark's door. It was open, but the key was on the outside. The temptation of making a Yankee prisoner was too strong to be resisted, and, yielding to the impulse, I quietly locked in the "Special Correspondent" of the *New York Herald*.

After this feat I hurried to the balcony, and, by the aid of my glasses, descried the advance-guard of the Confederates at the distance of about three-quarters of a mile, marching rapidly upon the town.

To add to my anxiety, my father, who was at that time upon General Garnett's staff, was with them. My heart beat alternately with hope and fear. I was not ignorant of the trap

* This American cant term is exactly rendered into English by the phrase "to hook it." Slang is now so well understood that I apprehend few of my readers require to be told that "to hook it" signifies to make off, to run away. Our Transatlantic expression can boast, I believe, of the earlier derivation. The meaning of Σκεδάννῦμι, the root of which is *skeda*, was, I am told, understood in that early age in which were recorded the wrath of Achilles and the patriotism of Hector.

the Yankees had set for my friends. I was in possession of much important information, which, if I could only contrive to convey to General Jackson, I knew our victory would be secure. Without it I had every reason to anticipate defeat and disaster.

The intelligence I was in possession of instructed me that General Banks was at Strasbourg with four thousand men, that the small force at Winchester could be readily re-inforced by General White, who was at Harper's Ferry, and that Generals Shields and Geary were a short distance below Front Royal, while Fremont was beyond the Valley; further, and this was the vital point, that it had been decided all these separate divisions should co-operate against General Jackson.

I again went down to the door, and this time I observed, standing about in groups, several men who had always professed attachment to the cause of the South. I demanded if there was one among them who would venture to carry to General Jackson the information I possessed. They all with one accord said, "No, no. You go."

I did not stop to reflect. My heart, though beating fast, was not appalled. I put on a white sun-bonnet, and started at a run down the street, which was thronged with Federal officers and men. I soon cleared the town and gained the open fields, which I traversed with unabated speed, hoping to escape observation until such time as I could make good my way to the Confederate line, which was still rapidly advancing.

I had on a dark-blue dress,* with a little fancy white apron over it; and this contrast of colors, being visible at a great distance, made me far more conspicuous than was just then agreeable. The skirmishing between the outposts was sharp. The main forces of the opposing armies were disposed as follows : —

* This dress was afterwards cut up into two shirts for two wounded Confederate soldiers.

The Federals had placed their artillery on a lofty eminence, which commanded the road by which the Confederates were advancing. Their infantry occupied in force the hospital buildings, which were of great size, and sheltered, by which they kept up an incessant fire.

The Confederates were in line, directly in front of the hospital, into which their artillerymen were throwing shells with deadly precision; for the Yankees had taken this as a shelter, and were firing upon the Confederate troops from the windows.

At this moment, the Federal pickets, who were rapidly falling back, perceived me still running as fast as I was able, and immediately fired upon me.

My escape was most providential; for, although I was not hit, the rifle-balls flew thick and fast about me, and more than one struck the ground so near my feet as to throw the dust in my eyes. Nor was this all: the Federals in the hospital, seeing in what direction the shots of their pickets were aimed, followed the example and also opened fire upon me.

Upon this occasion my life was spared by what seemed to me then, and seems still, little short of a miracle; for, besides the numerous bullets that whistled by my ears, several actually pierced different parts of my clothing, but not one reached my body. Besides all this, I was exposed to a cross-fire from the Federal and Confederate artillery, whose shot and shell flew whistling and hissing over my head.

At length a Federal shell struck the ground within twenty yards of my feet; and the explosion, of course, sent the fragments flying in every direction around me. I had, however, just time to throw myself flat upon the ground before the deadly engine burst; and again Providence spared my life.

Springing up when the danger was passed, I pursued my career, still under a heavy fire. I shall never run again as I ran on that, to me memorable day. Hope, fear, the love of life, and the determination to serve my country to the last, conspired to fill my heart with more than feminine courage, and to lend preternatural strength and swiftness to my limbs. I often marvel, and even shudder, when I reflect how I cleared the fields, and bounded over the fences with the agility of a deer.

As I neared our line I waved my bonnet to our soldiers, to intimate that they should press forward, upon which one regiment, the First Maryland "rebel" Infantry, and Hay's Louisiana Brigade, gave me a loud cheer, and, without waiting for further orders, dashed upon the town at a rapid pace.

They did not then know who I was, and they were naturally surprised to see a woman on the battle-field, and on a spot, too, where the fire was so hot. Their shouts of approbation and triumph rang in my ears for many a day afterwards, and I still hear them not unfrequently in my dreams.

At this juncture the main body of the Confederates was hidden from my view by a slight elevation which intervened between me and them. My heart almost ceased to beat within me; for the dreadful thought arose in my mind, that our force must be too weak to be any match for the Federals, and that the gallant men who had just been applauding me were rushing upon a certain and fruitless death. I accused myself of having urged them to their fate; and now, quite overcome by fatigue, and by the feelings which tormented me, I sank upon my knees and offered a short but earnest prayer to God.

Then I felt as if my supplication was answered, and that I was inspired with fresh spirits and a new life. Not only despair, but fear also forsook me; and I had again no thought but how to fulfil the mission I had already pursued so far.

I arose from my kneeling posture, and had proceeded but a short distance, when, to my unspeakable, indescribable joy, I caught sight of the main body fast approaching; and soon an old friend and connection of mine, Major Harry Douglas, rode

up, and, recognizing me, cried out, while he seized my hand—
"Good God, Belle, you here! What is it?"

"Oh, Harry," I gasped out, "give me time to recover my breath."

For some seconds I could say no more; but, as soon as I had sufficiently recovered myself, I produced the "little note," and told him all, urging him to hurry on the cavalry, with orders to them to seize the bridges before the retreating Federals should have time to destroy them.

He instantly galloped off to report to General Jackson, who immediately rode forward, and asked me if I would have an escort and a horse wherewith to return to the village. I thanked him, and said, "No; I would go as I came;" and then, acting upon the information I had been spared to convey, the Confederates gained a most complete victory.

Though the dépôt building had been fired, and was burning, our cavalry reached the bridges barely in time to save them from destruction: the retreating Federals had just crossed, and were actually upon the point of lighting the slow match which, communicating with the bursting charge, would have riven the arches in pieces. So hasty was their retreat that they left all their killed and wounded in our hands.

Although we lost many of our best and bravest—among others the gallant Captain Sheetes, of Ashby's cavalry, who fell leading a brilliant and successful charge upon the Federal infantry—the day was ours; and I had the heartfelt satisfaction to know that it was in consequence of the information I had conveyed at such risk to myself General Jackson made the flank movement which led to such fortunate results.

And here let me pause a moment to do justice to the memory of a brave enemy, Colonel Kenly, who commanded the Federals, and who fought at their head with the courage of desperation, until he fell mortally wounded.

The Confederates, following up their victory, crossed the

river by the still standing bridges, and pushed on by the road which led to Winchester.

General Banks was startled from his lair at Strasbourg, and leaving everything but his own head and a handful of cavalry behind him, with the victorious Confederates in hot pursuit, rushed through Winchester and Martinsburg, and finally crossed the river at Williamsport, Maryland; and it is said that he and his command have never stopped running since.

During this hasty flight General Banks halted for a few minutes to take breath in the main street of Martinsburg. Upon the sidewalk were standing many children and young girls, among whom was my little sister.

One of these girls, recognizing General Banks's aide-de-camp, walked up to him and said—

"Captain, how long are you going to stay here?"

"Until Gabriel blows his horn," replied he.

To this mistimed vaunt my sister quietly rejoined, looking full in his face as she spoke—

"Ah, Captain, if you were to hear Jackson's horn just outside the town, you would not wait for Gabriel's."

Nor did they wait; for the echo of the Confederate General's bugles had little less terror for them than the sound of the archangel's trump.

When I first returned from the battle-field, tired, or, to say the truth, utterly enervated and exhausted, the Confederates were filing through the town, and the enthusiastic hurrahs with which they greeted me did more than any thing else could have done to revive my drooping spirits and restore my failing powers. The dead and wounded were now being brought in, and our house soon became a hospital.

Notwithstanding my fatigue, I contrived to render some assistance in dressing the wounds and alleviating the sufferings of our poor soldiers, who consoled themselves in their agonies with the reflection that they had done their duty nobly, and that their pangs were not imbittered by the sting and remorse with which defeat always torments a true soldier.

Among the dead who were brought next day to our house for interment were Captains Sheetes, Baxter, and Thaxter, all of Ashby's cavalry, and Major Davis, of Louisiana.

To my great joy my father came safe out of the battle, with but a very slight wound in the leg.

All the Federals left in Front Royal were captured; among them my particular friend, Mr. Clark, who, upon endeavoring to leave his room unseen during the confusion, found himself locked in.

I afterwards heard an amusing account of the manner in which he extricated himself, by letting himself down from the window; this, however, was unfortunately a work of time, and the delay was the cause of his capture. He was being escorted a prisoner down the street when, catching sight of me as I stood upon the doorstep, he shouted out —

"I'll make you rue this : it's your doing that I am a prisoner here."

During the battle, and while Colonel Fillebrowne was preparing to remove his effects from Winchester, a gentleman of high social position and Southern proclivities stepped into his office and said, "Colonel, how on earth did you get into such a trap? Did you know nothing of the advance of the Confederates?" Colonel Fillebrowne turned, and, pointing to the bouquet I had sent him only a day or two before, he said, "That bouquet did all the mischief : the donor of that gift is responsible *for all* this misfortune."

I could not but be aware that I had been of some service to my country; and I had the further satisfaction of feeling that neither a desire of fame nor notoriety had been my motive for enacting the *rôle* I did in this sad drama. I was not prepared, however, for that recognition of my services which was received on the very day they were rendered, and which I here transcribe : —

                                        "May 23d, 1862.
    "Miss BELLE BOYD,
    "I thank you, for myself and for the army, for the immense service that you have rendered your country to-day.
                "Hastily, I am your friend,
                        "T. J. JACKSON, C. S. A."

This short note, which was written at Mr. Richards's house, very near Front Royal, was brought to me by a courier, and I am free to confess, I value it far beyond any thing I possess in the world.

The object General Jackson had in view was too important to admit of his leaving behind him an adequate force for the protection of Front Royal; one regiment, the Twelfth Georgia Infantry, was all that could be spared; and thus Front Royal was retaken by the Federals, just one week after its brilliant capture by our troops.

During our short possession of the town, there was, among the prisoners taken in the pursuit beyond the river and sent back into our custody, a woman who represented herself to be the wife of a soldier belonging to the Michigan cavalry. She was handed over to me, and I furnished her with clothing, and did all that lay in my power to make her comfortable and happy.

Upon the arrival of the Federals under General Geary, most of the Twelfth Georgia were taken prisoners, together with all the sick and wounded.

The woman of whom I have just spoken was of course liberated; and the first use she made of her freedom was to report me to General Kimball as a most dangerous rebel, and a malignant enemy to the Federal Government.

The General immediately placed me under arrest, and surrounded our house with sentries, so that to escape was actually impossible. Within a few hours, however, after my incarceration, General Shields arrived; and, being senior in the service to General Kimball, naturally superseded him in the command of the army. He at once released me, and I thank him for his urbanity and kindness.

Rumors soon reached us to the effect that the Confederate army was retreating up the Valley, and once more all this portion of the country fell into the hands of the Yankees.

Chapter VII

Tone of the Northern Press towards me.—General Banks refuses to pass me South.—How I procure Passes.—The two Confederate Soldiers.—I write to "Stonewall Jackson".—Novel Method of conveying Information.—My Letter is Intercepted.—I am warned to depart South without delay.—I prepare to leave.

The Northern journals vied with one another in publishing the most extravagant and improbable accounts of my exploits, as they were pleased to term them, on the battle-field of the 23rd May.

One ascribed to "Belle Boyd" the honor of having directed the fire of the Confederate artillery throughout the action; another represented her as having, by the force of her genius, sustained the wavering counsels of the Southern generals; while a third described her as having, sword in hand, led on the whole of the attacking line to the capture of Front Royal; but as I believe that the veracity of the Yankee press is pretty well known and appreciated, I shall give no more extracts from their eloquent pages.

At the conclusion of the last chapter, I mentioned that General Shields released me from the arrest under which General Kimball had placed me, upon the report of the un-

169

grateful *ci-devant* prisoner; and, after a short time, finding no further persecution was resorted to, I thought the opportunity favorable for making an attempt to get south.

Meanwhile, General Banks had returned, and encamped close to the town, making my aunt's house his head-quarters.

It was to him, therefore, I applied for permission to depart.

"Where do you wish to go?" he asked.

"To Louisiana, where my aunt resides."

"But what will Virginia do without you?"

"What do you mean, General?"

"We always miss our bravest and most illustrious, and how can your native State do without you?"

I laughingly thanked him for the compliment, and he conversed with the utmost good-nature and pleasantry upon the part that I had taken in his recent defeat. Though a rabid Abolitionist, the General was certainly one of the most affable gentlemen I have ever met.

Several weeks passed by in peace and quiet, unmarked by any incident worthy of record, and at the expiration of this period, Front Royal was again evacuated by the Federal troops, with the exception of the Third Delaware Infantry, which corps was left in garrison. Their colonel was a very large, coarse man, with the manners and appearance of a butcher rather than of an officer.

On the other hand, Major McEnnis and Lieutenant Preston, who officiated severally as Provost and Assistant Provost-Marshal, were upon all occasions not only courteous, but kind, the natural consequence of which behavior was, that they were both highly respected and esteemed by us "rebels."

In the court-yard of the General's headquarters, and at a few yards only from our cottage, they had pitched a flag-tent, which served the purposes of their office, and here it was that all passes for the South were granted or refused, as the case might be. How many of these were procured upon false

pretences and transferred to recruits on their way to join the
Southern army, or by whom this ingenious *ruse* was practised,
I shall not here say.

I was one morning sitting in the drawing-room, when I
noticed two men, dressed as Confederate soldiers, standing
near the Provost-Marshal's tent. At my request, my grandmother sent for the Major, who obeyed her summons without
loss of time.

We asked him who the men were. He told us they were
paroled Confederate soldiers procuring passes to go south.
We then asked if they might be permitted to dine with us,
and received a ready assent. In the mean time they had disappeared; but one of them shortly reappearing, I accosted
him thus : —

"Won't you dine with us? The Major says you may."

"With pleasure, if you dine shortly; I have only two or three
hours allowed me to get beyond the pickets."

"Poor fellow!" said I; "but I am glad that you will soon
be free. Won't you take a letter from me to General Jackson?"

Upon his assenting to this request, I went off towards my
own room to write my dispatch; but, as I was passing by the
kitchen-door, one of the servants stopped me suddenly, and
exclaimed : —

"Miss Belle! who's dat man yose-a-talkin' to?"

"I know no more about him than that he is a paroled rebel
soldier, going south."

"Miss Belle, dat man ain't no rebel; I seen him 'mong de
Yankees in de street. If he has got secesh clothes on, he ain't
no secesh. Can't fool Betsy dat way. Dat man's a spy — dat
man's a spy. Please God, he am."

I, however, entertained a different opinion from that of the
negro woman, so I persevered in my intention, and wrote a
long friendly letter to General Jackson. At the same time, I
introduced a great deal of valuable information concerning

the Yankees, the state of their army, their movements and doings, and matters of a like nature.

Disregarding the warning voice of my sable Cassandra, I fancied the man was true and might be safely trusted; so as soon as dinner was finished, I called him aside and confided the letter to him with these words : —

"Will you promise me faithfully, upon the honor of a soldier, to take the utmost care of this, and deliver it safe to General Jackson? They tell me you are a spy, but I do not believe it."

He, of course, denied the soft impeachment, and swore, by all the host of heaven, to execute my commission with fidelity and dispatch.

Reader, conceive my feelings when, shortly after this man's departure, one of the officers came in and informed me that he was a spy, and was on his way to the Confederate lines at Harrisburg.

I immediately set about to rectify my unfortunate error, and, after some reflection, I decided upon the following expedient : —

I sat down and wrote Major Harry Gilmore, of the Confederate cavalry, a few lines, giving an accurate account of the man's personal appearance, and explaining the motive and circumstances of his journey south, and by what means I had been entrapped into trusting him with a letter for General Jackson. This note I dispatched by a conveyance, to which we rebels had given the name of "the underground railway."

The locomotive on this railway was an old negro, and the mail-car was an enormous silver watch from which the works had been extracted. I sent off my train, with orders that if, in passing the pickets, any one should inquire the time of day, the answer must be that the imposing-looking time-piece was out of order, and had ceased to mark the hours and minutes.

Our friend the spy, however, went neither to Harrisburg nor to General Jackson, but made his way straight to the

Federal General Sigel and gave him my letter. The General, in his turn, forwarded it to Stanton, the Secretary-at-War, who, I make no doubt, still retains it in his possession.

The fate of the spy, like that of so many of his fraternity, was tragic. He was soon after detected in the pursuit of his calling on the Rappahannock, and hanged. My readers, perhaps, may think I ought to congratulate myself upon having hitherto escaped a similar fate.

Shortly after this adventure an officer came and told me that further misconduct on my part might bring down upon me the severest punishment, and hinted that the Yankees, once thoroughly incensed, would not hesitate at the perpetration of any atrocity.

Entertaining these views, he recommended my immediate departure; and this kind advice meeting with the approval of my grandmother, I gave my consent, and immediately my maid had orders to prepare for a journey to Richmond. It was on a Tuesday that the officer promised to get a pass, and we were to be sent through the lines on the next ensuing Thursday. But fate had ordained otherwise.

Chapter VIII

I am Arrested by Order of Mr. Stanton, Federal Secretary of
   War.—My Room and Trunks are closely Searched.—
   Yankee Disregard for the Rights of Personal Property.—My
   Departure for Washington.—My Escort.—I arrive at
   General White's Head-Quarters in Winchester.

It was on a lovely Wednesday evening that our firm and
valued friend Lieutenant Preston, my Cousin Alice, and myself
were standing on the balcony, watching the last rays of the
setting sun as it sank behind the western hills.

Our conversation turned upon the divided and unhappy
state of our country. We recalled the peaceful scenes and
joyous days of the past, which were so painfully contrasted by
the present, and we were forced to agree that we had nothing
to expect from the future but a continuance, if not an aug-
mentation, of our calamities.

In such gloomy forebodings, and in the interchange of
apprehensions and regrets, we passed some time, and the
twilight was fast deepening into gloom, when we heard the
sound of horses' hoofs; and, straining our eyes through the
darkness, we discerned a large body of cavalry approaching
the house.

I immediately conceived the idea that it was a scouting-

174

party on their way to the mountains with the design of surprising Major Harry Gilmore's cavalry, and feared that their enterprise would prove successful unless the Confederate officer should have timely notice of his danger. I ran at once to my room and wrote a hasty note, in which I communicated my suspicions to Major Gilmore, and warned him to be on his guard.

This note I transmitted in the manner I have described in a previous chapter, by my "underground railway." After this feat I retired to bed, and slept quietly, undisturbed by any dream or vision of my approaching captivity.

Next morning I rose early and soon after breakfast I went to the cottage door, where I daily spent much of my time, watching the movements of the persons who, for various purposes, frequented head-quarters. I had not been long at my post when I observed several Yankee soldiers go into the coach-house. They immediately proceeded to drag out the carriage, and pull it up at the door of head-quarters, where they put to the horses.

There was nothing very extraordinary in all this; but in these anxious days the minds of all were in a perpetual state of tension, and a slight incident was sufficient to cause alarm.

This may account for the strange feeling that came over me — an irrepressible desire to ascertain who was to be the occupant of the carriage, which was on the point of starting for a destination of which I was ignorant.

I walked out upon the balcony; and, looking up and down the street, I saw that it was thronged with cavalry, the men dismounted, lounging about, and conversing with each other, in groups of twos and threes, evidently waiting for the expected order to mount.

While I stood looking at this scene, not without interest and curiosity, one of the servants came to me and said —

"Miss Belle, de Provo' wishes to see you in de drawing-room, and dere's two oder men wid him."

I immediately went down-stairs, and, upon entering the room, I found the Major, whose face wore an expression of excitement and nervourness. There were, as the servant had said, two other men in the room with him : one, a tall, fine-looking man, was introduced to me by the name and title of Major Sherman, of the 12th Illinois cavalry; the other was low in stature, coarse in appearance, with a mean, vile expression of countenance, and a grizzly beard, which, it was evident, had not made the acquaintance of water or a comb for weeks at least. His small, restless eyes glanced here and there, with an expression of incessant watchfulness and suspicion. All his features were repulsive in the extreme, denoting a mixture of cowardice, ferocity, and cunning. In a word, his mien was unmistakably that of a finished villain, who was capable of perpetrating any act, however atrocious, when stimulated by the promise of a reward in money.

This man was a good type of his order : he was one of Secretary Stanton's minions—a detective belonging to, and employed and paid by, that honorable branch of Mr. Lincoln's Government, the secret Service Department.

I had not been in the room more than a few moments when Major McEnnis turned to me and said—

"Miss Boyd, Major Sherman has come to arrest you."

"Impossible! For what?" I cried.

Major Sherman here interposed, and speaking in a very kind manner, assured me that, although the duty he had to perform was painful to his feelings, he was, nevertheless, forced to execute the orders of the Secretary of War, Mr. Stanton; and, as he finished speaking, the detective produced from his pocket the document, which I transcribe as nearly as I can recollect:—

" War Department.

"Sir :—You will proceed immediately to Front Royal, Virginia, and arrest, if found there, Miss Belle Boyd, and bring her at once to Washington.

"I am, respectfully,
"Your obedient servant,
"E. M. Stanton."

Such was the curt order that made me a prisoner; and, as remonstrance would have been idle and resistance vain, nothing was left for me but quiet, unconditional obedience.

The detective then informed me that it was his duty to examine all my luggage.

To this I could not do otherwise than assent, and only begged that a few minutes might be granted, to enable my servant to prepare my room, which was in great confusion, and that I might also be permitted to retire. I made this request to the detective, for it had not escaped my notice that Major Sherman was acting a subordinate part, and was virtually at the disposal and under the orders of the former.

As no answer was returned to my question, I took it for granted I had tacit permission to withdraw; but my disgust was great when, turning round upon the stairs, I saw my persecutor silently following at my heels.

I stopped short, and said —

"Sir, will not you wait until I see if my room is in a suitable condition for you to enter?"

The reply was characteristic, though not urbane.

"No, yer don't : I'm agoin' with yer. Yer got some papers yer want to get rid on;" and, with these words, he pushed violently past me, and hastily entered my room.

My clothes were first seized, and searched with the utmost scrutiny. My dresses were examined closely, and, after being turned inside out, and distorted into all sorts of fantastic shapes, were flung in a pile upon the floor, much to the horror and amazement of my maid, who had employed a great part of the previous night in packing them safely and neatly, and who was at a loss to understand the meaning of such treatment, which appeared to her, naturally enough, so strange and unseemly.

My underclothing next underwent an ordeal precisely similar to that which my upper garments had passed through; and, finally, my desk and portfolio were discovered; but here, very fortunately, my devoted servant came to the rescue with the promptitude and courage of a heroine.

She well knew the value I attached to the contents of my portfolio, and made a shrewd guess as to how far they would compromise me with my captor and his employers. Acting upon a sudden impulse, she made a swoop upon the repository of the greatest part of the evidence that could be adduced against me; and, rushing at headlong speed down-stairs, she gained the kitchen in time to burn all the papers it contained. But some important papers were, unfortunately, in my writing-desk, and these fell into the possession of the detective, who also, much to my regret, made prize of a handsome pistol, with belt and equipments complete, which had been presented to me, on the 4th of July, by a Federal officer on the staff, as a token, he was pleased to say, of his admiration of the spirit I had shown in defence of my mother and my home.

It had always been my hope to have some day an opportunity of begging General Stonewall Jackson's acceptance of a present made to me, under very trying circumstances, by a gallant and generous enemy; but this could not be done. The pistol now occupies a conspicuous place in the War Department at Washington, and is entered in the catalogue of spoils in the following words : —

"A trophy captured from the celebrated rebel Belle Boyd."

Not contented with the seizure of my own papers, the emissary of Mr. Stanton proceeded to break open the private *escritoire* of my uncle, who was a lawyer, and who had left it in my room for safe-keeping during his absence from Front Royal.

The detective, bundling up the law-papers with mine, bade me, in the roughest manner, and in the most offensive language, be prepared to start within half an hour.

I asked permission to be indulged with the attendance of my maid; but this request was refused, with imprecations, and she was only allowed to pack one trunk with apparel absolutely necessary to comfort, if not to decency. Brief time was granted for the packing; and, before many minutes, my solitary trunk was strapped to the back of the carriage.

I then nerved myself, and walking into the drawing-room, announced, in firm, unbroken accents, that I was ready to start.

I preserved my composure unshaken; although it was a hard trial for me to see my grandmother and cousin weeping piteously, and beseeching Major Sherman, in the most moving terms, to spare me. Their supplications were vain; and the detective, stepping up close to my side, ordered me to get into the carriage forthwith.

Then came the final parting — bitter enough, God knows; for I was being dragged from those to whom I was endeared by the associations of my happy youth, no less than by the ties of nature, and consigned to the safe-keeping of a man whose countenance alone would have immediately convicted him of any crime of which he might anywhere have been accused.

My negro maid clasped her arms round my knees, and passionately implored permission to attend me. She was torn from me, and I was hurried into the carriage without any opportunity of further expostulation on the part of myself or my relations.

The news of my arrest had spread quickly, and the streets were by this time filled with soldiers and citizens of the town.

As I stepped into the carriage, which for aught I knew was my funeral car, I cast a rapid but comprehensive glance upon the crowd collected to witness my departure and the demeanor I should sustain under such a trial.

Upon many, nay, upon most of the faces that met my gaze, sorrow and sympathy were written in unmistakable characters; but there were, nevertheless, some looks the expression of which was that of exultation and malignant triumph.

I knew how closely I was watched by friend and foe, and I resolved neither to make myself an object of derision to the one, nor of pity to the other. Though my heart was throbbing, my eyes were dry; not a muscle of my face quivered; no outward sign betrayed the conflicting emotions that raged within.

I could not guess what fate was in store for me; but I felt that, if I might judge of the clemency of my captors by the bearing of their delegate, it would be the part of wisdom to steel my mind against the worst that could ensue.

I was seated in the back of the carriage, and, just as we started, my evil genius mounted the driver's seat. In his hand he clutched a tin case, which held the papers he had taken from my room; and, as he turned his ugly features round from time to time to scrutinize my looks, my imagination pictured him to me as the ill-omened incarnation of Satan himself. I could not help associating him with the idea of Edgar Poe's raven, and asking myself if the fancy of the poet was to be realized in my case, and the companionship of the bird was to cease only with my life.

That these were the visions of a disturbed mind, I am now quite willing to allow; but, if my readers will bear in mind that I was young; that I had just been torn from my friends; that a long captivity appeared certain, and death not improbable; that while either fate was in abeyance, I was in the custody of a man whose character was clearly adapted to his odious calling — they will not be surprised that during a few hours my reason tottered, and horrible imaginings got the better of my fortitude.

My escort consisted of four hundred and fifty cavalry, the officer in command of whom observed all the regular precautions prescribed by military law for a march through an enemy's country. In addition to the ordinary advance and rear-guards, fifty scouts were detached in skirmishing order, to protect our right from surprise, and an equal number to guard our left; and in this order we advanced until about half our march was performed, and we reached an eminence which commanded a view of the country for several miles round.

Here, at a dreary spot, the cavalcade was brought to a halt. Field-glasses and signal-whistles were brought into requisition, and many other, to me, mysterious forms were gone through.

I had not yet shaken off my terrors, and I now resolved to collect my thoughts, and devote what I believed to be my last moments to prayer : for I could not then penetrate the motives which actuated the, to me, strange behavior of my escort, and I fully and firmly believed I should soon be dragged from the carriage and hanged from the bough of the maple-tree, the leaves of which were rustling over the carriage.

I afterwards ascertained that it was from fear of a rescue by Ashby's cavalry that all the precautions which alarmed me so much were taken; and I make no doubt but that that gallant Confederate, had he known of my situation, would have brought me off, or perished in the attempt.

After a long pause, the word "Forward" was given, and our march was resumed at a walk.

In due course, we gained the outskirts of Winchester, and were met by the remainder of the regiment by which I was escorted. The whole, amounting to five hundred and fifty sabres, some in front, some in rear of the carriage, marched in solemn procession down the main street of the town; and I believe the citizens, who rushed to the windows and doors, at first supposed that the carriage which conveyed my small but living person was the funeral-car of a general officer, bearing the warrior to his place of interment.

It was about six o'clock in the evening when I was brought to General White's headquarters, which were fixed about a quarter of a mile beyond the town.

I was immediately ordered to alight, and, without a minute's delay, I was ushered into his presence.

He received me with a graceful bow, and bade me welcome with marked courtesy.

I returned his salutation with as much ease as I could assume, and asked what he intended doing with me.

"To-morrow," replied he, "I shall send you on to the commanding officer at Martinsburg. He can best inform you what is to be done with you. You will rest here after your journey, for the night."

"But surely," I interceded, "you will at least allow me to remain with my friends in the village until the morning?"

"No, no," he rejoined, rather pettishly; "I cannot consent to that. It would take a whole regiment to guard you; for, though the rebel cavalry should not enter the town to attempt your rescue, I make no doubt that the citizens themselves would try it."

"But surely," I then pleaded, "you do not mean that I am to sleep here, defenceless and alone in a tent, at the mercy of your brigade? I never yet slept in a tent when I was present with our army, and how can I endure such a penance in the camp of my enemies?"

"My own tent," replied the General, with a low bow, "has been properly prepared for the reception of a lady. Whenever you wish to retire you can follow your inclinations; and you may rest assured you shall sleep in perfect security."

Supper was then brought in; and it did not escape my notice that the table was decorated with a dazzling display of rich silver plate, which I more than suspected had formerly been the property of some of our dear old Virginian families; and the thought that the rightful owners were at that moment miserable outcasts, probably in want of the bread my Federal lords despised, effectually destroyed any appetite my sufferings might have left me.

I said not a word until supper was finished, then, rising quietly from my camp-stool, I begged permission to retire to the tent which I had been informed was to be my dormitory.

The General rang a small bell, which was quickly answered by an "intelligent contraband," bearing two very massive silver candlesticks, which, like the spoons and forks, were doubtless the spoils of my native province, probably once the property of an intimate friend.

"Show this lady to the tent that has been prepared for her reception;" and these words, with the accompaniment of a bow, were all I had in exchange for the prayers and blessings I had been accustomed to carry with me to my bed.

No sooner had I entered the tent than the negro left me to sleep or to my own reflections.

For some time I listened to the tramp of the sentries as they paced to and fro outside; then I tried to distract my thoughts and forget my grief, in attempting to guess how many Yankee soldiers were told off to guard a single Confederate girl. But all would not do: for the time being I was conquered in body and spirit; my burden seemed heavier than I could bear. I sat down upon my camp-stool, and pressed my hands upon my aching brow, and before long the fatigue and anxiety I had undergone stood me in stead, and I fell asleep.

Chapter IX

About half-past three the following morning I was suddenly aroused from my comfortless slumbers by the beating of the long roll, and by the reports of several muskets fired in quick succession. Officers half dressed sprang to arms, rushed to their horses, and rode off to the outposts. Meanwhile, I had lighted my candle, my heart beating high with hope; for I persuaded myself that the alarm was caused by an attempt on the part of the Confederates to effect my rescue. I sat down anxiously awaiting the result, when one of the officers, who was rushing to the front, stopped opposite my tent and shouted, or rather roared out—

"Put out that light : it is some signal to the rebels. Do you hear me ?"

I of course obeyed the mandate, and a few minutes afterwards I heard the retreat beat; upon which one of the sentries explained the meaning of what had happened, and how it

came to pass that the camp had been thrown into such a state
of confusion. It appeared that an obtuse cow had strayed from
a neighboring field, and, not understanding the challenge of the
sentry, had disregarded the order to halt, although twice
repeated. Hereupon the sentry, who could not make out the
outline of the cow in the darkness, fired, and the other sentries
on his right and left, taking the hint, fired also, though at what
they aimed it would be difficult to say. However, fire they did
at random, as is the custom of undisciplined troops everywhere,
and thus all my hopes of a rescue were extinguished by a cow.

Dawn was hardly breaking when I was ordered to get ready
once more, as I was to be taken directly to Martinsburg.

My preparations were soon made, and with two hundred
for my escort I set forward. At eight o'clock we came to a halt
at a small farm-house standing by the road-side. Here breakfast
had been prepared, and I was informed the refreshment was
at my disposal. No sooner was my appetite satisfied — a consummation which was easy and rapid — than we resumed our
journey to Martinsburg, at which bourne I arrived about one
in the afternoon, tired and exhausted with the fatigue and
anxiety I had undergone.

Major Sherman, compassionating my forlorn condition,
very kindly stayed behind the cavalcade and prevailed upon
his wife to accompany me to the camp, which was pitched at
a short distance on the north side of the town.

I was forthwith conducted to the tent of the commanding
officer. My head was now almost bursting with pain; and I
implored him to have me taken to my home, which was close
by in a suburb of the village, there to rest and refresh myself
for a few hours, as I understood I was to start for Washington
at two o'clock next morning. I make no doubt my petition
would have been granted had not the detective here interposed
and informed the Federal Colonel that Mr. Secretary Stanton
would probably take exception to such an indulgence, which

would give me an opportunity of holding communication with persons inimical to the United States Government.

After putting this "spoke in my wheel," so to speak, my amiable custodian went himself to my home and ransacked all my father's private papers, under pretence of hunting for "communications" from myself to my mother. Fortunately, however, he found none, and his unwelcome visit was not crowned with the success he had anticipated.

To return to myself.

I was sitting on the camp-stool in my tent, gazing listlessly about me, when my attention was suddenly attracted to a carriage which was driving into the encampment. It stopped, and a lady rapidly alighted. She was dressed in deep mourning; a thick veil entirely concealed her face. But I recognized her at once, in spite of her disguise.

The feverish intelligence which accompanies danger and suffering was superadded to that natural instinct which, though no one can explain, all have experienced; and I *felt,* for I could not see, that the visitor was my mother.

I sprang from my seat, and rushed into her arms, with a cry of joy I have no power to repress.

"My poor, dear child !" she said, or rather gasped, and then sank fainting at my feet.

They carried her into the tent, and the first use she made of restored consciousness was to implore the Colonel, in the most moving terms, to allow her to carry me home. She begged him to trust to the evidence of his own senses, and to read in my haggard looks the bodily prostration to which I was reduced, no less than the mental anguish which was consuming me; and in very truth the iron had entered into my soul, and my sufferings were almost greater than I could bear.

The Colonel politely but firmly refused to grant my mother's prayer; and I am willing to believe that in this refusal he was actuated by a stern sense of duty, for his feelings so far prevailed as to induce him to authorize my removal to Raemer's Hotel, which is contiguous to the station from which the trains for Washington start. No sooner had I, a young girl, weak and ill, accompanied by my mother and Mrs. Sherman, set foot in the hotel than the building was girdled by a cordon of sentries, twenty-seven in number, in addition to whom, three were posted in the passage leading to my room, and one more was stationed just outside my door; and then, with these material guarantees for my security and good behavior, my little sister, my brothers, and my mother, were allowed to visit me.

It had been arranged that the detective who arrested me should be my escort as far as Washington; but I so loathed the sight of this man, that I sent for Colonel Holt, and implored him to substitute for the odious reptile any one of his officers who could be spared, and upon whom he could rely for my safe-conduct.

Colonel Holt kindly granted my request, and detailed Lieutenant Steele, of the Twelfth Illinois Cavalry, for "escort duty."

As the time for my arrival approached, my feelings overpowered my self-control, and, for once, I yielded to a passionate burst of grief. Nor was I without an excuse for my weakness. My nearest and dearest were lamenting around me, and within a few minutes I was to be torn from their arms and consigned to the doubtful mercies of strangers and enemies. My strength, too, failed me; and, just as the fatal moment drew near, I sank down in a stupor, from which I was suddenly and painfully awakened by the ominous screech of the railway engine. I nerved myself by a vigorous effort, and within a few seconds I found myself seated in the train. I say found myself, for I have never been able distinctly to recall how I reached the station — whether I walked or was carried, I know not. I was soon, however, conscious that Lieutenant

Steele was by my side, and that Washington was my destination. I felt grateful for the presence of an officer to whom I might reasonably look for protection, and the reflection that, come what would, I had escaped the clutches of the detective, roused my drooping spirits.

Alas! this infatuation was soon dispelled, for, upon looking about me, I was horrified to see my "evil genius" occupying the left seat of the carriage.

The image of Edgar Poe's raven arose in my mind, and my disturbed imagination whispered that I was doomed to the perpetual companionship of an incarnate fiend.

It afterwards transpired that this able minion of Mr. Stanton had telegraphed to the chief of detectives at Washington to meet us at the dépôt.*

Mr. Steele, who had no idea I was to be thrown into prison, observed that, upon our arrival at Washington, I should go to Willard's Hotel, and, after a short rest, proceed to the office of the Secretary-at-War. This plan, however, was by no means in accordance with the programme drawn up by the detective. He was one of Mr. Stanton's chosen and trusted agents. He, doubtless, well knew what was in store for me, and he did not scruple to presume upon his position, and use very sharp words to Lieutenant Steele.

It was about nine o'clock in the evening when we arrived at Washington; but, notwithstanding the lateness of the hour, a very large concourse of people had assembled in and about the dépôt, in order to catch a glimpse of "the wonderful rebel;" for the news of my arrest had preceded my arrival.

As I stepped upon the platform, the chief of the detectives, another kindred spirit of Mr. Stanton's, seized me roughly by the arm, and, in a gruff voice, shouted out—

"Come on; I'll attend to you."

He was then proceeding to push me through the crowd,

* In America, a railway terminus is called a dépôt.

when Lieutenant Steele, thrusting himself forward, protested vehemently against such usage, and declared that I should not be treated in so barbarous a manner; that I was a lady, and that my character and position should be respected.

The torrent of abuse that was poured upon him for thus endeavoring to take my part, was conveyed in words too horrible to bear repetition; and at that moment I would gladly have lain down and died, for the thought flashed across my mind —

"My God! if this is the beginning, what will the end be?"

Amongst the crowd I had many sympathizers; but they dared not interfere. At Washington might was indeed right; and I will venture to say, that the arbitrary exercise of power by the United States Government has cast into the shade all that we read of the Spanish Inquisition, and all that we hear of Russian domination in Poland. A word of encouragement, nay, a whisper of condolence, would have been sufficient to introduce an imprudent friend to that receptacle which was awaiting me — a prison cell.

I was thrust into a carriage; and the order, "Drive to the Old Capitol," was promptly given; but, before it could be obeyed, Lieutenant Steele, who had been very unceremoniously dismissed from further attendance upon me, stepped up and politely begged permission to wait upon me to prison. To a gruff refusal he firmly rejoined —

"I am determined to see her out of your hands, at least."

The carriage was driven at a rapid pace, and we soon came within sight of my future home — a vast brick building, like all prisons, sombre, chilling, and repulsive.

Its dull, damp walls look out upon the street: its narrow windows are further darkened by heavy iron stanchions, through which the miserable inmates may soothe their captivity by gazing upon those who are still free, but whose freedom hangs but by a slender thread.

Such is the calm retreat provided by a free and enlightened community for those of its citizens who have the audacity to express their disapproval of the policy adopted by the Government of the hour.

In the days of old France the victims of royal indignation were seized under cover of night, and buried with secrecy and dispatch in the impenetrable recesses of the Bastille; the most jealous care, the most unceasing vigilance, was observed, in order that the mystery of their doom should never be elucidated; the *lettre de cachet,* which was the implement of their destruction, was in its very nature a proof that such acts of violence and injustice were a source of fear and shame even to the despot who committed them.

Many a dark deed has been perpetrated within the old walls of the Tower of London; its stones have more than once been stained with the blood of the innocent; but here, again, tortures and death were studiously concealed, and, when detected, amply avenged.

The autocrat of Russia does not exhibit to the world the instruments with which he chastises his naughty children; the clank of Siberian chains is not heard in any other quarter of the globe.

It has been reserved for the Government of the United States of America, the Apostles of Liberty, the tender-hearted emancipators, who shudder at the bare idea of the African's wrongs, to cast into a dungeon in open day, without accusation or form of trial, any one of their fellow-countrymen and countrywomen whom they may suspect of disaffection to the clique which retains them in power and office.

One of the greatest authors, ancient or modern, when speaking of our forefathers, said —

> "They left their native land in search of freedom, and found it in a desert."

Could "Nominis Umbra," wrapped in his old veil of mystery, revisit our world, he would be appalled to find how completely the men of this generation have parted with that freedom without receiving so much as a mess of pottage in exchange for their glorious birthright.

To return to my narrative.

Upon my arrival at the prison, I was ushered into a small office. A clerk, who was writing at a desk, looked up for a moment, and informed me the superintendent would attend to my business immediately. The words were hardly uttered when Mr. Wood entered the room, and I was aware of the presence of a man of middle height, powerfully built, with brown hair, fair complexion, and keen, bluish-gray eyes.

Mr. Wood prides himself, I believe, upon his plebeian extraction; but I can safely aver that beneath his rough exterior there beats a warm and generous heart.

"And so this is the celebrated rebel spy," said he. "I am very glad to see you, and will endeavor to make you as comfortable as possible; so whatever you wish for, ask for it and you shall have it. I am glad I have so distinguished a personage for my guest. Come, let me show you to your room."

We traversed the hall, ascended a flight of stairs, and found ourselves in a short, narrow passage, up and down which a sentry paced, and into which several doors opened. One of these doors, No. 6, was thrown open; and behold my prison cell!

Mr. Wood, after repeating his injunction to me to ask for whatever I might wish, and with the promise that he would send me a servant, and that I should not be locked in as long as I "behaved myself," withdrew, and left me to my reflections.

At the moment I did not quite understand the meaning of the last indulgence, but within a few minutes I was given a copy of the rules and regulations of the prison, which set forth that if I held any communication whatever with the other prisoners, I should be punished by having my door locked.

There was nothing remarkable in the shape or size of my apartment, except that two very large windows took up nearly the whole of one side of the wall.

Upon taking an inventory of my effects, I found them to be as follows : — A washing-stand, a looking-glass, an iron bedstead, a table, and some chairs.

From the windows I had a view of part of Pennsylvania Avenue, and far away in the country the residence of General Floyd, ex-United States Secretary of War, where I had formerly passed many happy hours.

At first I could not help indulging in reminiscences of my last visit to Washington, and contrasting it with my present forlorn condition; but rousing myself from my reverie, I bethought myself of the indulgence promised me, and asked for a rocking-chair and a fire; not that I required the latter, for the room was already very warm, but I fancied a bright blaze would make it look more cheerful.

My trunk, after being subjected to a thorough scrutiny, was sent up to me, and, having plenty of time at my disposal, I unpacked it leisurely.

Upon each floor of the prison were posted sentries within sight and call of each other. The sentry before my door was No. 6, and when I had occasion for my servant I had to request him to summon the corporal of the guard. My attendant was an "intelligent contraband," who was extremely useful to me during my enforced residence in the Old Capitol.

I had not unpacked my trunk, when dinner was served; and here I shall do plain justice by transcribing the bill of fare; and it will be allowed I claim no commiseration on the plea of bread-and-water diet, though such had been ordered for me by Mr. Stanton : —

BILL OF FARE

Soup—Beef Steak—Chicken—Boiled Corn—Tomatoes
—Irish Stew—Potatoes—Bread and Butter—Cante-
lopes—Peaches—Pears—Grapes.

This, with but little variety, constituted my dinner every day until released.

At eight o'clock, Mr. Wood came to my room, accompanied by the chief of the detectives, who desired an interview with me on the part of the Secretary-at-War.

I begged this worthy to be seated — a request he immediately complied with; and he then delivered the following graceful exhortation, which I transcribe verbatim : —

"Ain't you pretty tired of your prison a'ready? I've come to get you to make a free confession now of what you've did agin our cause; and, as we've got plenty of proof agin you, you might as well acknowledge at once."

"Sir," I replied, "I do not understand you; and, further-more, I have nothing to say. When you have informed me on what grounds I have been arrested, and given me a copy of the charges preferred against me, I will make my statement; but I shall not now commit myself." Thereupon the oath of allegiance was proffered, and I was harangued at some length upon the enormity of my offence, and given to understand the cause of the South was hopeless.

"Say, now, won't you take the oath of allegiance? Remember, Mr. Stanton will hear of all this. He sent me here."

To this peroration I replied—

"Tell Mr. Stanton from me, I hope that when I commence the oath of allegiance to the United States Government, my tongue may cleave to the roof of my mouth; and that if ever I sign one line that will show to the world that I owe the United States Government the slightest allegiance, I hope my arm may fall paralyzed by my side."

This speech of mine he immediately took down in his note-book, and, growing very angry at my determination, he called out—

"Well, if this is your resolution, you'll have to lay here and die; and serve you right."

"Sir," I retorted, "if it is a crime to love the South, its cause, and its President, then I am a criminal. I am in your power; do with me as you please. But I fear you not. I would rather lie down in this prison and die, than leave it owing allegiance to such a government as yours. Now leave the room; for so thoroughly am I disgusted with your conduct towards me, that I cannot endure your presence longer."

Scarcely had I finished my defiance, which I confess was spoken in a loud tone of voice, when cheers and cries of "Bravo!" reached my ears. Until that moment, I was not aware that the rooms on the floor with my own were occupied; for, having kept my door shut all day, I had no means of noticing what was passing around me.

My door, however, had been left open during my interview with the detective, consequently my neighbors, whom I after-wards ascertained to be Confederate officers and Englishmen, had overheard our whole conversation, and hailed with applause the firmness with which I had rejected Mr. Stanton's overtures of liberty, conditional as they were upon my renunciation of the Confederacy and on my allegiance to the Federal Government. And now, Mr. Wood, taking pity upon me, withdrew the detective, saying—

"Come, we had better go : the lady is tired."

Within a few minutes of their departure, I heard a low, significant cough, and, as I turned in the direction from whence it proceeded, something small and white fell at my feet. I picked it up, and found that it was a minute nut-shell basket, upon which were painted miniature Confederate flags. Round it was wrapped a small piece of paper, upon which were traced a few words expressive of sympathy with my misfortunes. I afterwards found out that the author of this short communication was an Englishman; and I can assure him that his kindness was like a ray of light from heaven breaking into the cell of a condemned prisoner. I wrote a hasty reply, and, watching my opportunity, threw it to him. I then lay down on my bed in a tranquil—I had almost said a happy—frame of mind; and I closed my first day in a dungeon by repeating to myself, more than once—

> "Stone walls do not a prison make,
>   Nor iron bars a cage :
> A free and quiet mind can take
>   These for a hermitage."

Chapter X

MY FIRST NIGHT IN PRISON

The first night in a convent forms the subject of a melancholy, but beautiful picture. My first night in a prison must be painted in dark colors, unrelieved by the radiance that plays upon the features of the sleeping devotee, who has of her own free will cast aside the world, exulting in the belief that the voluntary sacrifice of youth, love, and all the ties of nature, will be more than recompensed by an immortality of bliss.

Her dreams are of paradise : enthusiasm comes to the aid of religion, and gives her a foretaste of eternity.

"Her soul is gone before her dust to heaven."

Prophets, angels, and saints people her silent cell; a vision of glory streams in through her narrow window; and the first night in the convent is the night of ecstasy.

I said, at the conclusion of my last chapter, that I was comforted by the spontaneous proof of sympathy given by my unknown correspondent; but my situation was too painful to admit of real, lasting consolation. The medicine administered was at best but a momentary stimulant; the reaction soon set in; and, as my fatigue gained ground, the sense of my miserable condition prevailed against my bodily energies.

I rose from my bed and walked to the window. The moon was shining brightly. How I longed that it were in my power to spring through the iron bars that caught and scattered her beams around the room!

The city was asleep, but to my disordered imagination its sleep appeared feverish and perturbed. Far away the open country, visible in the clear night, looked the express image of peace and repose.

"God made the country, and man made the town," I thought, as I contrasted the close atmosphere of my city prison with the clear air of the fields beyond.

What would I not have given to exchange the sound of the sentry's measured tread for the wild shriek of the owl and the drowsy flight of the bat!

The room which was appropriated to me had formerly been the committee-room of the old Congress, and had been repeatedly tenanted by Clay, Webster, Calhoun, and other statesmen of their age and mark.

A thousand strange fancies filled my brain, and nearly drove me mad. The phantoms of the past rose up before me, and I fancied I could hear the voices of the departed orators as they declaimed against the abuses and errors of the day, and gave their powerful aid to the cause of general liberty. They never dreamed that the very walls which re-echoed the eloquence of freedom would ere long confine the victims of an oligarchy. Theirs was the bright day—ours is the dark morrow, of which the evil is more than sufficient. Those great men (for great they unquestionably were) lacked not the gift of prophecy, for they did not fail to discern the little cloud, then no bigger than a man's hand, which was gathering in the horizon — that dark speck which was so soon to generate a tempest far blacker than that from which the chariot of Ahab made haste to escape.

Throughout that long dreary night I stood at the window watching, thinking, and praying. It seemed to me that morning would never come.

> " Methought that streak of dawning gray
> Would never dapple into day,
> So heavily it rolled away,
>   Before the eastern flame."

But the morning came at last — the herald, let me hope, from a brighter world of another morrow to us. No sooner did the first faint light find its way through the windows, than I threw myself again upon my bed, and almost immediately sank into a deep sleep.

It was about nine o'clock, I believe, when I was aroused by a loud knocking at my door.

"What is it?" I cried, springing up.

"The officer calling the roll, to ascertain that no one has escaped."

"You do not expect me to get through these iron bars, do you?"

"No, indeed," was the chuckling rejoinder; and immediately afterwards I heard the officer's retreating footsteps as he passed on in the execution of his duty.

Soon after the servant who had been assigned to me came to make preparations for breakfast; and, as my morning meal was no less ample and choice than my dinner of the preceding evening, I will not detain my readers with a second prison bill of fare.

It was but a few minutes after breakfast when the sentry directly outside my door was relieved.

I listened attentively to catch the orders given to the relief. They were —

"You will not allow this lady to come outside her door or talk to any of those fellows in the room opposite; and if she wants any thing, call the corporal of the guard. Now don't let these —— rebels skear yer."

There was no more information to be gained for the moment; so I sat down and amused myself with the morning papers, which had been brought to me with my breakfast.

They all contained an account of my capture, and a summary of my career. The subject-matter was, of course, personally interesting, although in every instance my motives were misconstrued, and my character was aspersed. I must, however, admit that many of the most bitter calumnies then published of me were contradicted not many days afterwards in the very same journals which had originally circulated them.

There was a narrow space behind the prison which was reserved for the prisoners' exercise — an indulgence they were granted at stated hours. On their way to their playground most of them had to pass my door, and in the procession I recognized, on the second day of my imprisonment, several of my old friends and acquaintances who had formerly belonged to the army of Virginia.

The tedious day wore on, and a shudder passed over me as I recalled the hideous thoughts which had banished sleep throughout the previous night.

Late in the evening, when my servant came with my tea, she told me that many prisoners had been brought in during the day, and that two of the newly-arrived captives had been consigned to the room adjoining mine.

By this time it had become known throughout the length

and breadth of the prison-house that I was no other than that persecuted young lady, "Belle Boyd."

Acting upon this knowledge, my neighbors, who were the friends of happier days, devised a scheme by means of which they were enabled to make themselves known to me.

At about eleven o'clock I sat down and opened my Bible. I selected a chapter, the promises contained in which are peculiarly consoling to the captive; but I had not read more than two or three verses when my attention was distracted by a knock against the wall. I listened with attention, and presently felt sure that the next sound which reached my ears was that made by a knife scooping out the plaster of the wall.

Within a few minutes the point of a long case-knife was visible; and I was not slow to co-operate with those pioneers of free communication — the inmates of the next room.

I made use of the knife that remained on my supper-tray; and before long the two knives had conjointly made an aperture large enough to admit of the transmission of notes rolled tight and of the circumference of a man's forefinger. The clandestine correspondence that was thus carried on was, on either side of the wall, a source of much pleasure, and served to beguile many a tedious hour.

In the room immediately above mine, and in which Mrs. Greenhow had been incarcerated and suffered so much for five long, weary months, were confined some gentlemen of Fredericksburg. They had contrived to loosen a plank in the floor, and to make an aperture through which the occupant of the room beneath them might receive and return letters.

Whenever I desired to communicate with the prisoners whose rooms were on the opposite side of the passage, I adopted the expedient of wrapping my note round a marble, which I rolled across, taking care that the sentry's back was turned when my missive was started on its voyage of discovery.

I have described how I established a post between my room

and the room on my right; the same system was applied, with equal success, to the one on the left, which was then the abode of Major Fitzhugh, of Stuart's staff, and Major Morse, of Ewell's. This room, which joined with many others, became a medium of communication with all; and we were soon enabled to transmit intelligence to each other throughout the prison.

It was on the fourth morning of my imprisonment, as I was watching from my door the prisoners going down to breakfast, that a little Frenchman handed me, unobserved, a half-length portrait of Jefferson Davis. This I forthwith hung up in my room over the mantel-piece, with this inscription below it —

"Three cheers for Jeff. Davis and the Southern Confederacy!"

One of the prison officials, Lieutenant Holmes, passing by my door, caught sight of the hostile President's likeness, and the words with which I had decorated it. Rushing like a madman into my room, he tore it down with many violent oaths. "For this," he said, "you shall be locked in;" and he was as good as his word, for he turned the key in the door as he left the room.

My offence was severely punished. I was kept a close prisoner; and so little air was stirring in the sultry month of July that I grew very ill and faint, and at times I really thought I should have died from the oppressive heat of the room; and this misery I had to endure for several weeks. At last Mr. Wood paid me a visit, and, observing how pale and ill I had become under such rigorous treatment, took pity upon me, and gave orders that my door should be once more left open. Soon after I was granted the further indulgence of half an hour's walk daily in that portion of the prison yard which had been assigned to ladies for exercise.

One day, whilst standing in the doorway, my attention was attracted to an old gentleman almost bent double with age; his long white hair hung down to his shoulders, whilst his beard, gray with the heavy touch of old Father Time's fingers, reached nearly to his waist.

A feeling of pity took possession of my soul, and I could not but help thinking, as I gazed upon him, "Poor old man! what an unfit place for you; even I, the delicate girl, can better stand the hardships of this dreary, comfortless place, than you." And what was his crime? This—he was designated a traitor to the Northern Government because he firmly believed that the Constitution as it was should remain unaltered. I afterwards learnt that he was Mr. Mahony, the editor of the *Dubuque* (Iowa) *Crescent,* and who, when released, published a book, "The Prisoner of State," which was, however, suppressed by the Secretary of War, Stanton.

The rules of the prison, of course, inter-dicted all intercourse between the prisoners, but, alas! I was on one occasion taken so completely by surprise as to obey my first impulse and commit a flagrant breach of orders.

I was walking up and down my "seven feet by nine" promenade, when I suddenly recognized one of my cousins, John Stephenson, a young officer in Mosby's cavalry. So glad was I to see him that I never thought of consequences, but rushed up to exchange a few words with him. The charged bayonet of the sentry soon checked my impetuosity, and I was summarily sent back to my room, although "play-time" had not expired. My unfortunate cousin was at once removed to the guard-room.

It was late one evening, and I was sitting reading at my open door, when Mr. Wood came down the stairs exclaiming—

"All you rebels get ready; you are going to 'Dixie' to-morrow, and Miss Belle is going with you."

At this joyful news all the prisoners within hearing of the tidings of their approaching liberation joined in three hearty cheers. For my part, I actually screamed for joy, so suddenly had my return to freedom been announced.

The next day all the prisoners whose turn for exchange had come were drawn up in line in the prison yard.

Soldiers were stationed from the door of the prison half-way across the street, which was thronged by a dense crowd, brought together by curiosity to witness the departure of the rebel prisoners.

Two hundred captives, inclusive of the officers and myself, were then passed beyond the prison walls, and formed in line on the opposite side of the street.

I stepped into an open carriage, followed by Major Fitz-hugh, who had been "told off" to convey me to Richmond.

I carried concealed about me two gold sabre-knots, one of which was intended for General Jackson, the other for General Joe Johnston.

As we drove off, the Confederate prisoners cheered us loudly; their acclamations were taken up by the crowd, so that the whole street and square resounded with applause. When we arrived at the wharf, we were sent on board the steamer *Juanita,* which lay at her moorings all that night.

I shall conclude this chapter with two or three prison reminiscences, which will, I hope, give my reader some idea of the *ménage* of the "Old Capitol."

On one occasion my servant had just brought me a loaf of sugar, when it occurred to me that the Confederate officers in the opposite room across the passage were in want of this very luxury. Accordingly I asked the sentry's permission to pass it over to them, and received from him an unequivocal consent in these plain words — "I have no objection."

This, I thought, was sufficient; and it will hardly be believed that, while I was in the very act of placing the sugar in the hand of one of the officers, the sentry struck my left hand with the butt-end of his musket, and with such violence was the blow delivered that my thumb was actually broken. The attack was so unexpected, and the pain so excruciating, that I could not refrain from bursting into tears.

As soon as I could master my feelings, I demanded of the sentry that he should summon the corporal of the guard; and upon his refusing my just demand, I stepped forward with the intention of exercising my undoubted right *in propriâ personâ*.

But my tyrant was now infuriated; he charged bayonets, and actually pinned me to the wall by my dress, his weapon inflicting a flesh-wound on my arm.

At this moment, fortunately for me, the corporal of the guard came rushing up the stairs to ascertain the cause of the disturbance. The sentry was taken off his post, and, unless I am grievously mistaken, a short confinement in the guard-room was considered sufficient punishment for such outrageous conduct.

Not long after this adventure, my aunt called to see me. Permission was given to me to pass down-stairs for the purpose of an interview with my relation, and I was proceeding on my way, when one of the sentries, with a volley of oaths, commanded me to "halt."

"But I have permission to go down and see my relation."

"Go back, or I'll break every bone in your body;" and a bayonet was presented to my breast.

I produced the certificate which authorized me to pass him; and I think, from his manner, he would have relented in his intentions towards me, and returned to a sense of his own duty, but he was encouraged in his mutinous behavior by the cheers of a roomful of Federal deserters, who called upon him to bayonet me. In this predicament I was saved by Major Moore, of the Confederate States Army, and the timely arrival of Captain Higgins and Lieutenant Holmes, two prison authorities, who secured me from further molestation.

This man's crime, which was neither more nor less than open mutiny, was visited by a slight reprimand. This leniency was perhaps intended for a personal compliment to me. If so, let me assure the Yankee officers, I duly appreciate both its force and delicacy.

Mr. Wood, the superintendent, will, I am sure, forgive me for relating one characteristic anecdote of him.

It was Sunday morning when he came stalking down the passage into which my room opened, proclaiming in the tones and with the gestures of a town-crier—

"All you who want to hear the Word of God preached according to 'Jeff. Davis' go down into the yard; and all you who want to hear it preached according to 'Abe Lincoln' go into No. 16."

This was the way in which he separated the goats from the sheep. I need not say which party was considered the goats within the walls of the Old Capitol.

Chapter XI

At early dawn, the *Juanita* cast off from her moorings, and
late in the evening of the same day we dropped anchor at the
mouth of the Potomac, where we passed that night. Next day,
about 4 A.M., we proceeded on our way up the river, arriving
at Fortress Monroe late in the evening; and here we were
boarded by Lieutenant Darling, of General Dix's staff. On
each side of us lay General McClellan's transports, filled with
soldiers; about half a mile distant was the "Rip Raps," a fort
quite equal to Sumter in strength. Notwithstanding our
position, which was exposed to the fire of this splendid fort,
our people indulged their feelings by singing from time to time
"the songs of the sunny South," and these they interspersed
with loud cheers for Jeff. Davis.

At one time a Yankee officer on board one of the transports, irritated evidently by these repeated expressions of animosity to his Government, hailed us with the words—

"Three cheers for the Devil!"

"It is only natural you should cheer for the advocate of your cause," was the ready retort; "and we will cheer for ours." And so these shouts and counter-shouts were kept up until we got under way again, and steamed up the muddy waters of the James River.

As we rounded a bend in the stream we caught sight of the glorious flag of our country, the Stars and Bars. It was waving in the evening breeze from a window in the house of Mr. Aikens.

Until that well-known and beloved emblem met my eyes again, I had but imperfectly realized my freedom. Now it was present and visible in its chosen symbol. If our men had cheered before, their shouts, when surrounded by the transports and under the guns of the fort, were as nothing to those with which they hailed the emblem of "Dixie's" resolution to uphold its independence, defend its natural rights, and resist force with force.

At the wharf we were met by Colonel Ould, who held the office of Commissioner of Exchange at Richmond. He was attended by his assistant, Mr. Watson; and it was under the supervision and by the direction of these gentlemen that the exchanged soldiers were marched on shore. I passed that night very agreeably under Mr. Aikens's hospitable roof, and enjoyed myself thoroughly in his society and that of his family. Next morning Colonel Allen sent his carriage and horses from Richmond, to convey me at my ease into the city. I decided, without hesitation, to drive to the Ballard House, where, in fact, I had been informed rooms were prepared for my reception. My route lay close by the encampment of the Richmond Blues; and I confess to the mixed feeling of pride and pleasure I derived from the high compliment paid me by them.

The company was drawn up in review order, and presented arms as I drove by. In the evening I was serenaded by the city band; in short, my reception at the hands of all classes was flattering in the extreme.

After a sojourn of ten days at the Ballard House, I removed to Mrs. W.'s boarding-house in Grace Street, where I enjoyed the delightful society of many old and warm friends.

At the period of which I speak not a few of the notorieties of Richmond were assembled at Mrs. W.'s excellent establishment; among others, General and Mrs. Joe Johnston, General Wigfall and his family, and Mrs. C., that celebrated leader of *ton* at Washington, equally and justly renowned for her wit and charms. Her conversation attracted around her, wherever she appeared, crowds of admiring listeners; and I feel sure that many of my American readers will recognize the fair lady to whose name I have, for obvious reasons, placed the initial letter only.

I was engaged one evening in a desultory conversation, when an officer who had been one of my fellow-captives in Washington came up to me and placed in my hands a note and small box. Upon opening the latter I found that it contained a gold watch and châtelaine, both handsomely enamelled, and richly set with diamonds; and upon reading the note I discovered that the beautiful and useful ornament was offered to my acceptance "in token of the affection and esteem of my fellow-prisoners in the Old Capitol."

For a few moments I could not find words to thank their delegate, so overpowered was I by this striking and unexpected mark of the feelings entertained for me by my countrymen.

I had been in Richmond but a short time, when my father came to take me home. The battle of Antietam had been fought, and Martinsburg was once more in the hands of the Confederates.

The very day after my return home I rode out to the

encampment, escorted by a friend of my family, in order to pay a visit to General Jackson. As I dismounted at the door of his tent, he came out, and, gently placing his hands upon my head, assured me of the pleasure he felt at seeing me once more well and free. Our interview was of necessity short, for the demands upon his valuable time were incessant; but his fervent "God bless you, my child," will never be obliterated from my memory, as long as Providence shall be pleased to allow it to retain its power.

In the course of our conversation the General kindly warned me that, in the event of his troops being forced to retreat, it would be expedient that I should leave my home again, as the evacuation of Martinsburg by the Confederates would, as on former occasions, be rapidly followed by its occupation by our enemies, and that it would be unwise and unsafe for me to expose myself to the caprice or resentment of the Yankees, and run the risk of another imprisonment. He added that he would give me timely notice of his movements, by which my plans must be regulated.

Very shortly after the interview I have just noticed the General rode into the village and took tea with us, and on the very day after his visit I received from him a message to the effect that the troops under his command were preparing for a retrograde movement upon Winchester, and that he could spare me an ambulance, by aid of which I should be enabled to precede the retreat of the army, and thus keep my friends between my enemies and myself.

I must here explain that, when we had occasion to retire from the border, we were forced to look to the army for the means of transportation, it being the invariable practice of the Yankees, when they evacuated any place, to take with them every horse and mule, without the slightest discrimination between public and private property; and, should circumstances compel them to leave any animal behind, it was in these instances wantonly destroyed.

Acting upon General Jackson's advice, I removed to Winchester; and it was there and then that I received my commission as Captain and honorary Aide-de-camp to "Stonewall" Jackson; and thenceforth I enjoyed the respect paid to an officer by soldiers.

Upon the occasion of the review of the troops in presence of Lord Hartingdon and Colonel Leslie, and again, when General Wilcox's division was inspected by Generals Lee and Longstreet, I had the honor to attend on horseback, and to be associated with the staff officers of the several commanders.

While General Wade Hampton held possession of Martinsburg I seized the opportunity of paying many visits to my home, and upon one of these expeditions I narrowly escaped being again captured.

The party that accompanied me was a large one; and, upon our arrival at Martinsburg, we improvised a dance. We were informed that the Yankees were advancing, but we had suffered a similar alarm to disperse us without cause more than once before. We therefore easily persuaded ourselves it was only the old cry of "Wolf! wolf!" This time, however, the warning voice was a true one; and we were barely off when heavy skirmishing commenced at no great distance from us — in fact, at the very outskirts of the town. This was the last opportunity I had of seeing my mother for nearly a year.

The Yankees were advancing by way of Culpeper Court-House, and our people, leaving the valley, crossed the mountains to intercept them.

As the small-pox was raging fearfully at Stanton, it was, of course, dangerous even to enter that town. Accordingly I, in company with several officers' wives, among whom were Mrs. G., Mrs. W., Mrs. F., and others, avoided the pestilential spot, and adopted a different route.

We were well in advance of the army, but our servants were with our baggage, which was transported in the ordnance wagons of General W.'s division. Passing through Flint Hill — the inhabitants of which gave me a cordial reception — I went on to Charlottesville, where I remained some time.

At last, feeling very anxious to rejoin my mother, I determined to write to General Jackson and ask his opinion upon the step I so longed to take. I was prepared to run almost any risk; but, at the same time, I resolved to abide by the General's decision.

It was pronounced in the following note, which I transcribe verbatim, as there is a kind of satisfaction in noting down the words of a truly great man, however trivial the subject that may have called them forth : —

> "Head-Quarters, Army of Virginia,
> "Near Culpepper Court-House,
> "January 29th, 1862.
>
> "MY DEAR CHILD,
>
> "I received your letter asking my advice regarding your returning to your home, which is now in the Federal lines. As you have asked for my advice, I can but candidly give it. I think that it is not safe; and therefore do not attempt it until it is, for you know the consequences. You would doubtless be imprisoned, and possibly might not be released so soon again. You had better go to your relatives in Tennessee, and there remain until you can go with safety. God bless you.
>
> "Truly your friend,
> "T. J. JACKSON."

I lost no time in acting upon this sound and friendly advice, and was soon "on the road" once more.

Upon arriving at Knoxville, I was received with every mark of kindness and hospitality. The second night after my arrival

I was serenaded by the band, and the people congregated in vast numbers to get a glimpse of the "rebel spy;" for I had accepted the *sobriquet* given me by the Yankees, and I was now known throughout North and South by the same cognomen.

After one or two appropriate airs had been played, the people in the streets took it into their heads to call for my appearance on the balcony. I rather dreaded the publicity that would attend a compliance with their wishes, and I begged General J. to be my substitute and thank them in my name. But they would not be satisfied without a look at me; so I steadied my nerves and stepped forth from the window. Hereupon the shouts were redoubled, and I took the opportunity of concocting a pretty speech; but it did not please me, and I felt morally convinced I should break down were I to attempt any thing like an oration. So soon, therefore, as silence was restored, I addressed my kind-hearted audience in the following words, which contain an allusion to an expression once made use of in public by General Joe Johnston : —

"Like General Joe Johnston, 'I can fight, but I cannot make speeches.' But, my good friends, I no less feel and appreciate the kind compliment you have paid me this night."

I confess that I felt relieved when this harangue, brief and plain as it was, was over. It was followed by "Dixie's Land" and "Good Night." After which national airs the band marched off and the people dispersed.

Next morning the newspapers gave circumstantial accounts of the whole affair, in highly complimentary language, and, instead of being described as the "rebel spy," I was designated "the Virginian heroine." I now became the guest of my relative, Judge Samuel Boyd; and pleasant indeed was my visit to Knoxville. The city at this period was gay and animated beyond description. Party succeeded party, ball followed ball, concert came upon concert, and I took no thought of time.

When spring came round I made up my mind to make a tour through the South, and then return to Virginia.

I have said so much of the various receptions which I met with at different places that I almost fear I shall be accused of egotism rather than given credit for gratitude; but it should be borne in mind that the period of which I write had its perils and its pleasures, its griefs and its joys, exciting enough to justify outbreaks of feeling in a people naturally warm-hearted and sensitive. But, whatever criticism I expose myself to, I cannot refrain from expressing my warm thanks to that large body of my countrymen whose incessant kindness towards me made my progress through the Southern States one long ovation. My advent was anticipated by telegrams at each town through which I passed. Invitations of the most hospitable and delicate nature poured in upon me. Offers of assistance and assurances of regard and affection were innumerable. I accepted as many invitations as my time would permit, and was rejoiced at the opportunities I enjoyed of going over the famous and productive cotton plantations of Alabama.

After a long and delightful stay in Montgomery, I made the best of my way to Mobile, a city I had always wished to see, and one which existing circumstances made doubly interesting to all true Southern hearts.

Before arriving at the last-named port, a rumor had reached me that General Jackson had been wounded at the battle of Chancellorsville, but the rumor also affirmed that the wound was very trifling — so slight, indeed, as to be of no consequence. Conceive then the shock I experienced when this fatal telegram was put into my hand : —

"Battle House, Mobile, Alabama.
"MISS BELLE BOYD,
   "General Jackson now lies in state at the Governor's mansion.
                              "T. BASSETT FRENCH,
                              "A.D.C. to the Governor."

And this was all. These few words were the funeral oration of a man who, for a rare combination of the best and the greatest qualities, has seldom or never been surpassed.

It is not for me to trace the career and paint the virtues of "Stonewall" Jackson : that task is reserved for an abler pen; but I may be permitted to record my poignant grief for the loss of him who had condescended to be my friend.

The sorrow of the South is unmitigated and inextinguishable.

When Nelson fell, at the crowning victory of Trafalgar, it was given to England to engrave that thrilling epitaph —

           "Hoste devicto requievit,"

upon the tomb of her darling hero, whom she justly loved and reverenced beyond all the great sons that Providence had sent her with so lavish a hand.

Alas! it was not General Jackson's destiny to deliver his country; but future ages will not measure his fame by the shortness of his career.

"The lightning that lighteneth out of the one part under heaven shineth unto the other part under heaven." Yet no sooner do men see its brightness than it vanishes.

And such was the glory of Jackson. It had neither dawn nor twilight. It rose and set in meridian splendor.

During the next thirty days — the space of time allotted for the outward and visible sign of a soldier's sorrow — I wore a crape band on my left arm; then leaving Mobile with a heavy heart, I proceeded to Charleston, South Carolina, where I remained one day only. I found time, however, to accept an invitation to go on board the two gunboats which lay in the harbor, and from their decks, by the aid of glasses, I could make out nearly all the ships of the Yankee blockading squadron.

In the evening I dined on shore with General Beauregard and several of the officers of his staff; and shortly after dinner one of the officers kindly presented me with a large supply of fresh fruit, which was part of the cargo of a blockade-runner which had just run in safe and sound from Nassau. Besides the oranges, pine apples, and bananas, which were most acceptable, my kind friend gave me a very handsome parrot, which I contrived to take home with me.

When I made good my return to Richmond, I learnt, on the best authority, that the Confederate troops were making a second advance down the valley, their object being the recapture of Winchester. Being now very anxious to get home, I followed close upon the rear of our army, and when the attack upon Winchester commenced I was but four miles distant from the scene of action.

When the artillery on both sides opened fire, the familiar sound reminded me of my own adventures on a former battle-field, and I resolved to be at least a spectatress of this. I joined a wounded officer, who, though disabled from taking an active part in the fight, where, by his crippled condition, he would but have hindered his men, was yet able to accompany me some way.

Accordingly we rode together to an eminence which commanded an uninterrupted view of the combat. Here we sat some short time, absorbed in the struggle that was going on beneath us.

"The broken billows of the war,
And pluméd crests of chieftains brave,
Floating like foam upon the wave."

But this calm feeling was not of long duration. I was mounted upon a white horse, which was quite conspicuous to the artillerymen of a Yankee battery which had been pushed up to within three-quarters of a mile of the spot that we had selected for our watch-tower. A foolish report had been circulated through their army that in battle I rode a white horse, and was "invariably at General Jackson's side." Acting upon this mistaken idea, the guns of the battery were turned upon us.

By this time the officer of whom I have spoken and myself had been joined by several citizens, ladies and gentlemen, who were attracted by curiosity and anxiety to witness the fight. They were for the most part mounted on emaciated horses and mules which had been overlooked by the Yankees when they retired, and they one and all seemed to consider me as perfect security for themselves.

I shall never forget the stampede that was made when a shell came suddenly hissing and shrieking in among us. I joined, *con amore,* in the general flight; for I had seen enough of fighting to prefer declining with honor the part of a living target, when exposure, being quite useless, becomes an act of madness.

The battle was not of long duration. The terms were too equal to leave the issue long in doubt.

Milroy's "skedaddle" was even more disgraceful than that of Banks. The victorious Confederates, led on by General Lee, pressed hard upon the flying Yankees, of whom they killed many, and took more prisoners. The pursuit was not abated until the enemy were again in Maryland.

My father, whose health had been broken by the severe hardships of the campaign, was at home on leave; and I had

the double pleasure of being welcomed by both my parents
to poor Martinsburg.

Chapter XII

Elated by their continued successes, the Confederates, under
General Lee, marched on into Pennsylvania. A panic seized
the people of the North; for they knew of the depredations
that they had been committing in the South, and of course
could not expect much mercy from the invading army. General
Lee, however, issued an order to the officers under him not to
allow their men to burn, pillage, or destroy any property; if
they did, they were to be punished.

Though the hearts of the sympathizers with the South beat
high with hope—for rumor said that Baltimore and Washington were to be attacked—their hopes were blighted. The battle
of Gettysburg was fought. And, oh! how many of those brave

and noble fellows who went forward proudly to the front, eager to avenge the wrongs the South had suffered, who had left the beautiful shores of Virginia to defend their native soil, found a soldier's grave! Or, perchance, they were not even buried, their bodies lying upon the battle-field where they fell, with no covering save the blue canopy of heaven, their bones left to bleach in the sunlight, or gleaming ghastly white in the moon's pale beams.

Martinsburg soon became one vast hospital; for, as fast as they could be brought to the rear, the Confederate wounded of the great battle were sent back southward. There was no established hospital in my native village, it being too near the border; so that the churches and many of the public buildings were obliged to be used temporarily for that purpose. My time was constantly occupied in attending to the poor soldiers with whom our house was filled. Mrs. Judge McM., of Georgia, who had come to seek the dead body of her son, having heard of his untimely end, was also staying at my mother's.

Upon the retreat of the Southern army, after the battle of Gettysburg, they marched through Martinsburg, leaving the border again in the possession of the Confederate cavalry under General B., as General Wade Hampton had been severely wounded.

I had been from home so long, and my mother and father were so anxious that I should remain with them, that I hoped, by keeping quiet, to be allowed to do so. My mother was taken very ill just as the Confederates evacuated the town, it being found that they could no longer retain it in their possession, and for a short time all was quiet.

My little baby-sister was but three days old when, as I sat in my mother's room, I heard the servants exclaim, "Oh, here comes de Yankees trou' de town!" I went to the window, and, looking out, saw that a whole brigade had halted in front of my home. In a short time two officers approached the door, and one of them rang the bell. My father, who had gone to meet them, sent me word that Major Goff and Lieutenant —— wished to see me. I descended to the drawing-room and was introduced to them, when the Major said—

"Miss Boyd, General Kelly commanded me to call and see if you really had remained at home, such a report having reached headquarters; but he did not credit it, so I have come to ascertain the truth."

To this I answered—

"Major Goff, what is there so peculiarly strange in my remaining in my own home with my parents?" feigning perfect ignorance, as I spoke, that there was any danger to be apprehended from my so doing. He replied—

"But do you not think it rather dangerous? Are you then really not afraid of being arrested?"

"Oh no! for I don't know why they should do so. I am no criminal!"

"Yes, true," said he; "but you are a rebel, and will do more harm to our cause than half the men could do."

"But there are other rebels besides myself."

"Yes," he answered; "but then not so dangerous as yourself."

After a few moments' longer conversation he withdrew, bidding us "Good morning," as he left.

For some days we saw nothing of him, and began to hope that I should not be further annoyed. But, alas! my hopes were doomed to disappointment; for scarce four days had passed by before an order was issued for my arrest. My mother was very ill when they came to take me, and, fearing that if I were removed it might prove fatal to her in her delicate state of health, my father begged that they would let me stay at home, at least until she became convalescent. We hoped thus to gain time, and, through private influence, to procure my release from the department at Washington. To be just, although an avowed enemy of the Federal cause, I will state that they obligingly complied with this request, and placed me on parole, but at the same time stationed guards around the house; watching me so strictly that I was not even allowed to go out upon the front balcony.

It was amusing to hear the orders given to the sentries; for instance, "that they must not let me come near them, for I might give them chloroform, or send a dagger through their hearts."

This was in July; and, between my mother's illness, the warm weather, and my being a prisoner, I scarcely knew what to do. Without the necessary pass no one was allowed to go in or come out of our house. On one occasion, desiring to take a walk, I got a special permit from the commanding officer, which read as follows : —

"Miss Belle Boyd has permission to walk out for half an hour, at 5 o'clock this A.M., *giving her word of honor that she will use nothing which she may see or hear to the disadvantage of the U.S. troops."*

I had gone only a few blocks from home when I was arrested and sent back, with a guard on each side of me, their muskets loaded. In about an hour's time I received a note from the head-quarters of the general, informing me that, although on parole, *"I was not allowed to promenade freely in Martinsburg."* Vexatious and insulting to my feelings as this was, my troubles were not at an end.

Nearly a month passed away, during which period I was kept in a state of anxious suspense as to what would eventually be my fate. At last, one day, when we were all hoping that I should soon be at liberty to do and act as I pleased, Major Walker, the Provost-Marshal, called, with a detective, and informed me that I must get ready to go to Washington City; that the Secretary of War, Mr. Stanton, had so ordered it; and that I was to take my departure from home at eleven A.M. the next day.

There was no hope of escape for me, as the house was vigilantly guarded by the sentries. My poor mother, but just recovered from her grave illness, became seriously worse at the bare idea of my being again thrown into prison. My father, who was always so good and kind to me, determined that I should not go unaccompanied, trusting myself to the tender mercies of a detective. So, next day, when the time came for us to leave, I was attended by my fond parent; and, after bidding a tearful adieu to my poor mother, brothers, and sisters, who wept bitterly, we started once more for Washington City.

I shall pass over my dreary journey of one hundred miles. There was little of interest to commend it to the attention of my readers; for they can readily imagine the sad, tearful girl, and the father vainly attempting to comfort her.

When I arrived in Washington, tired and worn, I was immediately taken, not to my former quarters, but to the Carroll Prison. This large, unpretending brick building, situate near the Old Capitol, was formerly used as a hotel, under the name of Carroll Place, and belonged to a Mr. Duff Green, a resident in the city. But, since my first taste of prison life, it had been converted into a receptacle for rebels, prisoners of state, hostages, blockade-runners, smugglers, desperadoes, spies, criminals under sentence of death, and, lastly, a large number of Federal officers convicted of defrauding the Government. Many of these last were army-contractors and quartermasters, of whom I shall merely observe that they seemed to care very little about their ultimate fate, and evidently enjoyed the, to them, preposterous notion, suggested in the journals of the day, that Mr. Lincoln was Napoleonic in his idea of punishing them for their misdeeds.

At the guarded gates of this Yankee Bastile, I bade adieu to my father; and, once more, iron bars shut me off from the outer world, and from all that is dear in this life. I was conducted to what was termed the "room for distinguished guests" — the best room which this place boasts, except some offices attached to the building. In this apartment had been held, though not for a long period of time, Miss Antonia F., Nannie T., with her aged mother, and many other ladies belonging to our best families in the South. Again my monotonous prison routine began. It seemed to me that the world would never go round on its axis; for the days and nights were interminably long, and many, many were the hours that I spent gazing forth through the bars of my grated windows with an apathetic listlessness. Yet there were times when I wished that my soul were but free to soar away from those who held me captive.

Friends who chanced to pass the Carroll would frequently stop and nod in kindly recognition of some familiar face at the windows; unconscious that, in so doing, they violated prison regulations. When noticed by the sentries, these good Samaritans were immediately "halted;" and, if riding or driving, were often made to dismount by the officious and impudent corporal of the guard, and forced to enter the bureau of the prison — there to remain until such time as it should please their tormentors to let them depart. Can it be doubted that many went away with the unalterable opinion that a sterner despotism than existed in the United States was nowhere to be found? Defenceless women were not permitted to pass unscathed, because a drunken and brutal set, vested with a "little brief authority," saw fit to vent their spleen upon the weak.

A few days after my arrival at the prison, I heard the "old familiar sound" of a grating instrument against the wall, apparently coming from the room adjoining mine. Whilst engaged in watching to see the exact portion of the wall whence it came, I observed the plaster give way, and next instant the point of a knife-blade was perceptible. I immediately set to work on my side, and soon, to my unspeakable joy, had formed a hole large enough for the passing of tightly-rolled notes.

Ascertaining my unfortunate neighbors to be, beyond a doubt, "sympathizers," I was greatly relieved; for our prison was not without its system of espionage to trap the incautious. These neighbours were Messrs. Brookes, Warren, Stuart, and Williams; and from them I learnt that they had been here for nine months, having been captured whilst attempting to get South and join the Southern army.

But soon, alas! this little paper correspondence, that enlivened, whilst it lasted, a portion of my heavy time, was put a stop to by Mr. Lockwood, the officer of the keys, whose duty it was to secure our rooms, and who was always prying about when not otherwise engaged. Although it was well concealed on both sides, our impromptu post-office could not escape his Yankee cunning; and he at once had the gentlemen removed into the room beyond, and the mural disturbance closed up with plaster.

Several days subsequently I learned that I was to have a companion in a Miss Ida P., arrested on the charge of being a rebel mail-carrier. I was allowed to speak with and visit her as soon as she arrived, and she was placed in the room that had been occupied by the above-mentioned gentlemen.

Now, between her room and that to which the gentlemen had been removed, there was a door. This the workmen nailed up, and then boarded over; but I watched very attentively which plank was placed over the key-hole, and pointed it out to the new-comer. We then held a council of war as to the best way of getting the board off the key-hole. We tried several times, but our combined efforts produced no effect upon the stoutly nailed wood-work; and, having neither hatchet nor hammer, we were about to give it up, when I suddenly bethought me of the sentry outside. "Oh!" I said, "I will manage it!" and, going to the door, I bribed the sentinel with some oranges and apples, and, after talking to him for some time, asked him to "lend me his bayonet?" Pausing an instant, he finally unfixed it from his gun, then, with the whispered injunction of "Be quick, miss!" handed it to me. I ran into the room with it, and, whilst Miss Ida watched, I endeavored to wrench off the obstinate board.

But, at this critical juncture, the prison superintendent, Mr. Wood, came rushing up the stairway; and I only had time to thrust the bayonet under the camp bedstead when he entered the room. I was frightened, I will admit; for in a few minutes the sentries would be relieved, and of course the soldier would have to account for the loss of his bayonet. We wanted to free him from complicity in the affair; and woman's wit came to my assistance, as it had often done before.

I proposed that, my room being larger than Miss Ida's, we should go in there and sit down. Fortunately to this the superintendent agreed. After remaining for a short time, I said, "Oh! Miss Ida, I have forgotten my pocket-handkerchief!" and, running hastily into her room, I seized the bayonet, wrenched off the board, and returned the weapon to the scared sentinel.

Little did Mr. Wood imagine the part I had just played, as he sat glaring around him with his cat-like eyes, and boasting that "there warn't any thing going on in that prison that he didn't know of." For several days after this, Miss Ida and I whiled away our time by writing and receiving notes.

Miss P., however, did not remain here long, for, having given her parole that she would do nothing more against the Yankee Government, she was released.

Chapter XIII

A very Romantic Way of Corresponding.—The Prison Authorities for once are at a Loss.—My Confederate Flags.—They wave over Washington in spite of Yankee assertions to the contrary.—I become very ill.—Mr. Stanton in an unfavorable Light once more.—My Prisoner of Front Royal in her true Character.—Sentence of Court-Martial is announced to me.—A Relapse of my former Illness.—I am banished.—The Cry of "Murder" raised round the Corner. —Incidents in my Prison Life.

One evening, about nine o'clock, while seated at my window, I was singing "Take me back to my own sunny South," when quite a crowd of people collected on the opposite side of the street, listening. After I had ceased, they passed on; and I could not help heaving a sigh as I watched their retreating figures. What would I not have given for liberty? Rising from my chair, I approached the gas, lowered it, then resumed my seat, and, leaning my head against the bars, sank into deep thought.

I was soon startled from this reverie by hearing something whiz by my head into the room and strike the wall beyond. At the moment I was alarmed; for my first impression was that some hireling of the Yankee Government, following the

226

plan of Spanish countries, had endeavored to put an end to my life. I almost screamed with terror; and it was some minutes before I regained sufficient self-command to turn on the gas, so that, if possible, I might discover what missile had entered the room.

Glancing curiously round, I saw, to my astonishment, that it was an arrow which had struck the wall opposite my window; and fastened to this arrow was a letter; I immediately tore it open, and found that it contained the following words : —

"Poor girl! you have the deepest sympathy of all the best community in Washington City, and there are many who would lay down their lives for you, but they are powerless to act or aid you at present. *You have many very warm friends;* and we daily watch the journals to see if there is any news of you. If you will listen attentively to the instructions that I give you, you will be able to correspond with and hear from your friends outside.

"On Thursdays and Saturdays, in the evening, just after twilight, I will come into the square opposite the prison. When you hear some one whistling ' 'Twas within a mile of Edinbro' town,' if alone and all is safe, lower the gas as a signal and leave the window. I will then shoot an arrow into your room, as I have done this evening, with a letter attached. Do not be alarmed, as I am a good shot.

"The manner in which you will reply to these messages will be in this way : Procure a large india-rubber ball; open it, and place your communication within it, written on foreign paper; then sew it together. On Tuesdays I shall come, and you will know of my presence by the same signal. Then throw the ball, with as much force as you can exert, across the street into the square, and trust to me, I will get it.

"Do not be afraid. *I am really your friend.*

"C. H."

For a long time I was in doubt as to the propriety or safety of replying to this note; for I naturally reasoned that it was some Yankee who was seeking to gain evidence against me. But prudence at last yielded to my womanly delight at this really romantic way of corresponding with an unknown who vowed he was my friend; and I decided on replying.

It was an easy thing for me to procure an india-rubber ball without subjecting myself to the least suspicion; and by this means I commenced a correspondence which I had no reason to regret; for whoever the mysterious personage may have been, he was, without doubt, honorable and sincere in his professions of sympathy.

Through him I became possessed of much valuable information regarding the movements of the Federals; and in this unique style of correspondence I have again and again received small Confederate flags, made by the ladies of Washington City, with which I was only too proud and happy to adorn my chamber.

Little did the sentries below know of the mischief that was brewing above their heads; and where and how I had been enabled to obtain Confederate flags was a subject of much wonderment in the prison. It is almost needless to remark that I took care to keep the secret, though I must acknowledge that there was rashness in displaying the tiny Southern banners, and danger of subjecting myself to insult from the brutes who guarded me. But I could not resist the temptation!

On several occasions I fastened one of these ensigns to a broom-stick, in lieu of a flag-staff, and then suspended it outside the window, after which I retired to the back part of the room, out of sight of the sentinel. In a short time this would attract his attention — for, when on watch, the sentinels generally were gazing heavenwards, the only time, I really believe, that such was the case — and he would roar out at the top of his voice some such command as —

"Take in that —— flag, or I'll blow your —— brains out !"

Of course I paid no attention to this, for I was out of danger, when the command would generally be followed up by the report of a musket; and I have often heard the thud of the Minié-ball as it struck the ceiling or wall of my room. Before the sentinel had time to reload his piece, I would go to the window and look out, seemingly as unconscious as though nothing had occurred to disturb my equanimity.

Just after this episode of the "arrow-headed" correspondence — a green spot in my memory, to which I revert with pleasure — I was taken dangerously ill with typhoid fever. Can this be wondered at when I inform my readers that the room in which I was confined was low and fearfully warm, and that the air was fetid and rank with the fumes of an ill-ventilated Bastile ?

In this same room Miss McDonough died (as will be seen by referring to my husband's journal). The poor child was under the treatment of Doctor F., the surgeon of the prison — the same who attended me for some time, but under whose awkward treatment I grew daily, nay, hourly, worse. Nor did I begin to recover until I met with the kind attendance of a Confederate surgeon, who was a prisoner, like myself, in the Old Capitol; and it is to him that I feel indebted for my final recovery.

Years may roll by, but my sufferings in that prison, both mental and physical, can never be obliterated from my memory; and to attempt to describe them would be utterly impossible. There I was, far from home and friends — no soft hand to smooth my fevered brow, no gentle woman near me, save an humble negress, who nursed me through my illness as though she had been my own "black mammee." Relations and friends, who had heard of my attack of fever, as well as my immediate family, endeavored, time and again, to gain access to me; but they were referred, by his own orders, to Secretary Stanton, who, when application was made to him for me to be removed from the prison during my illness at least, would remark, "No; she is a —— rebel; let her die there!"

At the expiration of three weeks, passed under the treatment of my new physician, I was pronounced convalescent; and at the end of the fourth I was able once more to walk about.

It was at this period of my imprisonment that, one day, Captain Mix, of whom I shall have occasion to speak hereafter, came into my room and said—

"A most beautiful woman has arrived here to-day, and is in the room at the further end of the passage below you."

At the time, I took no notice of the remark, and had almost forgotten the incident, when, one morning, whilst walking in the passage, I saw our new inmate. Judge of my astonishment on recognizing in her my prisoner at Front Royal, who had requited my kindness to her when there by informing the general that I was a bitter enemy of the Yankees. She proved to be—alas! that I should have to write aught derogatory to one of my own sex—not what she had represented herself, the wife of a soldier, but a camp-follower, known as "Miss Annie Jones." She was said to have been insane; but how far this report is to be credited I know not.

Shortly after she was placed here, another arrival, a Frenchwoman, came in, who was charged with having sold her dispatches to the Confederate States authorities, enacting the "spy" for both sides. Neither of these women possessed that priceless jewel of womanhood—reputation. Yet it was with such that I was immured, though, thank Heaven! I was not thrown into immediate contact with them.

My trial by court-martial had meanwhile been progressing, under the fostering tenderness of the Judge-Advocate, L. C. Turner — as thoroughly unscrupulous a partisan as the United States Government possesses in its service.

One day Captain Mix came into the passage, and said to Miss Annie Jones, "Prepare yourself to go to the Lunatic Asylum to-morrow, as it is the Secretary of War's orders." She immediately commenced screaming hysterically, and rushed towards the spot where I was standing. I turned to leave, when he added, "Oh, you need not put on airs by getting out of the way, for you've got to go to Fitchburg Jail during the war. You have been sentenced to hard labor there."

Miss Jones's screams, coupled with this intelligence, completely unnerved me, and I fell fainting on the floor, whence I was conveyed to my room, only to suffer a relapse of the fever from which I had just recovered.

My father, who was in Martinsburg when he heard of my sentence and second illness, immediately came on to Washington, and, after untiring exertions in my behalf, succeeded in having the sentence commuted. What that commutation was he did not then know. It was "banishment to the South — never to return North again during the war."

Among the gentlemen who were retained as prisoners at the Carroll was Mr. Smithson, formerly one of the wealthiest bankers in Washington City. He was charged by the Yankees with holding correspondence with friends residing in the South, was arrested by the authorities, tried by court-martial, found guilty, and sentenced to five years' imprisonment in the Penitentiary at hard labor. All his property was confiscated, and his refined and delicate wife, with two little children, who had been reared in the lap of luxury, were obliged to see their residence taken from them and made into quarters for the Yankee officers. They were compelled to retire to a garret, with scarcely any of the necessaries of life whereon to support themselves.

Before leaving for the South, one of the imprisoned Confederate officers, Colonel ——, gave me letters of introduction to the Vice-President, the Honorable Alexander Stephens, and to the Honorable Bowling Baker, Chief Auditor of the Southern Treasury Department. In both of these letters he spoke of my untiring devotion to the Confederacy, of the zeal that I had shown to serve my country at all times, and of my kindness, as far as lay in my power, to my fellow-prisoners. The Colonel further commended me to his friends' "kind care and protection." These letters were, of course, contraband; and I intended, if I possibly could do so, to smuggle them through to Richmond.

It was agreed that I should leave for Fortress Monroe on the 1st day of December, 1863. My father was still in Washington, residing with his niece; but he was so ill that he could not visit me previous to my departure.

One evening, whilst I was looking out of my room-door, a significant cough attracted my attention, and, glancing in the direction whence it proceeded — the sentry's back being turned — I perceived a note, tightly rolled up, thrown towards me. I picked it up quickly, and, reading it, found that it was from Mr. K., of Virginia, begging me to aid himself and two friends to escape, and also asking for money to advance their object. I wrote, in reply, that I would do all that lay in my power, and, unobserved, I handed him forty dollars. By means of my india-rubber ball I arranged every thing, and the night when the attempt should be made was fixed.

Above Mr. K.'s room was a garret occupied by his two friends, who intended to escape with him; and it was so contrived that he should get into the garret with the others whilst returning from supper.

At one time I was afraid that this attempt would be frustrated, for the sentry, observing Mr. K. upon the garret stair-case, commanded him to "Halt!" adding, "You don't belong there; so come down." Standing in the doorway of my chamber at the time, I quickly retorted, "Sentry, have you been so long here and don't know where the prisoners are quartered? Let him pass on to his room." Taking the hint, Mr. K. declared that he "knew what he was about," which it was very evident he did; and the sentinel, thinking that he had made a mistake, allowed him to proceed upstairs.

This part of the scheme being satisfactorily carried out, I wrote a note to the superintendent, informing him that I was desirous of seeing him for a few minutes. He accordingly came, and I managed to detain him by conversing upon various topics. Suddenly, from round the corner of the prison that faced on the street, arose a startling cry of "Murder! murder!" I know that my heart beat violently, but I kept the composure of my face as well as I was able; for this sudden cry was the commencement of a *ruse de guerre* which, if it should succeed, would liberate my friends from thraldom.

Mr. Wood had, at the first cry of "Murder!" rushed to one of the windows and flung it open to see what was the matter; and some soldiers, who were lounging outside, waiting for their turn of sentry duty, ran hurriedly to the spot from which the cries proceeded. Meanwhile, those in the room above were not idle. Removing in haste a portion of the roof, they scrambled out upon the eaves, descended by means of a lightning-conductor into the street below, and made off, shel-tered by the darkness.

Of course, the next morning, when the roll was called, and the prisoners were mustered, Mr. K. and his companions were found to be missing. It was strongly suspected that I had connived at their escape, and knew more than I pretended about the affair; but as they could not prove any thing against me, I was not punished. I subsequently heard, to my great joy, that the fugitives had arrived safely in Richmond.

Shortly after my recovery from the severe illness which had prostrated me, I wrote to General Martindale (commandant at that time of the forces in and around Washington), asking him to grant me the privilege of walking for a while each day in the Capitol Square. This square lies in front of the Carroll; and I thought that a change, however slight, from the close confinement of my room, would greatly strengthen me. To my letter I received a gracious answer, with permission to promenade in the square, on condition that I gave a written promise that, on my word of honor as a lady, I would hold communication with no one, either by word of mouth or by letter.

I was glad to do anything to get once more a breath of pure air that did not come to me through prison bars. So I signed the promise; and every evening, when I felt so inclined, I was permitted to walk for half an hour, from five until half-past, in the square, followed by a corporal and guard with loaded muskets.

Even this limited enjoyment was not of long duration; for, when it became known in Washington City, through the public journals, that I walked in the square, Southern sympathizers — and their name was legion — both ladies and gentlemen, would congregate to see me; and often, when I passed, would they give utterance to pitying expressions on my account.

Intelligence of this eventually reached the ears of the authorities, through various channels, and ultimately led to an order from Mr. Stanton revoking the parole that had been granted. Thus my promenade became one of the things of the past, to which I often reverted with regret.

On one occasion a party of young girls, in passing me, dropped a square piece of Bristol board that had a Confederate battle-flag and my name worked upon it in worsted. The corporal detected the movement, and, before I could gain possession of this treasonable gift, picked it up himself. He commanded the whole group to "halt" immediately; and, had it not been for my earnest entreaties and supplications on their behalf, he would have arrested the entire party, who, terrified beyond measure at the turn affairs had assumed, added their appeals for mercy to mine. The corporal happening to possess that commodity, a heart, was merciful, and dismissed them with a slight reprimand.

Promising to say nothing that would implicate him should the flag ever be discovered upon me, I succeeded in procuring it from my guardian by a bribe of five dollars; and I wore it concealed long after I had left Washington for the South.

Had I been a queen, or a reigning princess, my every movement could not have been more faithfully chronicled at this period of my imprisonment. My health was bulletined for the gratification of the public; and if I walked or was indisposed, it was announced after the most approved fashion by the newspapers. Thus, from the force of circumstances, and not through any desire of my own, I became a celebrity.

Chapter XIV

On the first day of December, early in the morning, I started for Fortress Monroe, under the charge of Captain Mix and an orderly-sergeant. It was my poor father's intention to have accompanied me as far as Baltimore, and beyond, if he could get the necessary permission. Just before I left, however, a message was brought to me stating that my father, though not dangerously ill, was confined to the house by severe indisposition.

When I heard that I could not see my fond parent, it distressed me greatly; but I was powerless to act in the matter; and, though I entreated them to let me go to him, if but for a moment, it was refused.

After being subjected to the annoying and ungentlemanly

236

conduct of Captain Mix, who seemed to exert himself especially to make every thing as disagreeable as he possibly could for me, I arrived in Fortress Monroe about 9 A.M. on Wednesday morning. Captain Mix immediately went on shore to report to Captain Cassels, the Provost-Marshal and Aide-de-camp to Butler, to whose care I was to be committed until the "exchange boat" should start for Richmond.

Meanwhile all the passengers had landed, and I was left in the charge of the orderly-sergeant. Major (now General) Mulford, the exchange officer, returned on board with Captain Mix, and was introduced to me. I found him an elegant and courteous gentleman. In a short time I was escorted from the boat to the Provost-Marshal's office, passing between a company of negro soldiers, who were filed on each side. Thence I was taken into the fortress, to Butler's head-quarters, and, after waiting a short time, I was conducted into his august presence.

He was seated near a table, and upon my entrance, he looked up and said, "Ah, so this is Miss Boyd, the famous rebel spy. Pray be seated.

"Thank you, General Butler, but I prefer to stand."

I was very much agitated, and trembled greatly. This he noticed, and remarked, "Pray be seated. But why do you tremble so? Are you frightened?"

"No; ah! that is, yes, General Butler; I must acknowledge that I do feel frightened in the presence of a man of such world-wide reputation as yourself."

This seemed to please him immensely, and, rubbing his hands together and smiling most benignly, he said, "Oh, pray do be seated, Miss Boyd. But what do you mean when you say that I am widely known?"

"I mean, General Butler," I said, "that you are a man whose atrocious conduct and brutality, especially to Southern ladies, is so infamous that even the English Parliament commented upon it. I naturally feel alarmed at being in your presence."

He had evidently expected a compliment when I commenced to reply to his inquiry, but, at the close of my remarks, he rose, and, with rage depicted upon every lineament of his features, he ordered me out of his presence.

I was conducted to the hotel, and felt for the time being exceedingly uneasy lest, by my Parthian shot at an enemy whom I thoroughly detested, I should have laid myself open to his petty spirit of revenge. I feared that I should be remanded to a dreary prison cell : for General Butler was all-powerful in the North about this period.

Events have since clearly proved this man, even to the Yankees themselves, to be but a meretricious hero and a political charlatan. Like others who render themselves rather notorious than great, he first pleased a fickle populace by his acts of brutality, then disgusted his contemporaries, who feared that he might become to America what Robespierre had been to France. The tyrant of New Orleans, having failed most signally at Wilmington, was discovered to be a coward, and suspected of being a rogue. Well might the baffled New England attorney exclaim, *"Facilis descensus Averni!"* In the hope of being styled a modern Cincinnatus, he retired to Lowell, to live upon the ill-gotten gains extorted by threats or force from Southern people.

But to resume the thread of my story. I was obliged to give my parole that I would not leave the house until permitted to do so. Here I found the Misses Lomax, sisters of the Confederate General Lomax, and a Miss Goldsborough, of Baltimore, who were to be sent South. These ladies, however, were not the only sympathizers in the hotel; there were others whose names I dare not mention.

On Wednesday evening the order came for Miss Goldsborough and myself to be in readiness to start that same night for Richmond. The Misses Lomax, for some reason, were not allowed to proceed, but were sent back to Baltimore. When the time arrived for our departure, we were taken back to the Provost-Marshal's office; and here I found my luggage, consisting of two Saratoga trunks and a bonnet-box. The keys were demanded of me, and I complied with the request.

A man and two women immediately set to work to ransack my boxes, although I assured them that they need not search, as I had just come from prison. This appeal, however, was ineffectual, and they still continued their examination. Imagine their astonishment and my chagrin when they pulled from the bottom of one of my trunks two suits of private clothes, a uniform for Major-General W——, a dozen linen shirts, &c. These things I had succeeded in smuggling into prison by means of an underground railway, of which Superintendent Wood, sharp as he imagined himself to be, was little aware. I was interrogated as to how I had obtained the articles in question, but they did not succeed in eliciting any thing by their queries.

All the goods considered contraband, including several pairs of army gauntlets and felt hats, with a pair of field-glasses which had formerly belonged to General Jackson, and which I greatly prized, together with much clothing, were taken from me. I entreated them to let me retain the glasses; but this was flatly refused; and they were, to my mortification, given to General Butler.

When I saw how these Vandals were robbing me of nearly every thing, I strove in vain to restrain my tears; and my trunks having been thoroughly ransacked, I was informed that I must undergo a personal search. At this turn of affairs I began to feel very nervous, for I had concealed about me twenty thousand dollars in Confederate notes, five thousand in greenbacks, and nearly one thousand in gold, as well as the letters of introduction which I have previously mentioned. I earnestly appealed to their forbearance assuring them that I had nothing contraband; for I did not consider my money contraband.

As it was getting late, the captain said, "Well, if you will take an oath to the effect that you have nothing contraband upon you — no letters or papers — you shall not be searched."

As this was impossible, I told him that I could not make such a declaration, handing him my letters at the same time. He then asked if I had any money about me. To this I replied by giving him a roll of two or three thousand dollars in Confederate money, which I had placed in my pocket. This he regarded as valueless, and sneeringly informed me that I might keep "that stuff."

Upon opening my letters and finding mention of "my immense services to my country," "my kindness towards prisoners," "my devotion to the Southern cause," &c., he became very angry, and said, "I shall send this to General Butler in the morning. I would do so now, but it is after office hours."

Miss Goldsborough sat by meanwhile, a quiet spectator of the whole affair, she having undergone the ordeal of search in the morning. We were then conducted to the wharf, placed on board a tug, and sent off to the exchange boat, the *City of New York,* which lay at anchor in the stream. Upon our arrival on board we were kindly received by Major Mulford, who conducted us to the saloon and introduced us to his wife, a very charming, lady-like woman. Here we remained all night, and next morning, about seven o'clock, got under way. Shortly afterwards we ran aground, and it was not until eight A.M. that we succeeded in getting the vessel off again. Then, under a full head of steam, we steered for City Point.

About this time the little steam-tug that had brought us alongside the *City of New York* quitted the wharf, apparently in chase of us. My heart sank, for I felt intuitively that this pursuit had something to do with me, and that General Butler must have given an order for my detention. But the larger steamer had already waited so long that Major Mulford, angry and impatient at the delay, took no notice of our pursuers, and, to my great joy and relief, kept steadily on our course.

I afterwards learnt that my fears upon this occasion were not unfounded. When General Butler, smarting with the remembrance of my farewell sarcasm, had beheld the letters that Captain Cassels had taken from me, he commanded that I should be followed, and, if recaptured, should be sent at once to Fort Warren, in Massachusetts Bay. As he issued this order he remarked to those who surrounded him that he would take "a leading character in 'Beauty and the Beast.' " When the tug returned from her fruitless chase, he was almost beside himself with rage at being thwarted in his revenge. This I had from such good authority that I am confident the General will not feel it worth his while to contradict the statement.

At the mouth of the James River we passed the Federal blockading fleet, and were here boarded by a boat from the flag-ship *Minnesota,* commanded by Admiral Lee. In a few moments we had entered the James, whose waters are distinguishable from those of the Potomac by a yellow streak on the surface.

As we wended our way up the river we could see the signal-officers at the different stations busily announcing our approach, and occasionally we observed Confederate soldiers on picket duty. Every thing reminded me that I was once more drawing near to the capital of my own sunny South.

> "Amate sponde !
> Pur vi torno a riveder,
> Trema in petto e si confonde
> L'alma oppressa dal piacer."

Though exceedingly happy that I was again permitted to breathe the pure air of my native State. I did not feel completely free, for I was still under the Federal flag, and could scarcely count upon my liberty as being yet fully assured to me.

We arrived at City Point late on Friday evening. This place, which could hardly be correctly dignified with the name of village, is situate in a bend of the river. It was used as a dépôt by the Confederates, for the purpose of forwarding stores to those of their unfortunate countrymen who were prisoners in the North.

Whilst the *City of New York* was coming to an anchor, Major Mulford, his wife, Miss Goldsborough, and myself stood conversing on the hurricane-deck. Major Mulford remarked, pointing to what was apparently the Confederate flag-of-truce boat approaching, "After all, ladies, you will not have to remain on board here to-night."

Looking in the direction indicated, we distinctly saw a steamer, which, judging from the distance between us, would in less than ten minutes be alongside. Ten minutes, however, passed in fruitless expectation; then followed twenty more of hope deferred; when Major Mulford, who began to grow very impatient, went on shore to inquire the reason of her remaining as she did — he even sent a boat to her to ascertain the reason of her detention. Major Mulford was so confident that he had seen her that the Confederate officer commanding the "Point" telegraphed the news to Richmond. Judge of our great surprise when the telegraphic reply, brought to us on board shortly afterwards, announced "that the Confederate flag-of-truce boat had left Richmond exactly at the hour we had seen her." As Richmond was more than twelve hours distant from us at the then rate of travel over that route, we could only consider that we had been deceived by a "mirage." How often must such phenomena have given rise to stories of phantom ships!

A French corvette, which had been up the river to Richmond, lay at anchor near us. This evening, in acceptance of an invitation from Major Mulford, the French captain and his lieutenant came on board to spend the evening with us; and we enjoyed their visit heartily. The next morning, when I awoke, I found that the flag-of-truce boat had arrived during the night. Captain Hatch, the Confederate exchange officer, presently came on board. We were introduced to him, and very soon afterwards were, with our luggage, safely ensconced in the snug little cabin of the ——. Here, under my own country's flag, I felt free and comparatively happy.

On our way up the river to Richmond we had to pass the obstructions situated between Chapin's and Drury's Bluffs. These places take their names from the bold appearance that the shore here presents. The obstructions designed to impede a hostile squadron became accidentally hurtful to our Confederate vessel. She ran foul of them, and it was found utterly impossible to continue the voyage.

At Drury's Bluff, therefore, we went on board a tug, in which we proceeded to Richmond. When we arrived, at eight P.M., I went immediately to the Spottswood House, and, tired and worn out with the fatigues of my journey, I retired to rest, refusing to see any one that evening.

Chapter XV

When I came down to breakfast on the following day, my
many acquaintances and friends in the hotel were astonished
to see me, for few had expected that I should be released, and
none that I should so soon arrive at Richmond. The morning
papers announced my return in flattering terms; and, as it thus
became generally known, I was at once besieged with company, and every afternoon and evening I held a perfect
drawing-room, if I may be allowed to make use of the expression. My reception was every thing that I could wish; but,
alas! my happiness was of short duration, and my freedom
was dearly bought.

I was at a large dinner-party on a Saturday evening exactly
one week after the day I had arrived. I was joyous and light-
hearted, little dreaming of the blow that was to overwhelm
me with sadness—little dreaming that I should be so cruelly

244

reminded of the words of the Preacher, that "in the midst of life we are in death;" but so it was.

On Monday morning, the 14th, before I had risen, I received a little note from Captain Hatch, in which he expressed great sorrow at having to be the bearer of mournful tidings, and said that, as soon as I was dressed, he would call in person with the wife of the proprietor of the hotel. For one moment I could not imagine what he meant, but, dressing myself as speedily as I possibly could, I sent for them. They came: Captain Hatch held in his hands a newspaper. He approached me, saying,

"Miss Belle, you are aware that you left your father ill?"

In one moment I comprehended every thing, and exclaiming "My God! is he dead?" I sank fainting to the floor.

This swoon was succeeded by a severe illness; and I felt all the loneliness of my position. An exile (for the Yankees held possession of Martinsburg) and an orphan—these words described me; and, ah! how hard they seemed!

One of those strange warnings that are sometimes given to mortals, or that are, some would say, the imaginings of an excited brain shaken by sickness, ought to have prepared me for my sad bereavement.

> "Some say that gleams of a remoter world
> Visit the soul in sleep."

The night upon which my father died I had retired to rest somewhat earlier than usual. How long I slept I do not know, but I suddenly awoke, or seemed to awaken, from my sleep, although I had neither the power nor the wish to move. In the centre of the room I saw General Jackson, whose eyes rested sorrowfully upon me. Beside him stood my father, gazing at me, but saying nothing. I was dumb, or I should have spoken, for I did not feel alarmed. As I looked upon those two standing together, General Jackson turned and spoke to my father. I remember the words distinctly.

"It is time for us to go," he said; and, taking my father's hand, he led him away, adding as he did so, "Poor child!"

I afterwards learnt by a letter from my mother (the first and only communication received from her until my arrival in this country) that my beloved father, at the news of my being sent South, where I should have to battle alone with the world, had grown rapidly worse, and had expired the very next day after my arrival in Richmond. My mother and the children had been sent for, and reached my father just before he died. Although he retained his senses up to the last, he frequently spoke of me, declared that I was hovering around his couch, and would become quite restless if people in the room went to a certain spot near the bed, exclaiming that "I was being torn from him!"

Several of our senators and exchange officers, with many other influential persons, wrote to the Federal Government to try and obtain permission for me to return to my sorrowing mother. I myself wrote to the Northern President and Secretary Stanton, at the suggestion of my friends, and appealed to them as a Mason's daughter. But no, every appeal was refused.

My letters to and from my mother in Martinsburg were intercepted; and from December the 16th, until I arrived in London, and then not until the following October, did I receive one line from her, though she had written repeatedly.

My health was very bad and my constitution greatly undermined; so in February I went from Richmond farther south, visiting Mobile, Atlanta, Augusta, and other cities, whose names have since become historical.

I cannot express one-half the gratitude that I feel to the many kind hosts whom I met in my journey through the South. During my illness in Richmond I was well cared for;

and amongst the warmest of my friends must be ranked the wife of the world-renowned Captain Semmes, afterwards Admiral Semmes, of the ill-fated *Alabama*.

Mrs. Semmes treated me with as much attention as though I had been her own daughter, and invited me to visit them at their home in Mobile. I had always been termed "the child of the Confederacy," or "the child of the army;" and, no matter where I went, I was welcomed both by the gentry and the people.

In March I returned to Richmond, when, although somewhat recovered, my health still required care. I could not return home, and I felt, moreover, restless and unhappy at the death of my father. I determined, therefore, to visit Europe, so soon as I could arrange my affairs. When I made known this resolution to President Davis, he approved of the plan, considering me to need quiet and rest in some place remote from the dangers of our sorely-pressed country.

Orders were given to the Confederate Secretary of State to make me the bearer of dispatches. I commenced preparations for departure as speedily as possible.

The dispatches were ready for me on March 25th, but a brief return of illness hindered me from starting, and as these papers, being very important, could not be delayed, they were forwarded by some other hand.

At last, on March 29th, I was able to leave Richmond, having recovered sufficiently for travelling. Other dispatches were now ready, and of them I was made the bearer.

Owing to an accident on the railway, we did not arrive in Wilmington until several hours after the departure of the blockade-runner in which I was to have sailed.

This steamer would not be followed by another for at least a fortnight, because they did not run out during the brilliant nights of the full moon, lest they should fall an easy prey to Yankee blockaders. I was therefore obliged to await the arrival and departure of the next regular steamer, as, even putting aside all consideration of difficulties increased by moonlight, there was not a suitable craft in port.

One of the first vessels that arrived was the *Greyhound,* commanded by Captain Henry, formerly, it is said, an officer in the United States navy, and who had, at the commencement of the war, with many of his comrades, sent in his resignation to the United States Navy Department, and entered the Confederate service. Captain "Henry" had formerly been on "Stonewall" Jackson's staff; and, as I was acquainted with his family, I gladly accepted his kind invitation, and took passage on board the *Greyhound,* feeling doubly secure under such a skilful commander.

Chapter XVI

I leave Wilmington for Europe.—Running the Blockade.—Safe
Outside.—*Mal de Mer.*—The Federal Cruiser.—The Chase.
—The Yankee proves too fast.—The first Shell.—The Fire
grows hot.—Forced to surrender.—The English Sailor and
his Flag.

On the 8th of May I bade farewell to many friends in
Wilmington, and stepped on board the *Greyhound.* It was, as
may well be imagined, an anxious moment. I knew that the
venture was a desperate one; but I felt sustained by the great-
ness of my cause; for I had borne a part, however insignificant,
in one of the greatest dramas ever yet enacted upon the stage
of the world; moreover, I relied upon my own resources, and
I looked to Fortune, who is so often the handmaid of a daring
enterprise.

At the mouth of the river we dropped anchor, and decided
to wait until the already waning moon should entirely
disappear.

Outside the bar, and at the distance of about six miles, lay
the Federal fleet, most of them at anchor; but some of their
light vessels were cruising quietly in different directions. Not
one, however, showed any disposition to tempt the guns of the
fort over which the Confederate flag was flying.

There were on board the *Greyhound* two passengers, or rather adventurers, besides myself — Mr. Newell and Mr. Pollard, the latter the editor of the *Richmond Examiner*. We laughed and joked, as people will laugh and joke in the face of imminent danger, and even in the jaws of death.

Gentle reader, before you accuse us of levity, or of a reckless spirit of fatalism, reflect how, in the prison of La Force, when the reign of terror was at its height, the doomed victims of the guillotine acted charades, played games of forfeits, and circulated their *bon-mots* and *jeux d'esprit* within a few hours of a violent death. Remember also that the lovely Queen of Scots and the unfortunate Anna Boleyn met their fate with a smile, and greeted the scaffold with a jest.

About ten o'clock orders were given to get under way. The next minute every light was extinguished, the anchor was weighed, steam was got up rapidly and silently, and we glided off just as "the trailing garments of the night" spread their last folds over the ocean.

The decks were piled with bales of cotton, upon which our look-out men were stationed, straining their eyes to pierce the darkness and give timely notice of the approach of an enemy.

I freely confess that our jocose temperament had now yielded to a far more serious state of feeling. No more pleasantries were exchanged, but many earnest prayers were breathed. No one thought of sleep. Few words were spoken. It was a night never to be forgotten — a night of silent, almost breathless anxiety. It seemed to us as if day would never break; but it came at last, and, to our unspeakable joy, not a sail was in sight. We were moving unmolested and alone upon a tranquil sea, and we indulged in the fond hope that we had eluded our eager foes.

Steaming on, we ran close by the wreck of the Confederate iron-clad *Raleigh,* which had so lately driven the Federal blockading squadron out to sea, but which now lay on a shoal, an utter wreck, parted amidships, destroyed, not by the Federals, but by a visitation of Providence.

At this point we three passengers began to experience those sensations which, although invariably an object of derision to persons who are exempt from them, are, for the time being, as grievous to the sufferer as any in the whole catalogue of pains and aches to which flesh is heir. Reader, may it never be your lot, as it then was mine, to find sea-sickness overcome by the stronger emotion inspired by the sight of a hostile vessel bearing rapidly down with the purpose of depriving you of your freedom.

It was just noon, when a thick haze which had lain upon the water lifted, and at that moment we heard a startled cry of "Sail ho!" from the look-out man at the mast-head. These ominous words were the signal for a general rush aft. Extra steam was got up in an incredibly short space of time, and sail was set with the view both of increasing our speed and of steadying our vessel as she dashed through the water.

Alas! it was soon evident that our exertions were useless, for every minute visibly lessened the distance between us and our pursuer; her masts rose higher and higher, her hull loomed larger and larger, and I was told plainly that, unless some unforeseen accident should favor us, such as a temporary derangement of the Federal steamer's steering apparatus, or a breaking of some important portion of her machinery, we might look to New York instead of Bermuda as our destination.

My feelings at this intelligence must be imagined: I can describe them but inadequately. "Unless," I thought, "Providence interposes directly in our behalf, we shall be overhauled and captured; and then what follows? I shall suffer a third rigorous imprisonment." Moreover, I was the bearer of dispatches from my Government to authorities in Europe; and I knew that this service, honorable and necessary as it was, the Federals regarded in the light of a heinous crime, and that, in all probability, I should be subjected to every kind of indignity.

The chase continued, and the cruiser still gained upon us. For minutes, which to me seemed hours, did I strain my eyes towards our pursuer and watch anxiously for the flash of the gun that would soon send a shot or shell after us, or, for all I could tell, into us. How long I remained watching I know not, but the iron messenger of death came at last. A thin, white curl of smoke rose high in the air as the enemy luffed up and presented her formidable broadside. Almost simultaneously with the hissing sound of the shell, as it buried itself in the sea within a few yards of us, came the smothered report of its explosion under water.

The enemy's shots now followed each other in rapid succession : some fell very close, while others, less skilfully aimed, were wide of the mark, and burst high in the air over our heads. During this time bale after bale of cotton had been rolled overboard by our crew, the epitaph of each, as it disappeared beneath the waves, being, "By ———! there's another they shall not get."

Our captain paced nervously to and fro, now watching the compass, now gazing fixedly at the approaching enemy, now shouting, "More steam! more steam! give her more steam!" At last he turned suddenly round to me, and exclaimed in passionate accents—

"Miss Belle, I declare to you that, but for your presence on board, I would burn her to the water's edge rather than those infernal scoundrels should reap the benefit of a single bale of our cargo."

To this I replied, "Captain H., act without reference to me—do what you think your duty. For my part, sir, I concur with you : burn her by all means—I am not afraid. I have made up my mind, and am indifferent to my fate, if only the Federals do not get the vessel."

To this Captain H. made no reply, but turned abruptly away

and walked aft, where his officers were standing in a group. With them he held a hurried consultation, and then, coming to where I was seated, exclaimed —

"It is too late to burn her now. The Yankee is almost on board of us. We must surrender!"

During all this time the enemy's fire never ceased. Round shot and shell were ploughing up the water about us. They flew before, behind, and above — everywhere but into us; and, although I knew that the first of those heavy missiles which should strike must be fatal to many, perhaps to all, yet so angry did I feel that I could have forfeited my own life if, by so doing, I could have balked the Federals of their prey.

At this moment we were not more than half a mile from our tormentor; for we had luffed up in the wind, and stopped our engine. Suddenly, with a deep humming sound, came a hundred-pound bolt. This shot was fired from their long gun amidships, and passed just over my head, between myself and the captain, who was standing on the bridge a little above me.

"By Jove! don't they intend to give us quarter, or show us some mercy at any rate?" cried Captain H. "I have surrendered."

And now from the Yankee came a stentorian hail: "Steamer ahoy! haul down that flag, or we will pour a broadside into you!"

Captain H. then ordered the man at the wheel to lower the colors; but he replied, with true British pluck, that "he had sailed many times under that flag, but had never yet seen it hauled down; and," added he, "I cannot do it now." We were sailing under British colors, and the man at the helm was an Englishman.

All this time repeated hails of "Haul down that flag, or we will sink you!" greeted us, until, at last, some one, I know not who, seeing how hopeless it must be to brave them longer, took it upon himself to execute Captain H.'s order, and lowered the English ensign.

Chapter XVII

We are boarded by an Officer from the Yankee.—The U.S. Steamer *Connecticut*.—An Officer, but no Gentleman.—Strange State of Yankee Discipline.—Scenes on board of the *Greyhound* after her Capture.—"Ain't ye skeared?"—A proud Boast.

Before the acknowledgment of our surrender had been made, a keg containing some twenty or thirty thousand dollars, equivalent in value to about six thousand pounds sterling, had been brought up on deck and consigned to the deep; whilst all my dispatches and letters of introduction, of which latter I had many, were consumed in the furnaces very shortly afterwards.

We were boarded by a boat's crew from our captor, under the command of the executive officer, Mr. Kempf. Mounting the side, he walked up to Captain H. and said—

"Good day to you, Captain; I am glad to see you. This is a very fine vessel, and a valuable one. Will you be good enough to let me see your papers?"

To this Captain H. replied, "Good day to yourself, sir; but as to my being happy to see you, I cannot really say that I am. I have no papers."

The Federal lieutenant then said, "Well, Captain, your

presence is required on board the United States steamer
Connecticut, Captain Almy commanding; and, if you can
prove yourself all right, you will, no doubt, be permitted
to go."

To this Captain H. made no response, but, stepping into
the cabin, donned his coat, and, returning on deck, said, "Now,
sir, I am ready; shall we go?" Without further parley the two
stepped together into the boat which was lying alongside, and
immediately pulled for the *Connecticut.*

One Mr. Swasey was left in charge of our luckless *Greyhound* — an officer as unfit for authority as any who has ever
trodden the deck of a man-of-war. His subordinates were, I
imagine, well acquainted with his character and abilities; at
all events, they treated his orders not with respect, but ridicule.

"Now, sergeant," said he, addressing the sergeant of marines,
"look out for your men, and I will look out for mine. By-the-
way, though, station one man here to guard the spirit-room,
and don't let any one go below; the first man I catch doing
so I will blow his brains out, I will; I would not let my own
father have a drink."

He might possibly have resisted the solicitations of a thirsty
parent, but he proved quite unable to withstand those of the
men. He had hardly finished speaking, when a seaman, whom,
by his *illigant* brogue, I recognized at once for a true son of
Erin, approached and addressed Mr. Swasey with all the native
eloquence and pathos of his country —

"Ah, Mr. Swasey, will yees be afther lettin' me have a small
bottle of whiskey to kape out the could?"

The colloquy that ensued was ludicrous in the extreme,
terminating in a victory of the Irish sailor over the Federal
officer. This example of successful insubordination once set,
was soon followed; and in every instance Mr. Swasey yielded
to the remonstrances, or rather to the mutinous appeals, of
his men.

"Here," suddenly exclaimed he, catching a glimpse of myself, "sergeant of the guard! sergeant of the guard! put a man in front of this door, and give him orders to stab this woman if she dares to attempt to come out."

This order, so highly becoming an officer and a gentleman, so courteous in its language, and withal so necessary to the safety and preservation of the prize, was given in a menacing voice and in the very words I have used. I record them for the purpose of showing how admirably the Federal Government has selected its naval officers, and how punctually and gallantly they fulfilled the instructions of their superiors. *Parcere subjectis* must have been blotted out from the edition of the ancient poet read in those schools which had the honor of educating them.

Mr. Swasey then came to the cabin-door and introduced himself in these brief but delicate words—"Now, ain't ye skeared?"

My blood was roused, and I replied, "No, I am not; I was never frightened at a Yankee in my life!"

This retort of mine seemed to surprise him, as he walked away without another word. The effects of his displeasure, however, soon made themselves felt. To my ineffable disgust, the officers, and even the men, were permitted to walk at pleasure into my cabin, which I had hoped would have been respected as the sanctuary of a modest girl. In this hope, as in so many others, I calculated far too much upon the forbearance and humanity of Yankees; and these qualities were seldom exhibited when their enemies were defenceless, and, consequently, at their mercy.

Officers and men now proceeded to help themselves to the private wines of the captain, in spite of the protest of the sentry who had been placed in front of my door, and of whom it is but just to say that nature had qualified him to command when his superiors would have done well to obey.

While these scenes were being enacted, my maid, and a colored woman whom Captain H. was conveying to a lady in Bermuda, were subjected to the rude familiarities of the prize crew.

At this moment one of the *Connecticut*'s officers, a Mr. Reveille, walked up to me and said, "Do you know that it was I who fired the shot that passed close over your head?"

"Was it?" replied I. "Should you like to know what I said of the gunner?"

"I should like to know."

"That man, whoever he may be, is an arrant coward to fire on a defenceless ship after her surrender."

To this rejoinder of mine, more sincere, perhaps, than prudent, he made no reply, but left the cabin with an embarrassed laugh.

Chapter XVIII

An eventful Meeting.—A Gentleman at last.—A Wife's Apology.
—Mr. Hardinge.—I am disappointed.—A pleasant Ex-
change.—Farewell to Mr. Swasey.—A ludicrous Incident.—
Captain Henry's best Boots.—I am discovered through
Treachery.

Scarcely had the discomfited Yankee betaken himself, to my
intense satisfaction, to the deck, when I noticed a young
officer who had just come over the side.

He crossed the deck by the wheel, and approached the
cabin. I saw at a glance he was made of other stuff than his
comrades who preceded him; and I confess my attention was
riveted by the presence of a gentleman—the first, I think my
readers will allow, whom I had met in the hour of my distress.

A woman and a wife may, perhaps, be forgiven if, in a
work which treats of more serious adventures than those of
love, she indulges in a very brief reminiscence of the impression produced upon her by her future husband. Critics may
smile; but I flatter myself that Englishwomen, so widely and
so justly famed for conjugal devotion, will forgive me.

His dark-brown hair hung down on his shoulders; his eyes
were large and bright. Those who judge of beauty by regularity
of feature only, could not have pronounced him strictly hand-

some. Neither Phidias nor Praxiteles would have chosen the subject for a model of Grecian grace; but the fascination of his manner was such, his every movement was so much that of a refined gentleman, that my "Southern proclivities," strong as they were, yielded for a moment to the impulses of my heart, and I said to myself, "Oh, what a good fellow that must be !"

To my secret disappointment, he passed by the cabin, without entering or making any inquiries about me. I asked one of the *Connecticut*'s officers, who was close to me, the name of the new arrival in this party of pleasure. "Lieutenant Hardinge," was his reply.

Soon afterwards I heard the following conversation, which I perfectly well remember, and which I transcribe *verbatim,* between Mr. Swasey and Mr. Hardinge : —

Mr. Swasey. — "Hallo, Hardinge, any thing up? What is it?"

Mr. Hardinge. — "Yes, sir; by order of Captain Almy, I have come to relieve you of the command of this vessel. It is his order that you proceed forthwith on board the *Connecticut* : you will be pleased to hand over to me the papers you have in relation to this vessel."

Mr. Swasey. — "It is a lie ! it is a lie ! it ain't no such thing ! I won't believe it. You have been lately juggling with the captain. Confound it ! That is the way you always do !"

Mr. Hardinge. — "Mr. Swasey, I am but obeying my orders; you must not insult me. If you continue to do so, I shall report you."

Mr. Swasey cooled at once, I suppose, as I heard nothing further on his side. He promptly handed over his orders, as desired by Mr. Hardinge, jumped into the boat alongside, and I caught the last sound of his charming voice as he uttered the word of command, "Give way there !" to the boat's crew.

He returned to the *Connecticut,* and so passes out of this story. If its pages ever meet his eye, perhaps they may make him reflect that courtesy to a lady is compatible with the

sternest duties of an officer, and that forbearance to the vanquished has always been the attribute of a truly brave man.

Within a few minutes of the departure of our sometime
prize-master, Mr. Hardinge, now in command, issued his
orders to the sergeant of marines as to how the men were
to be posted; and I overheard, not without an emotion of
pleasure, the sergeant telling one of our officers that, although
Mr. Hardinge might be a strict disciplinarian on duty, there
was not a finer young fellow in the navy, and that his men
would follow him anywhere.

Before long, Mr. Hardinge came aft, and bowing to me,
asked permission to enter my cabin for a moment.

"Certainly," I replied; "I know that I am a prisoner."

"I am now in command of this vessel," said he; "and I beg
you will consider yourself a passenger, not a prisoner."

With the commencement of Mr. Hardinge's command—I
may safely say, from the very moment he came on board—the
conduct of the prize crew underwent a complete change; and
one of the Yankee officers remarked, in my hearing, that,
although Hardinge was young, he knew how to command
other men, and had learned, early in life, the secret and the
value of discipline.

Half an hour, or thereabouts, elapsed, and I was reconciling
myself to my captivity, when the return on board of Captain
"Henry" was the occasion of a ludicrous incident which amused
me more than perhaps my readers will suppose. I despair of
describing it as it appeared to me; perhaps the reaction of my
own feelings (such as we experience after passing safely
through sudden and serious danger) gave it a zest beyond its
real flavor.

It was on this wise. Captain "Henry," coming on board,
caught sight of a Federal sailor strutting about on the cotton-
bales in a pair of his (Captain H.'s) very best boots—boots
which the captain most particularly cherished.

"Here, you fellow, what are you doing with my boots? Take them off at once, or I shall report you to the officer in command for stealing."

"But, sir," said the sailor, loth to part with his contraband goods, "I bought them from a messmate of mine, and chucked my own into the sea."

This subterfuge, however, did not impose upon Mr. Hardinge's sense of honor and discipline. The ancient mariner had to remove the stolen boots, and return barefooted to his ship.

The officers and crew of the *Greyhound,* together with my fellow-passengers, Mr. Pollard and Mr. Newell, were taken on board the *Connecticut.* The captain, steward, cook, and cabin-boy, myself and my maid, remained prisoners on board the prize.

Before we were taken — indeed, when we sailed from Wilmington — it had been agreed that "Belle Boyd" should be for the time ignored, and that "Mrs. Lewis" should take her place. It was obvious that, in the event of capture, I should run less risk, suffer fewer privations, and be exposed to less indignity, under an assumed name. Conceive, then, my surprise and indignation when I found that my secret had been revealed through the treachery of an unworthy countryman!

Captain H. told me that the *Minnie,* a blockade-runner like the *Greyhound,* which had been captured the day before by the *Connecticut,* had been the means of our own mishap. There can be no doubt that one of her officers was a traitor to the cause of his country, and had, through fear, or actuated by some other unworthy motive, sacrificed those he should have defended with his life.

It is with reluctance that I record this instance of dishonor on the part of a Southerner; but I am resolved to be an impartial historian, and although often severe to the Yankees, by dint of telling plainly their short-comings, I will not shrink from the truth when it is unfavorable to my countrymen.

Chapter XIX

Bound North.—We are taken in tow.—Our first Evening at
Sea.—We arrive at Fortress Monroe.—Commodore Guerte
Gansevoorte comes on board in James River.—We are
paroled by him.—His Indignation against Mr. Hardinge
for flying the English Ensign.—The Commodore's Conduct
whilst on board.—Arrival at New York.—We go on Shore.
—I visit Niblo's Theatre.—Return aboard and departure
for Boston.—Love triumphant!

Boats were continually passing to and fro between the
"Prize," as she was designated, and the *Connecticut*, with
orders and counter-orders, until the proximity of the vessels
grew wearisome. I was relieved to hear that we were about to
start, and my pleasure did not diminish when, at eight P.M., the
command was given to get under steam and proceed northward, keeping just astern of the *Connecticut*, which would
accompany us. Heart-sick at the turn that the tide of fortune
had taken, I retired to my couch and endeavored to sleep. But
prison walls could not be banished from my imagination, and
the attempt was vain.

The next morning, at daylight, I was aroused by loud hailing
from the Yankee cruiser as she passed close to us, ordering
that we should "heave-to" whilst she sent a boat on board.

We presently learned that our destination was to be Fortress Monroe, and that we were to be towed thither behind the *Connecticut*. Hawsers were passed to us by means of boats, and, when these tow-lines had been well secured, both vessels steamed ahead.

It was the second evening after our surrender that Captain H., Mr. Hardinge, and myself, were seated together close by the wheel. The moon shone beautifully clear, lighting up every thing with a brightness truly magnificent; the ocean, just agitated by a slight breeze that swept over its surface, looked like one vast bed of sparkling diamonds, and the rippling of the little waves, as they struck the vessel's side, seemed but a soft accompaniment to the vocal music with which Captain H. had been regaling us.

> "Here will we sit, and let the sounds of music
> Creep in our ears; soft stillness, and the night,
> Become the touches of sweet harmony."

Presently Captain H. went forward on the bridge and conversed with Mr. Hall, the officer on watch. We two were left to ourselves; and Mr. Hardinge quoted some beautiful passages from Byron and Shakespeare. Then, in a decidedly Claude Melnotte style, he endeavored to paint the "home to which, if love could but fulfil its prayers, this heart would lead thee!" And from poetry he passed on to plead an oft-told tale. . . .

Situated as I was, and having known him for so short a time, a very practical thought flitted through my brain. If he felt all that he professed to feel for me, he might in future be useful to us; so, when he asked me "to be his wife," I told him that "his question involved serious consequences," and that "he must not expect an answer until I should arrive at Boston."

During our voyage, Mr. Hardinge was so kind and courteous that Captain H. took a great fancy to him, and swore eternal friendship to one of whom he afterwards spoke as "the most thorough gentleman from Yankeeland that he had ever met with."

The morning which succeeded the romantic episode slightly sketched above beheld the *Connecticut* and *Greyhound* lying-to off the Capes. A fog detained us in uncertainty as to our whereabouts for some time; and, when it lifted, we steamed up Hampton Roads.

I sat on the little deck aft, watching with interest all that I saw, and listening alternately to the captain and Mr. Hardinge as they conversed on various topics. From the latter I ascertained that General Butler was in command at Fortress Monroe, and from him I could expect but little courtesy.

As we neared our anchorage, I made out distinctly the grim outline of the fortress, rising in its majesty and strength. I compared myself to the fly nearing the cunning old spider, who was eagerly watching for the moment when it should become entangled in his intricate web.

My capture had been telegraphed to those in authority. The *Connecticut* had cast off from us about half way up the river, and had gone onward to the mouth of the James, where Admiral Lee then was; but the *Greyhound*, when opposite the pier of the Baltimore steamers, came to an anchor. Mr. Hardinge went on board the flag-ship *Minnesota* to report. He was absent about two hours, and when he returned we got under way, proceeding up-stream to join the *Connecticut*. Mr. Hardinge could tell me nothing of my probable destination, and I suspected that I was to be incarcerated in Fortress Monroe—there to remain I knew not how long—perhaps forever!

After about three-quarters of an hour we again anchored, this time close by the ironclad *Roanoke*, Commodore Guerte Gansevoorte, who was acting in the place of Admiral Lee.

The Admiral was then up the James River, ostensibly for the purpose of fighting the "rebels." But, much to the disgust of his officers and of the Federal naval department (if we may believe the journals of the day), he merely re-enacted the farce of sinking vessels and driving in spikes across the river from bank to bank, to prevent the "cowardly rebels" from doing what he dared not—giving battle.

Just after we brought up, it blew a perfect hurricane, followed by a drenching rain, which lasted for some time. Such weather was, in itself, sufficiently dreary and discouraging; nor did the sensation that we were dragging towards a lee-shore of uninviting appearance greatly comfort me. I felt, indeed, some pleasure when I thought that the Federals would, perhaps, lose their prize—a feeling which Captain H. fully shared. In this cheerful desire we were disappointed; for, as the captain afterwards remarked, "the vessel was admirably handled by Mr. Hardinge."

Amid whistling wind and pouring rain an English ensign had been flying from the stern, and the Federal flag, which had been hoisted when coming up the bay, was conspicuous at the fore. This seems to have excited the ire of the Commodore, who, when the storm had passed, boarded us, with solemn displeasure written upon his face.

I am positive that I should have had a better opinion of the man had he remained in his own vessel; for I now saw him far from sober. One of the officers remarked that "it was after four o'clock," by way of an apology to the "youngling," as he was pleased to term Mr. Hardinge.

Commodore Guerte Gansevoorte was not over-polite, and, upon reaching the deck, swore soundly and lustily, d——ing right and left, and was evidently

> "As *wild* a mannered man
> As ever scuttled ship or cut a throat."

But then, as it was a wet day, he had evidently been taking something hot within to guard him from the cold.

When the Commodore approached my cabin-door, I heard Mr. Hardinge say, "Sir, a lady is dressing there. Will you be kind enough to wait? She is my passenger, and I am responsible for her." I had finished, however; and the colored servant, opening the door, said to Mr. Hardinge, "De lady am ready, massa." On this the Commodore remarked, "Ugh! got to that, has it?"

His *entrée* into the cabin was truly imposing; for, stumbling over piled-up cotton, he staggered, then slipped, and made his descent and bow at the same moment. His aide, Mr. —— (executive officer, I believe) looked mortified, and seemed somewhat ashamed whilst following in the great man's rear, with less of the former's peculiar dignity.

"So," said the Commodore, "this is Miss Belle Boyd, is it?" Just then Captain H. came in, and, turning round, he then exclaimed, "What! by ——! George, old fel——;" then, remembering his official position, stopped suddenly in the midst of the exclamation. I do not remember much of the conversation which ensued, but noticed that the executive officer was sober, and apparently disgusted with the conduct of his superior.

The Commodore at first would not be seated, but did so after a few moments' further conversation. Champagne and glasses were brought in; and he soon became exceedingly communicative, and, with an oath, swore that Captain H. should have a parole extending as far as Boston. Asking for pen, ink, and paper, which I immediately procured, he bade the executive officer write the required parole, and signed it with his own hand. Mr. Hardinge asked for the document, or, at least, a copy of the same; but he would not comply, declaring that "his orders were sufficient."

As he rose to depart, he turned to me and said, in answer

to a request of mine, "You, Miss, when you arrive at New York, can go on shore, provided Mr. Hardinge accompanies you. And," he added, attempting some compliments, "I will not enforce a written parole with you, but will take a verbal promise. Don't be at all alarmed—you shan't go to prison." The Commodore then left us. His descent into the boat was executed in the same dignified and gentlemanly manner as had been his *entrée* into my presence; and I felt very thankful when Mr. Hall informed me that the great man had gone.

Half an hour may have passed, when a boat came from the *Roanoke* to inform Mr. Hardinge that the Commodore had ordered that the *Greyhound* should be brought under the lee of the iron-clad. My heart sank, for it seemed that, after all, he had been playing with us; still more so when, as we rounded-to under the *Roanoke's* stern, I heard the Commodore threatening through his trumpet to blow us out of the water. In his condition he might have done any thing; so our anxiety may well be imagined.

Reverting for a moment to the English ensign before mentioned as flying aboard the *Greyhound,* I may describe how the Commodore, when he saw it, shouted furiously, "Haul down that —— rag!" Mr. Hardinge ventured to suggest that this was a violation of the law regarding neutral vessels captured in time of war. To which the Commodore made answer by saying, "I don't want any sea-lawyer's arguments!" and he afterwards sent a written order to Mr. Hardinge, forbidding him to fly the English flag.

As we lay beside the *Roanoke,* vague threats were made, and contradictory orders given. Now we were told to be "off at once," then "not to think of moving at present;" until Mr. Hardinge grew restless at such constant supervision, and, taking advantage of a command to quit the station, steamed away, without waiting for any thing more. Right glad were we when the shades of night hid from our view the monster iron-clad, and yet, thankful to Captain Almy, of the *Connecticut,* who, *not* being drunk, stopped us somewhat farther down, delaying our departure for the very sensible reason that a gale of wind was blowing.

Early the next day a steam-tug from the fortress went along-side of the *Connecticut,* and the officers, passengers, and men of the *Minnie* and *Greyhound* were transferred to her, with the exception of Mr. Pollard, who was sent aboard of us to proceed to Boston. When the tug steamed by, handkerchiefs and caps were waved; and I was afterwards informed that they would have cheered me had they been permitted to do so. Fresh meat, vegetables, and ice (the latter of which we esteemed a luxury, as the weather was very warm) had been procured on shore for our consumption.

At length we proceeded to sea, bound for Boston, Massachu-setts, *viâ* New York, where it was intended that we should touch for coal. I will pass over this portion of the voyage, merely remarking that it was as pleasant as could be expected under the circumstances, and that the officers did all in their power to make things comfortable for us.

As we neared New York, thick fog completely enshrouded the coast, but our speed was not slackened. We pressed for-ward, often passing vessels so near as hardly to give them breathing room. Part of one night we lay off Barnegat; for the fog had become so thick that the pilot did not judge it safe for us to proceed. But when morning broke, a brisk wind sprang up, enabling us to see the outline of Sandy Hook. As we passed on up the harbor the motion became less disagreeable to me, and, a comfortable seat having been placed on the deck-house, I enjoyed a panorama of sea and shore scarce equalled in beauty by the approach to any other city in the world.

Off Quarantine we were boarded by the health-officer, who, after asking several questions, permitted us to go on our way; and we came to an anchor off the Navy Yard. Mr. Hardinge went on shore to report his arrival, while Mr. Hall proceeded to bring the vessel alongside the coal-hulk. When Mr. Hardinge returned in the afternoon, the dock was filled with gazers, who, excited by that morbid curiosity exhibited by the world in general, had come to witness, as they supposed, my debarkation. In this they were somewhat disappointed, for every thing had been arranged so nicely that not one of the many there assembled knew when I went on shore. A Navy Yard tug dropped alongside the *Greyhound*, and, with the assistance of Captain H., I was soon snugly settled in the tug's wheel-house.

Captain H. and Mr. Hardinge accompanied me. We crossed to the New York side of the river, and landed at the foot of Canal Street. Procuring a carriage, we drove to a friend's house, where I took from off my person the money which I had concealed about me, and the weight of which at times had almost made me faint. This money belonged to myself and Captain H., and was not, as Yankee papers averred, part of the ship's money we had thrown overboard previous to our capture. Captain H. placed our money in the bank, where it was safe from further molestation.

We visited Niblo's Theatre, to witness the performance of "Bel Demonio." What a contrast did the gay, wealthy city of New York afford at this period to my own sorrow-stricken land! Here there was no sign of want or poverty. No woe-begone faces could I see in that assemblage : all was life and animation. Though war raged within a short distance, its horrors had little influence on the butterflies of the Empire City; whilst, in my own dear native country, all was sad and heart-rending. We were sacrificing lives upon the altar of Liberty; while the North sacrificed hers upon the altar of Mammon.

Next morning Mr. Hardinge called for me, and, after having finished my shopping, we returned to the *Greyhound*, which now lay in mid-stream. Captain H. had gone on board before us, as also had Mr. Pollard. I forgot to mention that this gentleman had been paroled by Mr. Hardinge for the night.

For the rest of the time, above four hours that we remained at New York we were besieged by visitors — old acquaintances, who were allowed to see me. Amongst them were several naval and military officers. About four P.M. the pilot came on board, and, bidding adieu to the capital of "Shoddy," away we steamed for Boston.

The weather was lovely, the water smooth as glass, and the sky cloudless as that of Italy. On each side of us, along the shores of the Sound, were beautiful residences, whose owners, as they strolled over their lawns, or sat smoking on terrace or balcony, appeared to think little, and care less, about the war. We glided past many craft, which lay with white sails that flapped against their masts. I was melancholy; I hardly knew why. The face of Nature wore its very sweetest smile; every thing was propitious; yet I was not pleased, and sought the cabin.

Mr. Hardinge, in a few moments, followed me, and then he repeated a declaration on which I need not expatiate, as it concerned ourselves more than any one else. So generous and noble was he in every thing, that I could not but acknowledge that my heart was his. I firmly believe that God intended us to meet and love; and, to make the story short, I told him that "I would be his wife." Although our politics differed, "Women," thought I, "can sometimes work wonders; and may not he, who is of Northern birth, come by degrees to love, for my sake, the ill-used South?"

Then Captain "Henry" came into the cabin; and, when we told him all, he joined our hands together, saying —

"Hardinge, you are a good fellow, and I love you, boy! Miss Belle deserves a good husband; and I know no one more worthy of her than yourself. May you both be happy!"

Chapter XX

Arrival in Boston.—Our Plan for recapturing the *Greyhound* frustrated.—Captain H———'s Escape.—How it was managed.—Marshal Keyes comes on Board.—The Search for the Captain.—A false Report of his Arrest.—I communicate with him.—He leaves for New York.—I bid adieu to the *Greyhound.*—My Quarters on Shore.—I am paroled for the City.—Newspaper Rumors.—Mr. Hardinge proceeds to Washington on my behalf.—My Mother telegraphs to the Marshal.—She is not permitted to see me.—Politeness of the British Consul.—I write a Letter to the Secretary of the Navy.—Am pronounced Insane.—I am liberated.—Mr. Hardinge and his Officers are placed under Arrest.—Mr. Pollard is sent to Fort Warren.—I leave for Canada.

When we neared Boston, I saw the grim walls of Fort Warren; and a shudder passed over me as I inwardly wondered if that would be my home. All my bright dreams of "merrie England," of "bonnie Scotland," and of a tour on the Continent, were, for the time, banished. The future lowered dark and uncertain. Had not some good spirit whispered hope, I should scarcely have borne up against these gloomy impressions. But I was still "Mrs. Lewis," and might yet escape.

> "For, lo! the heavier Grief weighed down,
> The higher Hope was raised."

272

When we were first captured, it had been agreed that, on our voyage North, an attempt should be made to retake the *Greyhound*.

The project, however, had been abandoned, not from any lack of zeal, but from force of circumstances; for Captain Almy had refused to put on board of us our chief engineer and first officer, without whom the attempt could not possibly succeed.

Another plan, quietly prepared by us previously, and which had reference to the escape of Captain "Henry," had better luck. Whilst we were coming to an anchor off the Boston Navy Yard, and Mr. Hardinge was forward, giving orders to the men, Captain "Henry," Mr. Pollard, and myself were aft, seated in the cabin. I asked the two Yankee pilots if they would join us and partake of a glass of wine. To this they of course assented, and drank freely; for doubtless such wine but seldom passed their lips. I then nodded to Captain "Henry," who, carelessly putting on his hat, and taking his umbrella in his hand, walked up on deck and went aft, where he stood for some moments. Every thing seemed to favor us, for Mr. Hardinge had called a harbor-boat alongside, that he might go ashore to report his arrival.

Before starting, Mr. Hardinge came to me and asked "where his papers were;" when I replied that I thought they must be "in the lower cabin, where he had been dressing himself." He immediately went down to fetch them; and this was the golden opportunity for which we had waited. In less time than it takes me to write it, Captain "Henry" stepped into the boat, which dropped slowly astern with the tide; and when Mr. Hardinge reappeared, the Captain was safe on land.

The whole scene was amusing in the extreme to those who understood it, so well had it been managed. When Mr. Hardinge found his boat gone, he came to the conclusion that the waterman had grown tired of waiting and had pulled off;

so, calling another, he stepped into it and proceeded to report his prize.

In about three hours he returned, bringing with him the United States Marshal, Keyes, and several other gentlemen of position and influence in Boston, whom he introduced to me.

The Marshal then asked for Captain "Henry."

"I think he is on deck," I replied.

Mr. Hardinge went to find him, leaving the other gentlemen to converse with Mr. Pollard and myself. From me, however, they did not learn much, for I sustained the supposititious character of "Mrs. Lewis" with becoming gravity; and it was not until several days after that they became quite sure that I was none other than the celebrated "Belle Boyd."

In a few moments Marshal Keyes, followed by Mr. Hardinge, entered the cabin, the Marshal exclaiming, "Captain 'Henry' has escaped!"

"What!" said I; "it is impossible! Only a few moments ago he was here!" and I looked very serious, though all the while I was laughing in my sleeve, saying to myself, "Again I have got the better of the Yankees!" The vessel was thoroughly searched — nay, I believe that it was fumigated, or "smoked," to get the Captain out; for Marshal Keyes was "positive" that he was on board — so he informed me on his way to the hotel.

Captain "Henry's" escape caused much sensation. Detectives, great and small, were thrown into a flutter of excitement, and the Boston police, whom Marshal Keyes affirmed to be the "best in the world," were all astir, that the fugitive might be lodged in Fort Warren. These myrmidons of Northern power were, certainly, not favored with a very accurate description of Captain "Henry." Some declared that he wore a black hat, others that he had a white covering to his head; some that his nose was aquiline, others that it was decidedly *retroussé*. Such contradictions bewildered the police, whose efforts resulted in a wild-goose chase.

Late on the evening of the escape, Marshal Keyes was jubilant over a supposed capture at Portland, Maine, whither he had telegraphed to have any suspicious character arrested. The Portland captive proved to be not the gentleman of whom they were in quest, but a harmless English tourist, who was, no doubt, much aggrieved at his unlawful detention.

When the Marshal informed me of the Captain's arrest at Portland, I knew that there must be some mistake, and could hardly restrain my laughter; for all this time Captain "Henry" was lying *perdu* in Boston, under an assumed name. I was well aware of the Captain's residence, and through the medium of a friend received several communications from him. In my replies I assured him that he was already as good as free. For two days he stayed quietly at the hotel, and then I heard that he had set off for Canada, *viâ* New York. Detectives had been sent all over the country to intercept him, but it was one of the best-managed escapes from the toils of the "'cute" Yankees that ever took place. Captain "Henry" actually remained for some time at one of the largest hotels in Broadway, where he saw many of his old friends, who, fortunately, did not recognize him.

Many and various were the reports of this affair that found circulation; but, singularly enough, it was the United States officers on board the *Greyhound,* and not "Mrs. Lewis," who had to bear the brunt of suspicion, though I was really the one to blame. I was delighted at being a *non-suspect,* by way of a change, and could thoroughly appreciate the chagrin of Marshal Keyes. He had prophesied that this was a case of capture with which Lord Lyons, at Washington, would not dare to interfere, as Captain "Henry" — to use the Marshal's own words — "was an officer of the Confederate navy, and therefore not an Englishman." To this view of international law I politely assented, thinking that, if Captain "Henry" could only reach a place of safety, it would matter very little how the Marshal classified him.

The *Greyhound* was hauled alongside a wharf, and an immense concourse of people assembled to witness my coming ashore; for it had been telegraphed from New York, and then again from the station in Boston Bay, that "Belle Boyd" was aboard the prize. Marshal Keyes was most courteous, and stated that he had procured a suite of rooms for me at the Tremont House, where I was to remain until my fate was definitely settled. This, he added, would be in a very few days; when he should either have the "supreme pleasure" of taking me to Canada, or the "unpleasant task" of delivering me over to the tender mercies of the commandant of Fort Warren.

The public journals were indefatigable in noticing all my movements. The Sunday-morning papers informed their readers that "Miss Belle Boyd would attend Divine service at the Old —— Church during the forenoon." The week-day news-sheets gave notice that "Miss Belle Boyd, in company with her gallant captor, whose sympathies, no doubt, were with the South, were seen out driving the day before;" and, as a climax, the bulletin-boards announced that "Belle Boyd had been sent to the Fitchburg Jail!" Such were a few of the many *canards* that flew abroad during my stay in the "modern Athens."

I had been there about ten days, when Mr. Hardinge, fearing that the "Fitchburg Jail" story might be but the shadow of a coming event, proceeded to Washington, to procure, if possible, my release. Having letters of introduction to many of the leading and influential men there, he induced them to use their power in my behalf.

Although I was but thirty-six hours' railway-journey from my mother, who had telegraphed to the Marshal to allow her to come and see me, she was not permitted to do so; and none of her letters reached me, they being probably intercepted. But, if letters of affection were thus stopped, there were, happily, other channels than the postal department by which friendly comfort could arrive. Many Boston ladies and gentlemen visited me, despite the Government spies who hovered about my quarters.

After being kept in suspense for three weeks, I forwarded, through Marshal Keyes, a letter to Gideon Welles, Secretary of the Navy at Washington, telling him that "I really was Belle Boyd, and wished to go to Canada, that I might communicate with my mother."

The Marshal received a telegram in answer, saying that "Miss Boyd and her servants should be escorted beyond the lines into Canada, and that, *if I was again caught in the United States, or by the United States authorities, I should be shot.*" This was on a Sunday evening; and the Marshal advised me to depart with all convenient speed, as I had only twenty-four hours' grace. I promised to start on Monday, at five P.M. It was impossible to go sooner, no trains running through to Montreal on Sunday.

The *Washington Republican* got possession of my letter to Gideon Welles, and published it *in extenso,* with the remark that I was "insane," and had been, on that account, released by the Government. For this verdict of lunacy I thank them, if it contributed in any degree to mitigate my sentence. There certainly existed sufficient method in my madness to make me appreciate the advantage of having the promised shooting deferred until they caught me again; and I felt much obliged to members of Congress and others who used their influence in my behalf.

Mr. Hardinge was sent for early on Monday morning by Admiral Stringham, but he assured me that he would soon return. The day passed by, however, without any sign of him, and I began to wonder what had happened, when I received the following letter in his handwriting : —

"MY DEAR MISS BELLE,

"It is all up with me. Mr. Hall, the engineers, and myself, are prisoners, charged with complicity in the escape of Captain H——. The Admiral says that it looks bad for us; so I have adopted a very good motto, viz. : 'Face the music !' and, come what may, the officers under me shall be cleared. I have asked permission of the Admiral to come and bid you good-by. I hope that his answer will be in the affirmative."

This was written on board the receiving-ship *Ohio*. Its receipt made me feel very unhappy, for I feared that circumstantial evidence was against Mr. Hardinge, and that, ere long, he would, although perfectly innocent, share with poor Mr. Pollard a casemate in Fort Warren. But suddenly the object of my thoughts made his appearance. He informed me that the Admiral had allowed him and his officers to be paroled until sundown, and that he had availed himself of this privilege to come instantly to me.

Mr. Pollard, my fellow-passenger from Wilmington, against whom the Yankee journals were exceedingly vituperative, had on the Sunday morning been conveyed to Fort Warren, and there immured for the crime of being distasteful to those in authority. Suffice it to say of Mr. Pollard's subsequent adventures, that he was paroled to the city of Brooklyn, owing to his very bad health; since which I have not heard of him.

The time for my departure from Boston came at last. The Tremont Hotel was left, and the railway dépôt was reached. Marshal Keyes endeavored to make himself agreeable, and was very busy in getting my baggage checked and my ticket taken before the train moved away. The Marshal, I may add, was my courteous companion to the boundary-line between Canada and the United States. With a sad heart I had bidden good-by to Mr. Hardinge, although I trusted that he would soon rejoin me; and I enjoyed the delightful prospect of breathing free Canadian air.

Yes, I should be free! Free from prison bars and irksome confinement; but, alas! an exile! Each step towards freedom carried me farther and farther from my native land; whilst, did I turn back, a heavy penalty awaited me. My father dead, and my dear mother far away! Truly I was alone in the wide, wide world! And I had left one generous heart behind that I knew would miss me sorely.

Chapter XXI

Upon arriving at Montreal, I proceeded to the "St. Lawrence Hall." Captain "Henry" and his wife had proposed that
I should join them at Niagara; but, not having heard from
them for some time, I waited till I could ascertain their exact
whereabouts. In Montreal I met many Southern families,
refugees, and many Confederate sympathizers. The British
provinces were at this time a haven of rest for American
exiles—much as England has always been to the victims of
persecution on the European continent. I learned that my
friends at Niagara were expecting me, and accordingly set off
to join them, the Guards serenading me just before my
departure.

Niagara, with its sublime scenery, I will not attempt to
describe. We were stopping at the Clifton House, and from my
windows I could plainly see the Yankee side of the Falls. There,
lower down, was the Suspension Bridge, offering almost
irresistible temptation to cross from Canada to the States. We
heard, on good authority, that above a hundred thousand

dollars was being expended on the retaking of Captain "Henry" and myself. Spies were stationed on the bridge to watch, and, if possible, to entrap us, should we by chance be foolish enough to venture within their power.

About a week after our arrival at Niagara we noticed, at the *table d'hôte,* two very foppishly-dressed men, with thin, waxed mustaches *à la Napoléon,* and who apparently took great seeming interest in the movements of our entire party. We watched them closely, and were very soon convinced beyond doubt that they were Yankee detectives. Shortly after this discovery, we left for Quebec. It was in the morning, about eight o'clock, that we quitted Niagara and proceeded by rail to Toronto, where we arrived about noon. Imagine our surprise at finding the fair imitation dandies, whom we had left quietly at the "Clifton House," watching for us at the Toronto terminus! It transpired that they had seen us going, and had quietly entered another car in the same train.

The Canadian journals commented severely upon these fellows, and the system of espionage practised on us whilst we remained in the provinces.

The brace of detectives accompanied us in the steamer that left Toronto a few hours afterwards, and which plies regularly during the summer months between that place and Montreal. We noticed that they hovered round, eyeing us narrowly; and we determined to ascertain whether it was really our party that they were watching. When, therefore, we arrived at our destination, Captain "Henry" repaired to the "Donegana Hotel," whilst I went to the "St. Lawrence Hall." In a few hours I learned that one of these fellows had engaged a room at the same hotel where I was stopping; and, when Captain "Henry" called, he told me that the other detective had taken up his abode at the "Donegana"!

When we resumed our journey to Quebec, the spies still dogged us. Captain "Henry" embarked at once for Halifax. I remained some time in Quebec, previous to sailing for Europe; and when, at length, I quitted the American shores, one of the spies endeavored to secure a passage on board the same vessel! The Canadians, however, detesting this odious calling, insisted that he should be denied this opportunity.

My trip across the Atlantic was, on the whole, favored by calm weather and a smooth sea; so that I did not suffer much from my enemy, the *mal de mer*. Off the banks of Newfoundland we were, to make use of a nautical expression, "tied up" for more than a week by the fogs, amid fields and bergs of ice. The latter I had never before seen; and I gazed upon their majestic grandeur with feelings of awe and amazement. So near, at times, did we pass them, that it is no wonder that I felt somewhat nervous; for, had we struck, it would have been instantaneous death to us all. While crossing the banks we encountered a fearful storm, and for one entire night the steamer rolled and plunged with the force of the waves like some living creature.

> "It was midnight on the ocean,
>   And a storm was on the deep!"

But the storm in our case, though violent, did not last long. More moderate weather soon came, and the passengers felt greatly relieved.

When, after entering English waters and passing up the Channel, and my feet touched the ground once more, I thanked God for our safety. I remember for a long time after, in imagination, I could hear the whir-r-r, whir-r-r of the screw, the creaking of blocks, the flapping of sails, the hoarse, uncouth cries of the sailors, and the clear, distinct voices of the captain and his officers.

Arrived in Liverpool, I remained there for some days at the Washington Hotel, and then proceeded to London. I soon ascertained the address of Mr. Hotze, the Confederate commercial agent, to whom I had letters of introduction from the Secretary of State. I reported to the Confederate States Commissioner that the dispatches intrusted to me at Wilmington had been destroyed when the *Greyhound* was overhauled, that they might not fall into our enemy's hands.

This report terminated Belle Boyd's connection with the Southern Government for the time being.

> "So from the scene where death and anguish reign,
> And vice and folly drench with blood the plain,
> . . . . I turn!"

Mr. Hotze gave me a letter that had been left with him until I should reach London. Upon opening it, I found that it was from Mr. Hardinge, informing me that he had come to England, but not being able to learn my whereabouts, had proceeded to Paris, in the faint hope of finding me there. I was deeply touched at this new proof of his honest attachment, and immediately telegraphed a message to him, stating where he would find me in London. Gentle reader, you can, perhaps, imagine for yourself how joyful was our meeting, and in what manner a courtship, which had in it much of romance, was, at length, happily terminated.

Our marriage took place on August 25th, 1864, and journalists were pleased to treat the world to some portions of the romance in which we had taken part. The English press was friendly in its tone, but certain Yankee editors became marvellously indignant at the news, and even now they are subject to periodical returns of indignation.

(Le Moniteur Universel de Paris.)

UN MARIAGE A LONDRES.

"On écrit de Londres : Un mariage singulièrement romantique vient d'avoir lieu aujourd'hui, à onze heures, à l'église Saint-James. La fiancée était la célèbre Belle Boyd, l'héroïne de tant d'exploits aventureux pendant la guerre civile d'Amérique et surtout au moment des brillantes campagnes, du général Stonewall Jackson, dans la vallée de Shenandoah.

"Mlle. Boyd est à peine âgée de vingt ans, d'un caractère très-doux, douée de grands avantages personnels, et liée par la parenté avec quelques-unes des plus influentes familles du Sud. Il paraît que les scènes de la guerre, dont elle était témoin, depuis ces dernières années, avaient développé en elle une énergie et un courage qui se rencontrent rarement chez une femme.

"Les courses à cheval, au milieu de la nuit, à travers marais et forêts, jusque dans les lignes de l'ennemi, d'où elle rapportait aux généraux du Sud des renseignements d'une importance immense, forment le thème de nombreux récits autour des feux de bivouac dans toute l'armée confédérée.

"Elle était tombée entre les mains des fédéraux, mais un jeune officier lui donna les moyens de s'échapper et la suivit dans sa fuite. C'est lui qui, après l'avoir accompagnée en Angleterre, vient de lui donner son nom.

"Dans quelques jours, le jeune époux doit repartir pour les Etats confédérés, où il va s'enrôler comme simple soldat. Ceci a été une des conditions du mariage exigées par la fiancée, comme preuve du dévouement de son époux à une cause qu'il combattait dernièrement encore l'épée à la main.

"Le mariage a été célébré sans aucune pompe, mais ensuite un élégant déjeuner, préparé à l'hôtel de Bruns-

wick, rue Jermyn, a réuni les jeunes mariés et tous les
confédérés de marque et de distinction actuellement à
Londres.

"Dans l'après-midi, les deux époux sont partis pour
Liverpool, où le futur soldat du Sud va s'embarquer
pour les Etats confédérés. On assure que les autorités
fédérales ont mis sa tête à prix.

(Morning Post.)

"St. James's Church, Piccadilly, was yesterday the
scene of a romantic episode in the fratricidal war now
raging on the American continent; as, at the altar of
that sacred edifice, Miss Belle Boyd, whose name and
fame are deservedly cherished in the Southern States,
pledged her troth to Mr. Sam Wylde Hardinge, formerly an officer in the Federal naval service. The marriage
attracted to the church a considerable number of English and American sympathizers in the cause of the
South, anxious to see the lady whose heroism has made
her name so famous, and to witness the result of her
last captivity, the making captive of the Federal officer
under whose guard she was again being conveyed to
prison. Miss Boyd, it will be remembered, is the Virginian lady who, during the terrible scenes enacted in
the Valley of the Shenandoah, rendered such essential
service to General Stonewall Jackson, by procuring for
him information of great value as regards the position
and condition of the Northern forces, and who signalized her devotion to the cause of her country by so
many other services. Capture and imprisonment did not
damp her adventurous and patriotic ardor, as she was
twice immured; once for seven months, and once for
ten months. She was again seized, and, while on board
a Federal vessel, on her way to the North, made the
acquaintance of Lieutenant Hardinge, with whom,

having crossed the Atlantic, she has entered into the bonds of matrimony. Mr. Hardinge needs no excuse for the step he has taken in renouncing his allegiance to the Federal cause and espousing the fair 'rebel,' whom he has now sworn to love, honor, and cherish. Though, in obedience to the wishes of his father, he served for some time in the Federal navy, in which service he rose to be lieutenant, his Southern sympathies were notorious in the North, where it was well known that he had long tendered his resignation, which Mr. Secretary Welles refused to accept; and thus he was forced to continue in a service which he would gladly have renounced long since. Though more than suspected of Southern sympathies, he kept his word when he promised the executive of the Federal navy that the name he bore—a name which had descended to him from a long line of ancestors in Great Britain and America—should not be disgraced, and proved his readiness to perform his duty on many occasions.

"The bride was attended to the altar by Mrs. Edward Robinson Harvey, the bridegroom by Mr. Henry Howard Barber, and the marriage service was read by the Rev. Mr. Paull, of St. James's Chapel, in a manner which deeply impressed all present with the solemn nature of the contract entered into. Amongst the friends of the bride and bridegroom, and of the Confederate cause, who attended, were the Hon. General Williams, formerly United States Minister at Constantinople; the Hon. J. L. O'Sullivan, formerly Minister from Washington at Lisbon; Major Hughes, of the Confederate army; Captain Fearn, Confederate army; the Rev. Frederic Kill Harford (who gave the bride away); Mr. Keen Richards, of Kentucky; Mr. Henry Hotze, Mr. C. Warren Adams, Mrs. Paull, Madame Cerbelle, Mr. Reay, &c.

"At the conclusion of the ceremony, the bride and

bridegroom, and their friends, proceeded to the Brunswick Hotel, Jermyn Street, where a choice and well-
arranged breakfast was partaken of; and at a fitting
moment, towards the conclusion, Mr. Barber, in a most
eloquent speech, proposed the health of Mr. and Mrs.
Hardinge, eulogizing the services the lady had performed, and prognosticating that the bridegroom would
soon win fame in the service on which he is about to
enter. The toast, as may be anticipated, was received
with much delight, and was replied to by both bride
and bridegroom, who expressed their acknowledgments
to the many friends they had found in this country. The
toast of 'The Queen' was afterwards given by Captain
Fearn, who assured the English portion of his hearers
that her Majesty was greatly revered in all parts of the
Southern States of America—an assertion which was
most warmly corroborated by all present, who were
qualified to speak from experience. 'President Davis and
General Lee,' and many other toasts, followed in due
order, till the growing hours warned the bride and
bridegroom that it was time to depart for Liverpool. Mr.
Hardinge purposes in a few days to leave for the South,
whither, in spite of the blockade, he intends to convey
a goodly portion of the wedding cake, for distribution
amongst his wife's friends."

The journey referred to above was taken by my husband
very shortly after, for the simple purpose of communicating
with my family in Virginia. Its results will be shown in the
following chapters, in which he will tell his own story.

Chapter XXII

Lieutenant Hardinge's Journal.—Arrival at Home.—A Surprise.
—A silent Breakfast.—Visit to Martinsburg.—A pleasant
little Excitement.—A Negro Welcome.—"Miss Belle's Hus-
band."—A Portent.—A Sailor's Superstition.—Capture.—
Poor Pat in the Toils.—A high-bred General.—Lieutenant
Adams.—A Yankee Provost-Marshal.—The Guard-House.
—The Restaurant.—A Guardsman.—Ordered off again.—
Arrival at Washington.

Last November it became necessary for me to quit the
tranquil shores of England, and make, much to my disgust, a
trip across the Atlantic, rendered doubly disagreeable to me by
the fact that I was parting for an indefinite period from one
whom I loved fondly—my wife, and to whom I had been
married but two short months.*

On the Monday afternoon after my arrival, I left Boston
and proceeded to New York, where I arrived about 11 P.M.,
and put up at the New York Hotel. I did not sleep here, however, but went over to my mother's residence, in Brooklyn,
almost immediately.

---

* These papers were originally intended solely for the perusal of my
wife; but, upon second thought, they have been somewhat condensed in
material, and have been added to her adventures as an after-piece.

Gaining admittance to the house, and being, as you may suppose, thoroughly conversant with its internal arrangements, I mounted softly on tip-toe to my parents' room and entered. My father, aroused by the noise I made — for floors and doors will invariably creak at such times — called out as I opened the door, "Who is that?" "Martin," I replied; for I wished to surprise them as much as possible.

As soon as I had lit the gas I turned upon them and said, "Mother, how do you do?" For a moment she was struck dumb with astonishment, but the next she was in my arms, pressing me to her heart as only a mother can who loves her son devotedly.

We sat for a long time, conversing upon many topics — my wife, my future prospects, &c. About three in the morning, however, I left her and retired to my brother's room, who was at the time absent in Boston on business. I do not know why it was, but I felt like a stranger in a strange land — for my heart was with you, over the ocean, in merrie England.

All the rest of the night I sat framing a letter to you; and it was late in the morning, just as the faint glimmering streaks of dawn were flashing up from the east, and the distant hum of the city was becoming more and more audible, that I threw myself, tired, weary, and heart-sick, on the bed, and fell asleep to dream of you.

Sleep, did I say? ay, the sleep that the dog enjoys in his kennel. I think it was about nine in the morning when my mother awakened me. I sprang to my feet, and, hurriedly completing my toilet, descended, and entered the dining room. There was very little said — a monosyllabic breakfast, one of those dismal feasts where Death seems to reign supreme. With me it was soon over; and that same night I was *en route* for Baltimore, bound to Martinsburg, which I reached, after much delay and detention, after having enjoyed the nervous excitement of running off the track *only twice,* about 6.30 in the evening.

Here I was subjected, with the rest of the passengers, to a strict examination by the Provost-Marshal, of my passes and travelling-bag; but finally, after a quarter of an hour's delay, I was allowed to go on.

After passing several sentries and two barricades, I at length found myself at your mother's house. I did not announce my name to any one; but one of the girls rushed up to me, and, after gazing intently at me for a moment, flew out of the room.

Whilst I was revolving over in my mind this, to me, inexplicable scene, she returned, and, half laughing, half in doubt, said, "You's Miss Belle's husband, isn't you?" I of course assured her that I was. She again disappeared, but returned, accompanied by the whole sable household, who, crowding round about me, welcomed me to my home, inquiring affectionately after you, and evidently much disappointed at not finding that you were with me.

Greatly to my chagrin, your mother and sister were at Kennysville, about ten miles distant; but Mrs. G., who could not help shedding tears when she knew who I was, welcomed me as a son. All that evening we sat conversing together; and when, at last, I retired to sleep, it was in your own room; and, as I entered in at the door, I uncovered my head, and thought of you.

This was your room; here you had been held a prisoner, and had suffered the torture of an agonizing doubt as to your fate. Here lay your books just as you had left them. Writings, quotations, every thing to remind me of you, were here; and I do not know how long a time I should have stood gazing about me in silence, had it not been for my revery being disturbed by the little negro servant, who broke the silence by saying, "No one's ever sleep in dis room since Missy Bel' been gone — missus says you're de only purson as should."

So, when I retired to bed that night, and "Jim" had been dismissed from further attendance upon me, I lay for a long time thinking, looking into the fire, that glimmered and glared about the room, picturing you here, there, and everywhere about the chamber, and thinking of you sadly, far away from me in England—the exile, lonely and sad.

About midnight I fell asleep, and was only aroused from my slumbers late the next morning by Jim, who was making the fire. When I had finished dressing, I sat down near the fire-place. I hardly know what persuaded me to do so; but, if you will recollect, on the evening that we parted from one another, you placed upon my finger a small diamond-cluster ring,* telling me that there was a peculiar charm attached to it—viz., of forewarning the wearer when in danger, by dropping or being taken off. Without thinking, I did the latter.

Now we sailors are somewhat addicted to superstition; and I must confess that I felt nervously apprehensive about myself, which did not leave me, despite the endeavors that I made to allay my fears. I told Mrs. G—— of the circumstance when I met with her at breakfast, but she laughed at my credulity; but so firmly was I impressed with the belief, that I already began to feel that I was doomed—a marked man.

And I was. At half-past five—having previously procured a pass—I left for Baltimore; but at Monocacy station I was —judge of my surprise—arrested and kept confined all night under guard as a deserter. As a prisoner, I was of course searched; but, finding nothing upon me, the officer command-ing told me that I might retire for the night.

"Where?" I asked.

"Oh! on the floor, by all means," was the response, accom-panied with a horse-laugh.

The next day, at my earnest entreaty, I was sent to Point of Rocks, where I was treated more like a dog than a human

* This ring was once the property of an African princess.—B. B. H.

being; but, fortunately for myself, I was sent on to Harper's Ferry, under a guard of Irish emigrant soldiers, who were far kinder to me than their officers. During the journey they gave me a long history of their wrongs, asserting upon oath that they had been entrapped by the oily tongue of Federal agents in Ireland, who had given them gold and promised them a farm, and two hundred pounds apiece more in gold upon their arrival in the United States, if they would only emigrate for the purpose of tilling the land out West. Upon their arrival in New York, however, they were locked up as prisoners — not allowed to see any one — and were only, after an imprisonment of over three weeks, set free, their liberty having been purchased by their becoming Federal soldiers.

They were also promised eight hundred dollars bounty and three months' furlough, which they had never to this day received, although they had applied for it from time to time; for no sooner had they taken the oath of allegiance, than they were sent to the front.

At the conclusion of this narration, which they swore by the "Holy Vargin" was truth and nothing more or less, one of them informed me that they had orders to shoot me if I was *impudint* to them even. "But we won't do it, me bye," they chorussed; "and, if yes says the word, we're yer min to cut over the border with yes."

This, however, was an utter impossibility, for the country was full of Yankee cavalry, looking after Mosby and his men; so I declined their proffered kindness, much to their astonishment and fright, for they begged me for the love of Heaven not to expose them. This I faithfully promised and kept; and, as I bade them good-day, just before I was conducted into the presence of General Stephenson, one of them remarked to me, *sotto voce,* "Be my sowl! young fellow, it's too bad to see yes in this condition, when ye ought to be afther mountin' into a saddle."

When ushered into General S——'s room, the General, a grizzly, gray-haired, bearded man, scanned me closely for a short time. After enduring this as long at least as my patience could stand it, I said, "Is there any thing remarkable about me, or that you admire?"

"Yes, sir, your duplicity."

"Duplicity?" I reiterated, vaguely, seemingly unconscious of the meaning of the word.

"Yes, sir, duplicity; you are a spy, and ——"

I interrupted him somewhat sharply, but recollected myself, and held my tongue.

"Where are your papers, passes, dispatches?" he asked, angrily.

"Papers I have none, except the *New York Daily News* and the *World* of yesterday. Dispatches — excuse me, did you say dispatches?"

"Yes, sir, dispatches."

"I'll save you a pun," I remarked, savagely; "I have none. As for my passes, they are there," pointing to a formidable-looking official document that had been brought on with me.

"Ugh!" was the rejoinder to this.

Lieutenant Adams just then made his appearance, and a very nice and gentlemanly fellow he was too. In striking contrast with the General, was his adjutant, the lieutenant.

"You're the husband of Miss Belle Boyd, and you ought to be hung. By-the-way, we hung one to-day; didn't we, Adjutant?"

"What are you going to do?"

"Hang you, if you can't prove your innocence — send you to Washington, perhaps. That will do, sir;" and I left the room.

In a few moments Lieutenant Adams came out, and said, and very kindly, too, "Now, Mr. Hardinge, we'll go and get something to eat; and, if I can manage it, you shall sleep elsewhere than in a guard-house. Come into my office for a short time, until I write a letter, and then we will go."

Thanking him for his proffered hospitality, I entered the room and seated myself near the fire—for it was a rainy day, and very disagreeable—and listened with feelings of horror and disgust to the brutal boasts of a braggadocio Provost-Marshal (I wish I could recollect his name, for the sake of humanity), who boasted of having enacted the part of Jack Ketch to a Confederate soldier of "White's Battalion" that very day; remarking, "By —— ! didn't the fellow jump when the rope broke!" and he added, "Here's a piece of the rope, young fellow. Wouldn't you like to swing?"

"Not with you, at least, for a hangman," I said; and I did not attempt to suppress my disgust from appearing.

"D—— you! I'll give you a double allowance of dancing on nothing if I do!" was the reply.

Shortly after this light and entertaining conversation, Lieutenant A. and myself left them; and, after a good meal and a short tour about the town, we once more entered his office. But this time I did not stay long; for, although Lieutenant A. did all in his power to keep me from the guard-house, to that delectable place I went, under the tender auspices of the Provost, who endeavored to regale me with stories of men that he had "hung."

As for sleeping there, it was out of the question. A terrific fire roared and blazed up the chimney, flinging its heat into a room whose measurement might have been ten feet by twelve. In this space were packed some twenty steaming, drunken soldiers and citizens; and add to this the fact that other animals besides rats and mice were at play in the room, I think you will admit that I was at least uncomfortable.

The next morning, at a later hour, I was allowed to proceed under guard to a very seedy-looking cellar rejoicing in the name of a "Restaurant," where I succeeded in getting some stale oysters and bean coffee. Having finished this delectable breakfast, I was again reminded that I was a prisoner in the Yankees' hands by the sentinel, who carried, in addition to his gun, a watch, and who ostentatiously glanced at it, remarking, as he did so, "Time's up."

"Any news from the front?" I ventured to remark.

"No!"

"Is Mosby in the neighborhood?"

"I 'spose so."

"How often do the trains go northward in the course of a day?"

"Twice."

"Corporal," I said, "I am quite an amateur in my way. Come, you have excited my curiosity. Tell me, honestly, now, what you are; for you are the only one of the many soldiers that I have met in my intercourse with the tribe for the last three or four days who is rightly entitled to the name."

He evidently felt flattered, for it was the "Open sesame" of his tongue, and he flatly informed me that he was a deserter from the Guards, who had been stationed in Canada. "And I wish to the devil I was back out of the dirty rapscallion set that I've got into! They say birds of a feather flock together; but I'm —— if I am a bird of their stripe!"

Our conversation was brought to a close at this period by the door of the guard-house once more being closed upon me. For want of better amusement, I stood watching the farmers or their wives from the country round, who came to procure the necessary passes to return to their homes again; and I must confess that the brutal remarks that accompanied the pass, or oftener its refusal, were enough to make the blood of any father, brother, or son, boil with indignation.

At 5 P.M., just as I was beginning to despair of ever being sent away from Harper's Ferry, a detective came to me and said, "All humbug; you're the chap, are yer? Come on!"

To this tender appeal I merely said, "I am ready; lead on."

As I passed out, he significantly pointed to a six-shooter that was buckled to his side, and remarked, "None o' yer capers."

I could not help laughing in the fellow's face; and I hardly know what would have been the *finale,* if Lieutenant Adams, who was passing in at that moment, had not said, "Treat him like a gentleman,——," calling him by his name. And it is to this remark that I, no doubt, am indebted for the little kindnesses I received on my way to Washington.

We arrived in Washington about midnight, and the detective, having visited the Provost's office, I was relieved of his further attendance upon me; and at 1 P.M. on Sunday morning I was consigned to a horrible hole known as the Forrest Hall, filled with every thing that was infamous, low, and degraded.

Forrest Hall, or, as it is somewhat significantly designated by the fellows who board here at the Government's expense, "The Last Ditch," was without exception the most fearful realization of a prison that it was my misfortune ever to have any thing to do with; not that I would have you for one moment suppose that I am familiar with a convict's residence; but I have mentioned it merely from the fact, that until I was thus thoroughly convinced to the contrary, I had always entertained the belief that, in this age of improvement and luxury, prisons had been converted by science into luxuriously improvised hotels — watering-places where roughs and rogues retire for a while to recruit their wasting energies.

And in this respect I have always entertained the belief that in America "they know how to manage these things better than in Europe, you know;" but this foretaste of St. Giles and Billingsgate dispelled, and effectively too, any highly-colored and very romantic ideas that I had conceived of prison luxury; and the rose-color tinting with which I had in fancy painted such residences, gave way to a most sombre picture, edged with

black, that nearly crazed me as I walked gravely backward
and forward, picking my way daintily through dirty groups
of sleeping men or puddles of tobacco-juice with which the
floor of this place was saturated.

Situated in Georgetown, on the suburbs of the City of
Washington, Forrest Hall was, before the commencement of
this devilish struggle, used as a place of public entertainment,
where balls and suppers were held or given. A large square-
shaped room, it had nothing of beauty to recommend it even
then, much less at the present day, when its walls are defaced
with unseemly pictures, vulgar writings, or punctured plaster;
and even in its halcyon days it was such a room that one felt,
however warm one may have been, chilled upon entering.

Four immense windows, reaching from the top almost to the
bottom, bound with iron, looked forth upon the street, but
none of us ever presumed to gaze from them, for orders were
given to shoot dead the audacious wretch who should thus defy
the laws. Four others looked out upon what was known as
the "Promenade," a small enclosure where we were allowed
to walk for half an hour daily. One feature of this "yard,"
as it was called, was the hose; an instrument of torture
which was applied upon "suspects," who were supposed to be
deserters from the United States army. Whether it was so or
not, it was almost impossible to say. The manner of torturing
the unfortunate man was after the most approved method of
Yankee invention and ingenuity. You may doubtless somewhere have read of the prisoner who was tortured by being
fastened in an immovable position beneath a faucet that permitted to escape, every second, one drop of water, which fell
always in one spot upon the forehead, producing a most fearful
torture, resulting eventually in insanity. Well, although it was
not exactly the same thing, nevertheless it approached it very
nearly. For in this instance the victim was made to stand,
bound securely to a post, whilst a steady stream of water, whose

force was thirty pounds to an inch square, was played upon the small of the back.

It was often the case that the victim, unable to endure the torture, would, guilty or not, give in; and the consequence was, that the authorities, having witnessed the acknowledgment of his crime, would remand him in an exhausted state back to the "Hall," to be led out to execution, or conducted to the Penitentiary, where he had been sentenced for a lifetime.

Again, some, more obdurate and stubborn, would remain firm and unyielding, however fearful the torture, until fainting would ensue, or the medical attendant, who waited in person and watched closely the victim's wrist, would say, "Enough" — when he would be carried back to the room, only to be brought forth again to endure the same torture when he had sufficiently recruited his energies to be able to appear once more.

But, to revert once more to Forrest Hall. In a space little less than seventy-five feet square were crowded together over five hundred dirty, ragged, and filthy wretches, of all conditions and color, who had been immured here for many months, with the consoling remark, "Your case will be attended to." The dirt that filled the floor was something awful to reflect upon, and here they were obliged to live — here sleep. A space large enough for the promenade of the guards, who were relieved at the end of every four hours, was reserved for them; and whoever the poor wretch was that dared to invade the neutral ground — for such it was called by the residents — he was shot like a dog for his daring — murdered, coolly and deliberately. Right over the entrance to this room was a place called "The Lodge." Here a corporal and three or four sentries are placed, with the same humane orders to execute relative to the shedding of human blood. The place literally swarmed with vermin, and the air is corrupt, and vile with odors that are, at least, to be moderate, in one's language, disgusting and nauseating in the extreme.

It was early on a Sunday morning that I entered this sink, after having undergone a rigid examination of my person at the hands of the officers who were quartered at the Hall.

This over, I was handed over to a sergeant, and conducted by him to the room that I have endeavored to describe to you above. It was so late, that (fortunately for me) only some nine or ten out of the whole number that lay huddled together on the floor were awake. One or two stared at me for a short time, but went on again with their play at cards.

A sentry was once more my friend in this place. *He pitied me.* I was glad to have any one's pity, even, for I felt almost like the desperate suicide at times, and the future of my life was enveloped in gloom, so dark and obscure, that it was in vain that I attempted to penetrate it.

Having passed the spot where I was standing, wrapped up in my own thoughts, he stopped suddenly and said, "You surely are not a deserter, sir?"

"You have surmised correctly," I replied.

"What are you doing here, then?" he added, with some surprise.

"That is just what I would like to know myself; and if you will inform me, I shall thank you for the information."

"An' I suppose you are one of those fellows we call political prisoners; and if you are, by Jove! there's plenty more of your same stripe that would like to have the same information you're after wanting;" and he resumed his beat.

In a short time he came to me and said, "Why don't you sleep?"

"Sleep!" I said, in astonishment. He grinned at the manner in which I spoke the word *sleep*, and said —

"By ——! there'd only be a clean-picked skeleton of you in the morning."

"Then I will try to fancy myself on the quarter-deck for four hours;" and I commenced to promenade up and down with the sentry, and it was not until late the next morning that I gave up, and was forced to sit down; but I first took my handkerchief and brushed away the dirt on the floor as well as I could before I did so.

As the morning wore on apace, the rascals, who by this time were thoroughly awake, came and stared at me, or asked me questions of myself, business, &c. To the former I affected a perfect indifference, but to the latter I kept my tongue, which brought down innumerable left-handed blessings from these fellows, who saw in me, as they did not abstain from informing their comrades, "a —— aristocrat."

Taking my silence for fear, they became bolder. One of them, a wall-eyed, villainous scoundrel, knocked my hat off. Picking it up, I replaced it on my head, without apparently noticing the offender. Growing bolder, the cries of "Toss him! toss the swell cove! mash him! jam him!" were raised on all sides. A blanket was getting stretched for my special benefit, and I determined to act instantaneously.

Near the stove was a goodly-sized stick of wood, that was used for supporting the door when opened. I determined to get possession of it; so I walked up quietly, and, gaining possession of the instrument that was soon to decide my fate, I retreated to a corner, and waited for them.

It was not long. A party advanced, and then halted, when the wall-eyed man, who was known as "the Gouger" — a name that he had won from his prowess in tearing the eyes from out the sockets of others — came as near as was prudently safe; for I swung the stick defiantly as he advanced, and said —

"Now, young 'un, if yer don't give in, I'll bite yer nose off! Come, now, are yer goin' to?"

To his tender and merciful intentions as regarded my nose, I paid no attention.

"Oh, yer ain't agoin' to, then, are you? Well, I'll have a fresh-meat breakfast, by ——! this morning, at any rate. Come on, bullies."

I only remember one thing until the whole affair was over; and this is the picture : the gouger and his second advancing as I swung my trusty weapon in a circle about me, the pointed edge of the stick cutting into the bridge of the "gouger's nose," and effectually closing an eye for him, and the remaining force of the blow being received by his second on the temple, who fell like a lump of lead by his leader. Then it was that I sprang forward, slashing right and left as I went; but there was no necessity to do murder, for they gave way before me; and the sentry, who had been watching the battle, received me with the remark, as I gained his side, panting from the exertion, "By —— ! if I hadn't have liked you, I'd have shot you for mutiny; but you did that well; they won't trouble you any more, I'll bet."

Nor did they. On the contrary, a "select committee," to my great surprise, waited upon me about 10 A.M., and their spokesman informed me that, by a unanimous vote, I had been chosen their president, and, if I would accept the leadership of "the Owls," it was at my command.

To their astonishment, I refused them; but, not wishing to make them my enemies, for I had no idea how long I was to remain here, I did so as politely as possible.

Fortunately for me, in the afternoon I was sent for; and, under guard, I was conveyed to the Provost-Marshal's office, in Washington City. Here I was kept for over an hour, in a place that was partitioned off for rebels, a ferocious-looking aspirant for military honors guarding me the while. Several of the clerks, who had ascertained from their superior who I was, attempted to converse with me, but in this they failed most decidedly.

Shortly after this, I was taken, under the surveillance of

Captain —— and four of his satellites, to the Old Capitol. On my way to that place, I was kindly permitted to partake of some food—the first that I had eaten for over twenty-four hours—at "Hanmack's," and to the proprietor of that place I was indebted for much attention.

Resuming my journey once more, after running "a muck," so to speak, of the curious loungers, for the churches were fast pouring forth their inmates upon the street, and the terrific fire of conversation from the Captain, which was by far the worst torture I had to endure.

On my arrival at the Old Capitol, I was welcomed by a one-armed lieutenant, who had "seen service," but when he did not say, and whom I ascertained to belong to that body of men known as the "invalid corps." I was ordered to sit down, and, after a running fire of questions, I was sent off to the Carroll Prison, under the guard of two soldiers.

I was not long in reaching it, for the political Bastile is situated not far from its prototype, the Old Capitol. I was received by the Under-Superintendent, who, having registered my name, age, occupation, height, business, ancestry, &c., was good enough to relieve me of some money—not all, for I had been deprived of most by "the gallant knights of the greenwood," through whose merciless fingers I did not pass unscathed, and who certainly have a taking way about them. A diminutive penknife, which was also captured, although I begged to retain it as a favor, was refused, on the plea that I might injure myself.

This over, I was conducted to "Room No. 35," to keep company with a spy and a blockade-runner. On its walls, rudely executed with a piece of charred wood, I wrote our names, one day, and drew above it the English and Confederate flags, which, coming under notice of the sentinel outside, drew down upon my devoted head a whole mouthful of curses, loud and deep. Some wag, a previous inmate of this room, had written *à la* Jack Sheppard, over the door, the following very curious misnomer: "Piety Hall!"—"Piety Hall" is certainly a most deplorable spot. Four bunks, filled with bedding of a most suspicious character, occupy one-third of the space. I very foolishly slept in one of these "beds," as they are designated here, but I can assure you that I regretted it exceedingly long before morning.

It was almost an utter impossibility to tell the time correctly in this place, for the window, that opened on a passage-way without, is so completely enclosed with the cell, that has evidently been added to the building since the commencement of the war, and which is reserved exclusively for "close confinement," that it is not until a very late hour in the forenoon that daylight favors us with his presence at all. A stove in the centre of the room is used by us to cook whatever we choose to buy from the sutler, Mr. Donelly, who has had the monopoly of this prison since the beginning of the rebellion.

The morning after my arrival at the Carroll, in company with the blockade-runner, I descended into the yard, when, after refrshing myself with a hearty wash at the pump, I entered the *salle à manger* for my breakfast! I could eat nothing. The coffee is a mixture of—but I will not attempt to describe it—whilst the "hard-tack," as the old inmates call it, is the flintiest kind of flour that was ever baked and honored with the appellation of biscuit. So I walked out into the yard, and strolled listlessly about, wondering, as prisoners will, when I should be released.

About 11 A.M. I again went up to my room, and received from the sentinel a reprimand for remaining below in the yard, accompanied with the remark, that "if I didn't mind my eye, I'd have old Wood after me."

One of my room-mates said, "What was that old fool saying?"

I repeated the above remark to him, when they both

laughed derisively, and said, "Don't you believe all they tell you : if you do, you will have a surfeit of gasconade, and a troublesome indigestion."

The second day after my arrival the "Colonel" entered the room and said, "Ho, ho, here we are ! so you're the husband of the famous Belle Boyd, are you? Well, we haven't got her, but we've got her husband, that's next to it;" and before I had time to reply, he was out of the room; and this was the way that I first made the acquaintance of William P. Wood, the Superintendent of the Old Capitol and Carroll.

Chapter XXIII

5th December.—Having procured some paper from the
sutler, I wrote to Mr. Stanton, with a simple statement of
my case.

This document I forwarded to Judge Turner, who *attends*
to all the cases of the prisoners held here. That gentleman,
after the expiration of three days, sent for me; and having
asked me, in the presence of witnesses, if I had written it, to
which I answered in the affirmative, then swore me as to the
truthfulness of it, and dismissed me from his awful presence,
with the assurance that he would attend to it in the proper
course of time.

I shall not readily forget my introduction to the inmates of Rooms 25 and 26, to which I was now transferred. I was introduced into my new quarters by Captain Mark T. "Gentlemen," he said, "allow me to introduce to this select and distinguished company, Lieutenant S. Wilde Hardinge, formerly of the United States navy, now of England, but just at present boarding with the freemen of the city at the Old Carroll Prison." (A momentary pause.) "Allow me, sir — Captain McD., of Philadelphia, a counterfeiter, sir; brought here, not for an attempt to counterfeit himself, but for the crime of counterfeiting United States greenbacks, and buying Southern horses with them" — "Mr. Parker, sir" (as I was somewhat unceremoniously pushed round in front of him), "a blacksmith, not of anvils, but of the City of Brotherly Love, a forger by trade. He was brought up at the forge; and how could such an apt scholar end otherwise than in forging the United States Government?" — "Ah, H." (familiarly), "two distinguished 'colonels,' from New York, charged with ballot-box stuffing, and having the presumption to vote for McClellan; a bad case, sir, I assure you, as they [the authorities] keep putting their trial off for further evidence, which they cannot procure. However, they have an idea that they are sulky, and so they intend to keep them here. Ah, sir, this is a glorious country! nothing like it; in fact, a country whose institutions one ought to esteem, for they hang you first and try you afterwards."

Captain T. having finished his somewhat lengthy harangue, I ventured to remark, "And what, sir, may I ask, is your crime?" "Ah! mine," said he, winking complacently, "is *nothing!* but, as out of nothing came something, I presume they'll make it out of my case."

Here the introduction suddenly ceased; for, dinner being announced, every one rushed for a seat, and devoured, somewhat ravenously, it must be confessed, every thing, except what was not eatable, upon the table; an example which I was not slow to imitate, for it had been over two weeks since I had the good fortune to get a mouthful of anything really eatable.

December 7th. — I woke up very early this morning, and, having dressed myself, strolled about the yard below for awhile, in conversation with two or three others incarcerated here — for nothing; at least, that is the invariable answer.

By way of explanation to this, one of them said to me, "It don't do, Mr. H., to know too much in a place like this. You are a newcomer : let me advise you to ask no questions, and answer fewer. I don't mean to say there are spies here, but I wouldn't trust my own father in here;" and having finished his sentence, he left me.

I can see the ladies in the different rooms in that portion of the building devoted to them, gazing down, through their iron bars, into the yard, upon the prisoners, who are allowed to walk about here at stated intervals. I accomplished the prison feat of exchanging notes with a "close-confined" prisoner, an exploit which was executed when the Hessian sentry had his back turned upon us, and which would have been punished with bread and water in the guard-house for forty-eight hours, had it been discovered.

It is quite worthy of notice that one seems to take an indescribable pleasure in eluding the vigilance of the sentries at all times, not so much for any particular reason, but merely for the purpose of passing away the time, and proving that such a thing can be done, in spite of the "Rules and Regulations."

Captain Marsh left Room 26 to-day. He had been prisoner here for some time, but eventually was released without a trial or any satisfaction being accorded to him. His arrest was very ingeniously managed, Secretary Stanton ordering him to report for examination for colonel at Washington, Captain M. was "at the front," *i.e.,* before Richmond, when he received this mandate; but judge of his surprise when, upon his arrival, instead of being promoted, he was ordered to the Carroll, and detained there !

December 9th. — This evening, as we were seated, conversing or playing cards, for want of some better occupation, we were somewhat startled by the cry of "Officer of the keys ! corporal of the guard ! Post No. 7 !" and almost simultaneously with it came the report of a musket, that sent whist-players and every one else to their feet. Officers and men rushed to their different stations, and the general belief, for the moment, was that some one had been shot in attempting to escape. Such, however, was not the case; it proving to be only the accidental discharge of a fire-arm, through the carelessness of a sentinel who had just come off post, and was placing his piece in the rack, when it fell, the jar causing it to go off. The ball passed upwards through the floor, going through a bed in 26, but fortunately without wounding its inmate. This is not the first instance of this kind that has occurred.

Said Colonel Wood, who at that time was playing Inspector of the rooms, "That reminds me of a good story." The *good story* was as follows : —

"There was a fellow, an officer in the Confederate States Army, who received some money from a lady who was held in my residence for stubborn people. With this he bribed the sentinel who was in the yard beneath to let him attempt an escape. The sentinel agreed; but I got wind of the affair an hour before it took place; and, walking up to the sentinel, I said, 'Now, you —— ——, I've got you in my power; and, if you don't shoot that —— rebel, I'll have you hung.' So when Mr. Rebel gets out of the window, Mr. Sentinel blazes away at him, and down he drops kerflummuxed."

"What became of him?" asked one of his audience.

"Why, —— him, he died in the hospital, several days afterwards."

December 11th. — A captain in the Massachusetts 8th was

sent into 26 to-day. He had been arrested and imprisoned in the Baltimore Jail for six weeks. In about an hour after his appearance amongst us, he was ordered out, and put into close confinement.

Captain McD., an incarcerated prisoner in 26, received the news of his sentence of court-martial through the *Star* of this evening. He was convicted of passing counterfeit money, and was sentenced to ten years' imprisonment in the Clinton Prison, New York, has been cashiered the service, and disqualified from holding any office of honor, trust, and profit, under the United States Government, and to pay a fine of $5,000 : this latter item, fortunately for him, is in "greenbacks."

He is a stout-built, thick-set, brawny-looking man, with black eyes and hair, and has lost a finger in the service of the Union. I watched his countenance closely as his eyes met the paragraph containing his sentence. Every one had seen it, but none cared to break the intelligence. He gave a sudden, spasmodic start, and sat for as much as ten minutes gazing at it. How he must have felt inwardly at that time, none can know but himself. It made one feel cold and nervous to see him sit there so quietly. Ten years! a lifetime for him. His hopes for the future were blighted. Farewell for him to all life's charms : he is dead henceforth and forever to the world. I would not have been in his place for thousands.

There he sat, without moving, and Room 26 was very quiet, for the occupants of it were looking at him. He evidently and suddenly became aware of this fact, and, looking up from the fatal *Star,* he said, "I'm in for it. They've done for me. Well, ten years' imprisonment! Humph!" (and he laughed), "I'm glad of that : I'll get out sooner." Then he got up and walked out of the room, and we all of us somehow felt relieved when he had gone.

December 15th. — Glancing up at the windows of Room 40, I saw this afternoon, whilst walking up and down the yard, a poor little child—a girl—about four years old, and standing close beside her was her mother. She clasped the iron bars of the window with childish glee, and did not seem to be aware that the cold, repelling touch of the iron that encircled her present abode was that of prison bars, that held her captive from the outer world. Her merry little laugh was truly painful to listen to.

"Aunt Lizzie" was in the sutler's at this time, so I asked her who it was.

"Who dat lady, massa? Dat's Mrs. K."

"What is her crime?" I asked.

"Oh, her husband was drafted, and she connived at his escape out ob de country, so they arrested her; an' now she's drefful feared that he'll guv hisself up in her place."

December 17th.—The ladies in Room 42 sent me a note, smuggled by ——, in which they thanked me for presents, at different times, of wine and delicacies for the table, that I had procured; for I have followed the business of blockade runner very successfully since I have been in here; no matter if I have ill-luck for an attendant outside in that dashing and very exciting business.

December 20th—I cannot imagine why I can hear no news of you. Mr. Wood says, "You are very foolish, Mr. H., to fret: every thing is fair in love and war;" so I am forced to construe out of the latter portion of his sentence that others are employed in reading my letters. What a jolly thing military surveillance is!

December 21st—I was introduced to the ladies in 42 to-day, and spent a very pleasant half hour in their society; and so quickly did the time slip away, that I was only reminded that the thirty minutes were gone by the officer of the keys, who, looking at his watch, said, "Time's up!" Mrs. Colonel M. spoke of you, and said "that you were undeniably the pet of the Confederacy, and would always be looked upon as its child as long as the Confederacy existed and had a name."

December 23rd. — No signs of my being released yet. Mrs. Colonel M. remarked, and in the presence of Mr. Wood, to-day, "I have material enough of Bastile life, as exemplified in my treatment here, for a book."

"Mrs. M.," said Wood, and he laughed, "no one will ever be able to write a truthful account of the Capitol and Carroll Prisons. I have a reminiscence-book, where I put every thing that occurs of note within these walls. If published, it would equal any of Reynolds's novels of the Tower of London."

Then he spoke of Mrs. Horns. "I did that girl an injustice. By —— ! she was no traitor to the South. It was I who got the papers that condemned her friends, without her knowledge and consent; and Mrs. G., when she went to Richmond, ruined and completely crushed her." Turning to Mrs. Colonel M., he added, "You may believe me or not, but Mrs. G. used to write me notes, until I fairly got sick of her, and afterwards she came out with a vengeance against me. But, as I rather glory in my origin, it didn't hurt me."

December 24th. — My poor mother-in-law, in a letter to me to-day, says : "What have I done, a weak, defenceless woman, weighed down with sorrow and care, that they will not permit me to come on to Washington, and see you ?"

Had an interview with Judge Turner in the afternoon. Judge Turner, *loquiter,* his back to the fire, hat over his eyes (probably from very shame), a cigar in his mouth : —

"Good-morning, Mr. H."

"Good-afternoon, sir."

"Your business, Mr. H. ?"

"This, sir : can you inform me when I am to be released ?"

"Oh, one of these days."

"Are there any charges against me ?"

"None, sir; that is, perhaps there may be."

"Then why am I held prisoner here?"

"Because it pleases the Government."

"Ah! but do you call it justice?"

Judge Turner (frowning): — "Be very careful what you say, sir. You are held here because it pleases Mr. Stanton; besides, your wife won't destroy any more of our army than she has done, Mr. H., if you are held as a hostage; and Mr. Stanton has an affectionate regard for your future welfare."

What could I do? I was like the mouse, a prisoner in the cage, and at the mercy of the lion.

"I repeat my question," I said: "is it justice?"

"Justice or not," said that worthy judge, "we keep you here to make a patriot of you."

Mr. M. told me to-day two stories: one of them was of Sherman's march through Georgia. Mrs. M—— was tied to her chair and flogged, her clothes first being stripped to her waist. Leather straps were used for the purpose. A negro informed the officer that her husband had buried $20,000 in gold, and that she was aware of its hiding-place; so, finding that threats could not extort the secret, they used force.

As she stood there writhing in her agony, she appealed to the fellow, who was a "capting," for mercy; but the ruffianly scoundrel's only reply was, "D—n you! tell us where the gold is hid, and I'll let you up." But this she could not do, and the infuriated wretches continued until she fainted, and the brutes then left her.

The other story was this, and not the less worthy of comment, as it came from the lips of a lady, both in position, as regarded her standing in society, and in wealth and accomplishments. I have no reason to urge you not to publish it to the world. Near the Rio Grande a Mrs. —— lived quietly and undisturbed, though the civil war raged about her, until a band of these "patriots for the restoration of the Union" took possession of the place for a few hours. Several of them entered her house in the night-time and ascended to her room, where she lay sick with rheumatism, and unable to move. Her servant, a young quadroon, who was waiting upon her, concealed herself in the bed; but she was dragged from her hiding-place, and these less than men, rendered furious with drink, and in the presence of the agonized and terrified lady, and in spite of her protestations and appeals for mercy, committed upon the unhappy girl the worst of outrages.

Christmas Eve. — About nine P.M. I sat down to a game of cards, and I am sorry to say that it lasted far into the morning — Sunday morning, and Christmas too; but you must excuse me, for you know that I was a prisoner. I retired to my bed about four A.M., and fell asleep almost immediately, waking up with the winter sun streaming into my face, unwell and low-spirited.

In "our room," 25, hangs, suspended from the ceiling, an evergreen wreath, with two figures pendant from it, the only thing here, in this dismal place, to recall to one's mind Christmas, save that the bells are already beginning to ring out merrily. No greetings from those you love meet your ears. Some few bid you "Merry Christmas," as you pass them by; but the look which accompanies it is low and melancholy, betokening that the one who gives the "God's greeting" says so mechanically.

Egg-nog has already commenced to flow freely in our room. Mr. Donelly's shop is much patronized this morning for whiskey and weiss-beer (the latter drink decidedly doctored, and a late importation, I should judge), eggs, and other necessaries that he doles forth, for money, to us. A glorious day, yet every one is down-hearted. I chew the bitter cud of reflection as I smoke my cigar.

Many of my fellow-prisoners have already drowned their sorrows in drink. An occasional maudlin carol comes from the barred window of some caged bird. As the day wears on apace, so does the state of intoxication increase. The sentries are maudlin, the prisoners noisy or sullen, as the liquor which they have drunk may affect them. Several are insulting. Without, drunken men and women reel through the streets. Why should I grumble, after all? There is misery and sorrow without, in this world, as well as within. I have not smiled to-day, but two or three times my eyes have been filled with tears; for I have been thinking of you, Belle, a stranger in a strange land, waiting sad and lonely for my return.

So the day creeps slowly along. The sentries are drunk, and many of the prisoners are dozing off the effects of whiskey, made up of morphine and other slow poisons.

A few moments ago one of the sentries asserted his authority with me.

Sentry (intoxicated) : — "Say ! where in the —— are you going to?" crossing his gun before me at the same moment.

"Are you addressing your conversation to me?" I ask.

"I don't want none of your —— palaver. Get back into that room, or I'll shoot you !"

I could stand this no longer; but I folded my arms, and, looking him straight in the eyes, I said, "I am unarmed. Shoot, if you dare; but, by Heaven ! if you miss me, I shall not you."

The muzzle of his piece dropped, and, as I walk away, three cheers are given for me by the prisoners who were witnesses of the affair.

Several of the inmates of Carroll Prison have been locked up in their rooms for being noisy; cheering for Jeff. Davis and the Southern Confederacy, and groaning for Sherman and Governor Brown, of Georgia.

Dinner is announced at last; goose, and turkey, and mince-pies, for Room 26; bean-soup and bread for the other prisoners. The former dinner passed off in silence. Every mouthful one takes seems like lead. Nobody laughs or smiles : some few curse and swear.

The dinner is over. At the latter every one scowls, grumbles, or swears, and leaves the room—the *salle à manger* of the Carroll Prison—chewing, by way of dessert, "hard tack."

I ask permission to see the ladies in 42. Wood is gracious to-day, and the request is granted, and for a few brief minutes I feel differently. Suddenly, with a bang, the door is flung open. In rushes Wood, utterly regardless of the poor sick girl who lies writhing with pain upon her bed—the same bed in which you slept, in the same room; and fancy made me always picture you as the sufferer, as you suffered here months before —and roars out in his loudest tones as he discourses upon Atheism; then off; before you are quite sure that you have not made up your mind to knock him down, or show him the door.

As I stood in No. 42 this afternoon, despite myself, the tears sprang to my eyes. There, on the bed, lay poor Miss Mollie McDonough, groaning and moaning with pain, sick and delirious; for close imprisonment had, with its iron grasp, taken hold upon her delicate frame, and, after a brief struggle, she had succumbed before it.

"The doctor says she must be removed," whispers Mrs. Colonel M. to me.

"Why, then, is it not done?" I rejoin.

"Because that renegade Virginian refuses to let it be done."

Poor Mollie! I thought of you, Belle, as I gazed upon her this evening, and the blood rushed to my temples, and I clinched my hands in silent wrath.

Mrs. Colonel M. tells me that Wood rushed into the room this morning, and yelled out at the top of his voice, "Hooray, Mollie! I've got your father a prisoner." She gave one shriek, and cried out in her agony, "My God! what will become of my poor mother now?"

Pretty scene! pretty language was that, to be used in a sick girl's room! Mrs. Colonel M., who had stood by, a silent witness of the scene, said to Mr. Wood, "For God's sake, sir, do you want to finish your work by killing her?"

"Madam, you can't ride a high horse here." "No, sir," said Mrs. M.; "I leave that for Mr. Wood to do." Bang went the door, and he was gone, and in a few minutes he returned with Mr. McDonough.

It was at muster-roll in the evening I left for Room 25, where Colonel Wood was, swearing as usual, and holding forth upon some argument that was engrossing the attention of a crowd of tobacco-smokers lying on the beds in every conceivable position: a choice party for Sunday evening; and, in their intercourse with one another, oaths made up what their ideas lacked in the formation of their sentiments.

Finally, Wood sang a song. Give him his due: he sang it well, and with feeling. Then he left us, for which I fervently thanked Heaven. The moment that he went out, singing commenced. Every one who could not sing was compelled to make a speech, and in this manner we managed to pass the time away quickly. When it came my turn to sing, I gave them the following verses, which I had hastily written for the occasion; and, as I went on, one by one, the members who formed the company of Rooms 25 and 26 joined in the strain, until every one who could sing had done their part to swell the volume of song; and, at its conclusion, long applause greeted me from all sides. The following was the song, sung to the tune of "God Save the Queen": —

I.

> " 'Land of the Pilgrims' pride,
> Land where our fathers died,'
>   Thy doom is read.
> From every hill and glen,

In lowland, marsh, and fen,
Thy fate is written there,
　　Thy glory fled.

II.

"Ambition holds her sway;
Injustice rules the day:
　　Save us, O God!
Spies paid by those who reign,
Belie the freeman's fame,
And terror reigns supreme:
　　Help us, good Lord!

*　　*　　*　　*

IV.

"Arise, ye men who dare,
Who for your rights 'do care:'
　　Uphold the laws.
Uphold them as they were,
Not as at present are:
Prove freemen as of yore—
　　Uphold your cause,

V.

"What! are ye silent still?
Have ye no manly will
　　To battle them?
Yes, yes! ye will, ye come:
I hear the fife and drum!
Hark to th' increasing hum
　　Of fearless men!

VI.

> "Strike! for the old times gone;
> Strike! for your slaughtered sons,
>   And honor fled.
> Down with the feudal horde,
> Who irritate and goad,
> With prison, debt, and sword,
>   And scoff the dead!"

You know that I do not claim to be a poet; so that should you, in glancing over these scraps, have your attention directed for a moment to their errors, forbear, if you please, from laughing at them, and recollect that they were thrown off hastily in my prison-home, and served to while away a few heavy moments on Christmas evening.

Chapter XXIV

On the 30th day of December, as I was busily engaged in writing, Mr. Wilson, the superintendent, called me down into the office to see my father and mother, who had come on from New York to visit me.

Previous to their coming to the Old Capitol they had gone to Secretary Stanton to procure the necessary pass. That gentleman expressed himself astonished at their coming, but, after some considerable delay, having ascertained that the purport of their visit was purely such an one as two fond parents would be supposed to pay their son in "durance vile," gave them the necessary order, without which they could not have seen me.

Whilst we were seated together, conversing upon various topics, Mr. Wilson entered the room and said, addressing his remarks to me —

319

"Mr. Hardinge, you must get ready, sir."

"For what?" I said. "Is it then indeed true that I am to be sent to Fort Delaware?"

"I presume so, sir," was the reply to my inquiry.

Of course I was powerless to do aught for myself to prevent it. The scene that ensued was very affecting. My poor mother wept bitterly, and, unable to endure it unmoved any longer, I hastily quitted the room.

Whilst engaged in packing together what few articles of clothing I possessed—I do not imagine I was more than five minutes about it—I was again interrupted by Mr. Wilson with—

"Come, sir!"

"But I have not got my things together yet," I said.

"Well, if you haven't, there ain't no time to spare; so come along with you."

Seeing no possible way of obtaining a brief respite, I hastily bade adieu to those of my room-mates who were about me, and, taking my few clothes, I followed my jailer.

Down-stairs my poor mother again saw me; she was still weeping, and at times sobbed audibly. Near her, my father stood looking at me sadly.

My mother pressed forward and flung her arms round my neck, saying, as she did so, "God bless you, my son!" and then, blinded by her tears, she staggered rather than walked from the room, my father following.

I was immediately searched, then gruffly ordered to "Fall in and be d——d to you!" with the rest of the prisoners, seven in number.

The orders were then given to "Right face! Forward, march!" and away we went. In front of this modern Bastile we were again halted. Guards were then stationed on each side of us, a lieutenant marching in front with a drawn sword.

We were, upon our arrival at the depot, again halted and

drawn up into line, where we remained for some time, the rain descending upon us in torrents, drenching us to the skin. We asked permission of our guards to seek shelter under a roof where they themselves were standing, but we were gruffly refused.

When the rain had ceased, we were marched into one of the railway-carriages. Lieutenant C., belonging to Major Harry Gilmore's command, sat on the same seat with me. He was, as I afterwards found, very loquacious, and, though a perfect stranger, entered into a spirited conversation, that was kept up nearly the whole way. As I have before stated, he did not, of course, know who *I* was, nor my name; and once, during a lull in our discussions, he said : —

"By-the-way, did you ever hear tell of Miss Belle Boyd?"

I smilingly assented that I had.

"Well," he said, "there isn't a Southerner who would not lay down his life for her. When I was at the battle of Winchester, I was wounded, and she came into the hospital where I was, and inquired if there were any Maryland boys there. Amongst other delicacies, she gave me some very nice peach-brandy. She and Mrs. G. were in the fort, if I err not, cheering us on when we made a charge and drove the Yankees back. When she was in Montgomery Hall, Alabama, in 1863, she attended a ball held there, and was *the* belle. She stopped a duel between two Frenchmen who were going to fight in the garden attached to the hotel. When she came back from her imprisonment she brought me a splendid uniform. You have no idea how every one loves and respects her," he added; "however, she married a Yankee, so I understand. But Miss Belle would never marry a Yankee, I am certain; I'll bet he was a rebel : indeed, I am confident of it; and ——"

"And the gentleman who sits beside you is her husband," I added, interrupting him; "and, like yourself, sir, I am a prisoner held by the Yankees."

I never in my life saw a person so thoroughly dumbfounded and confused for the moment, but finally he said —

"Well, I trust that you will pardon me for what I have said; upon my honor I did not know who you were, or I would never have done as I have."

"You have said nothing," I replied, "that a gentleman could construe into an insult; and I am happy to make the acquaintance of one who knew my wife so well." And for the rest of the way we were the best of friends.

We arrived in Philadelphia about midnight; the same systematic process of guarding us was gone through with, and as we were marched out of the carriages, sleepy passengers rubbed their eyes, and stared at the "Johnnies" as we passed by them. We were quickly moved over opposite the station. Here we were halted for a few moments, the lieutenant leaving us in charge of the sergeant whilst he went off to ascertain further information in regard to our movements. He returned, however, in a few moments; and, again taking up our line of march, we filed to the left, then to the right, in through a gateway, under an arch, through what had once been a door-way, then down through a long corridor, whose sides were filled with camp-bedsteads, and finally a dismal slave-pen, where there were no windows, only a narrow grated door. This, we were informed, was to be our quarters for the night. Our beds were the hard boards; our covering, what we stood in; our pillows, knapsacks or valises.

Sleep was out of the question; so, for the consideration of ten dollars in "greenbacks" (about two pounds sterling), I purchased, from a calculating specimen of Yankeedom, about *tenpence* worth of tobacco, and tried to drown my cares and sorrows by smoking; but, although the "smoke" vanished, my woes and sorrows still clung to me. I felt very sore, stiff, cross, out of temper, and indisposed every way, which was in a measure increased the next morning by a breakfast off tin-ware of *something*. I know that I was very hungry, and ate and drank it!

Could any one be more miserable than we, under the circumstances? Soldiers, sailors, flunkeys, women, &c., came and stared at us.

"So that is him! oh, my!" was the sentiment of a very stout, red-faced woman, staring in upon me. "Who'd a-thought it of him? What a wicked man!"

"What will they do with him?" I heard one ask of another.

"Oh, hang him," was the reply.

"Roasting's too good for him," said the other, with a laugh.

"I wonder if I can get a button or piece of his coat?" I heard some one else say.

"Ask him," said another.

This species of degrading torture I endured until noon-time, when we were ordered out, and conducted, still under guard, to the cars that we had occupied the night before on our way from Washington, now on our way to Wilmington, Delaware, where we arrived in about two hours' time.

Once more we were ordered out of the carriage. I obeyed the command with an apathetic listlessness, for I had lost all spirit, as had the rest of our party, two of whom were old gentlemen, men who already had one foot in the grave — political prisoners, like myself; men who had refused to take the oath of allegiance to the United States Government.

This time we had a journey of eight miles on foot to make. True, apparently, this was not long; but to us it was indeed so. The roads were very bad; and almost all of the way we were over our ankles in mud and slushy snow; and it was not until after three hours of this torture that we marched into Newcastle. As we passed through the principal streets, women and men rushed to the windows and doors to see us, whilst a guard of honor (?), extemporized from all the small boys and girls in the village, attended us in the front and rear, gazing at us in wonderment.

Arriving at the steamboat landing, much to our disappointment and surprise, the steamer was not to be found, and we were ordered to right about; and this time, as if to add insult to injury, we were conducted to the Newcastle jail, and confined in a convict's cell.

In this horrid place we were left to our meditations until far into the evening, when we were marched out : and this time it was with a sensation of relief that I passed on to the deck of the *Osceola*. About 8 P.M., the *Osceola* got under way and proceeded down the river, *en route* for the fortress, about twelve miles distant. Several officers stationed at that place were on board, and came aft, questioning us, scanning our attire, features, &c., and, in fact, doing every thing but poke us with sticks to make us roar.

Upon our arrival at the landing, about 10 P.M., the same routine of guarding was gone through with as I have before described. At last we reached the provost-marshal's office. Here our names were registered, our age, State, when born, profession, whether citizen or soldier, &c.; and, this accomplished, it being late, we were conducted into the "Private Barracks," and lodged in the Virginia division, in which were confined some thirteen hundred privates — a place that a gentleman-farmer in this country would not have permitted his pigs to live in, much less human beings.

As we entered the doorway, yells and shouts from every side greeted us, of "Fresh fish ! fresh fish !" Men and boys crowded around us to find out from "whence we came," "what we were held for," "who we were;" and last, but not least, "had they gone through us," in other words, and more plainly speaking, 'had the sentries outside searched us."

To this last inquiry I assured my questioners that the Yankees outside had done so most effectively.

Several of them proposed "tossing us in a blanket," by way of diversion to the rest, and many were evidently in favor of it, when suddenly Sergeant B——, of the division, sprang forward, and shouted at the top of his voice —

"By Jove, boys! this gentleman is Miss Belle Boyd's husband; you wouldn't wound her feelings by insulting him, would you?"

In an instant the shout that was raised was perfectly deafening. I was received with *empressement* by the whole body of Confederate prisoners.

In spite of this, however, I passed a miserable night, and awoke more dead than alive with the excessive cold, having no covering to shield me from the weather, the hard floor for my bed. At 9 A.M. I ate my initiatory meal at Fort Delaware, consisting of a piece of flinty bread and the smallest morsel of pork yellow with age. The latter delicacy I gave away, not having been here long eough to appreciate such dainties and eat anything that was placed before me.

Jan. 1st, 1865. — I passed a dreadful New Year's Eve; cowering over the fire until far into the mid-watch, with my gloomy thoughts for sole companions — fitting company, though, for such a place as this. The floor is my bed again to-night, and I sleep as the dogs sleep — half waking, half sleeping. Once I awoke, hearing some one engaged in prayer; deep silence prevailed around about; and whoever he was — the speaker, I mean — he spoke impressively. Before I retired for the night I called upon General Vance and his staff, and passed a very pleasant evening.

Jan. 2nd. — Some of the "boys" gave me a blanket, and another handed me his overcoat; so that I managed to sleep warmer than usual. Found several friends of mine here from Mobile, Alabama. Captain W. gave me a very good cup of coffee for my dinner. The days drag wearily by, God knows.

Everybody treats me kindly. I have found warm friends. Am getting accustomed to my "feather bed of boards."

Jan. 2nd. — Two letters. Very gloomy, and dull, and cold. In the evening heard some very fine singing; Captain —— sang an *aria* from "Norma" that he rendered excellently well.

Jan. 3rd and 4th. — Wrote to my friends outside the prison to-day. Whilst engaged in this occupation, one of General Vance's aides brought me an invitation from the General to dine with them. Passed a pleasant afternoon in their society; and was introduced to Captain M., brother of General M., the distinguished Kentucky cavalry officer, and we became very warm friends afterwards.

Jan. 5th. — I attempted my first cup of tea this morning. Gods! fancy my having turned cook! My friends laughed heartily at my handiwork; *for I put the tea in the cup, then the snow upon that,* waiting for that to melt into water and boil. Meanwhile the tea suffered the natural result of such stupidity, by being burnt.

Jan. 6th — Saw an account in the paper of my friend Mrs. Colonel —— having been sent South. Thank God, she is free!

Jan. 8th. — Received a letter from one of my friends outside to-day, smuggled in by the underground route; there is hope for me yet in Rome with Nero. Saw an account of my removal from the Carroll Prison here, headed —

> "THE HUSBAND OF BELLE BOYD. — The husband of Belle Boyd, the famous Rebel Spy, took refreshments in the guardhouse of the Citizens' Volunteer Hospital on Friday afternoon, on his way to Fort Delaware. Dr. (?) Kenderdine was *careful to provide secure quarters for this noted individual.*"

Jan. 9th and 10th. — Damp weather. Afflicted with the "blues." My feet so swollen that I cannot put my boots on.

Jan. 11th. — Whitewashed our division to-day. The guard kept us out in the snow that had fallen heavily. Passed the time away by snow-balling one another. One of these frozen missiles falling near a sentry, that menial deliberately fired upon us, but fortunately without doing any mischief, although the ball ploughed the snow up very near one of our party.

The places where the prisoners are held here are called "pens;" and they are correctly designated, for they are nothing more. Any one who may at any period of his life have attended a "cattle-show," can readily portray to himself the places we inhabit. These habitations, boarded and roughly put together, remind one very forcibly of old-fashioned farmhouse barns, where, in the old times, your poor horse shivered the night through, standing uneasily in his stall, whilst his master slept comfortably within the chimney-corner. Officially and by courtesy they were denominated "barracks," of which there are three distinct kinds upon this island, viz., the Officers' Barracks, the Privates' Barracks, and last, but not least, the Allegiance Barracks; or, as they are commonly termed, the "Whitewashed," or "Galvanized Barracks."

In the Officers' Barracks are held some fifteen or eighteen hundred officers and political prisoners — about 150 in all of the latter.

In the Privates' Barracks, which occupy a little more space, and whose divisions are somewhat larger than those of the former, are crowded together, in their misery, some nine or ten thousand soldiers, from almost every regiment and command in the Southern Confederacy. Many of these poor fellows are but half-clad, and suffer terribly from the cold, inclement winter of the North. Many of them, by far the largest portion, are without friends in the North to whom they could apply, and are therefore indebted to the Yankees for the very little clothing that is at times given to them, but which is never given unless every vestige of the original garment has entirely disappeared, and common decency demands it. Many of them are young scions of some of the noblest and proudest families in the South; men who before this war knew naught of want and trouble; men who had from infancy been reared in the lap of luxury, and are now enduring every thing — insult, imprisonment, and starvation — willingly, and without murmuring; patriots whose names will yet live to be handed down to posterity as noblest among the noble.

And, lastly, the Galvanized Barracks. These are domiciled by Southern soldiers who have taken the oath of allegiance to the United States upon being imprisoned here. These "patriots" remain in this delectable spot for one year, and are made to work for the Government, to prove their devotion to Mr. Lincoln's Administration, by hauling wood and doing the disagreeable duties of the prison. These fellows are allowed to draw rations daily, and to live the same as the garrison in every respect as regards their food. Moreover, they are permitted to receive boxes containing clothing and luxuries which those who choose to remain constant to their principles cannot, unless they are fortunate enough to possess the influence of outside friends.

As regards their love for the "old flag," and devotion to the Union, I can hardly deem myself competent to pronounce judgment correctly. But an excellent story is told of these individuals, which is not unworthy of attention, as it may in a measure serve to show how far these *patriots* should be trusted.

General S—— and his staff once paid them a visit. Upon entering their abode the General stated to them that there was to be an exchange of prisoners, and that all those who still desired to go back to the South might do so.

"Now," he added, "all those who feel inclined to do so, step over on the left of the division."

*Every one of them went over; not a man remaining of the
many who had grown to love the Federal Government as at
present conducted.*

It is said General S—— laughed, and remarked, "Well, that
will do; I only wanted to find out whom I could trust—to
ascertain if any of you were really sincere."

These barracks or pens are divided into divisions, each
division having a stove for the purpose of heating, in a manner, quarters that would otherwise be untenable. They range
in length from eighty to one hundred feet, and in breadth
measure about thirty feet. They are separated from one
another by thin partitions of boarding, so that really they are
quite connected, as conversations carried on in one can be
distinctly heard in the other. On each side of these places,
wide structures of wood are built, two stories in height, which
are reached by means of wooden chats nailed to the supports.
Upon these elevated platforms, each prisoner is apportioned
off so much space for his sleeping and cooking purposes.

At night calcium lights, placed at one end of the barracks,
throw their broad glare upon the square of something less than
an acre of mud and boards. Delectable spot in rainy weather,
with its ditches filled with muddy yellow water! Splendid
place in the summer for disease; and many a poor fellow has
looked his last upon this earth, dying here, far away from his
home, struck down by the small-pox or some virulent, fearful
malady!

Escapes during the summer months are not unfrequent;
but in winter all such attempts were put an end to from the
inclemency of the weather, the floating ice in the river, and
the utter impossibility of any one, however bold and daring
a swimmer he might be, living any length of time in the water.

The regulations for the prevention of escape, &c., are
rigorous enough, but they are still more rigorously carried out.

One of the prisoners in the private barracks, rising one

morning, carelessly, and without thinking of the consequences that might ensue, threw some dirty water out of the pigeon-hole, which answered the purpose of a window, and served to lighten up in a manner the gloom within.

The water, splashing on the ground, attracted the attention of a sentinel who was standing guard about twenty paces distant; and, without warning, he brought his musket to a "ready," and fired hap-hazard in the direction from whence the water was thrown, hitting, not the aggressor, but an innocent youth who had just awakened, and was gazing out upon the dreary scene that presented itself before him, perfectly unconscious of his danger, or how near unto death's door he was passing.

Chapter XXV

A piteous Spectacle.—The Old Men's Petition.—Our Guardians.
—Colonel W.—Mr. W.—Tom S. the Toady.—How Tom
got his Situation.—The Ladies' Attendants.—Aunt Lizzie.
—Mr. L.—The Spy discomfited.—The Prison Building.—
Fort Delaware.—The "Galvanized Barracks".—Galvaniza-
tion and its Results.—The Prison by Night.—A Reckless
Sentry.—Our Cuisine.—Scrap Pudding.—How the Prison
Officers made their Profit.

About the middle of January I saw one of the most piteous
spectacles, I think, that I ever had the misfortune to witness.
Four men, old and decrepid, one of them tottering on the
entrance to the valley of shadows, men whose gray beards and
venerable aspects ought to have commanded at least sympathy
from the presiding powers at Washington, were brought in as
prisoners. They were to be held here until exchanged—men
who could not possibly be of any benefit whatever to either
side, North or South. These men were arrested on the 3rd of
August last by a captain in the United States navy, who was
on shore, in command of a raiding-party, and who brought
them back prisoners on board his vessel. They were confined
in the hold for five months, and then transferred to the supply
steamer *Massachusetts,* and sent to Philadelphia, and from
thence, upon her arrival, were forwarded to Fort Delaware.

Truly, if this was the sole result of the brave captain's raid, he had nothing to feel proud of.

Upon their arrival here they excited the "commiseration" even of Adjutant Ahl, who informed them, if they would take the oath and draw up a petition to the Secretary of War, that he himself would forward it for them to the proper authorities. Below I subjoin the letter that they had written, by friends who volunteered their services in the barracks, and to which they respectively signed their names. One of them recounted to me his misfortunes and those of his comrades, and I confess that, as I sat listening to his recital, I felt moved. "We have been treated very badly, very badly," he said, in conclusion — "confined in the hold of the vessel for most of the time; and we are all of us very old men, sir, and we never did them any harm."

"*Jan. 16th,* 1865.

"Capt. Geo. H. AHL, A. A. A. Genl.
    "SIR,
        "In accordance with your request, we enclose you the written petition to the Secretary of War, and we solicit your kindness to have it forwarded at your earliest convenience. You have seen our condition, and can appreciate the truthfulness of our statements. If, therefore, you find it consistent with your views of duty and humanity to add thereto the recommendation of the Commanding General of this post, or such other good word in our behalf as you may deem best, you will add greatly to the obligations we are already under for your considerate attention.

"THE PETITIONERS."

PETITION.

"*Jan.* 16*th*, 1865.

Hon. E. M. STANTON, Secretary of War.

"SIR,

"The Petition of the undersigned humbly sheweth, that they are citizens of the State of Georgia, and residents of McIntosh County, whence we were seized and taken on the 3d of August last, by a raiding-party under the command of Captain Colverconerris, of the United States Navy, and, after five months of close and severe confinement on board vessel, have been transferred to the military prison at Fort Delaware, where we are at the present writing of this. We were, at the time of our capture, peaceable citizens, engaged in the pursuit of our several civil occupations, non-combatants, having never been engaged in any military service or duty to the Confederate authorities, and are, from our advanced age and physical disabilities, wholly incapable of such service as the field, neither of us being less than fifty, some of us over sixty years of age, and one of us being deprived of a leg, which was lost by accident many years ago. Being thus incapable of contributing any thing towards the continuance of this war, or the result of this unfortunate struggle between the sections of our once common country, and having, in the course of nature, but few remaining days to look for on this earth, we indulge the hope, and appeal to the humanity of the enlightened Government in whose hands we are placed, that those days shall not be shortened by the terrific rigors of an imprisonment which cannot otherwise be endured. To this appeal of our extreme age and helplessness, and our entirely civil and non-combative character, we have to add that our homes are now within your military lines as recently established by the forces under the command of Major-General Sherman. Under this state of affairs, we humbly beg to

be, as soon as practicable, released from confinement
and returned to our homes, where we engage to remain
as heretofore, and, as our physical condition compels,
quiet and peaceable citizens. To this end we are willing
and ready to subscribe to the usual oath of allegiance
to the United States Government. Trusting that the
petition and appeal may receive a speedy and favorable
response, we shall, as in duty bound,

"Ever remain, your obedient servants,

"WM. JAMES CANNON,
"CHARLES LINGOAUT,
"WM. RILY TOWNSEND,
"WM. SOMERLIN."

Yankees generally are very susceptible to flattery, at least
those in authority at Washington; and let us hope that the
few masterly touches of the ingenious, if not diplomatic author,
will not fail to have its desired effect upon hearts that are
proverbial for their adamantine qualities. Since my sojourn
here I have had ample opportunities of observing the spirit of
piety and godliness amongst the Southern soldiery. A Young
Men's Christian Association was organized some time ago, and
prayer-meetings are held nightly in some one of the divisions,
whilst prayers and readings from the Bible take place in each
division every evening about half an hour before the lights are
put out, either conducted by some chaplain or Confederate
officer.

In their pious regard for the Sabbath day and God's command to keep it holy, I know of no nation which approaches
nearer to the marked devotion of the English people than the
Southerners. The Sabbath day is always passed in a quiet and
orderly manner, service being held in different parts of the
barracks. It was my very good fortune to attend the meeting
held by the Rev. Mr. Kinsolving, in Division 23. His service

was attended by all grades of rank, and he certainly spoke and read with — and what is very rare with the public speakers of the present day — much feeling and pathos, so different from the rant and fume of a certain sensational preacher of the word of God that I once had the misfortune to hear in the "City of Churches."*

You will like to hear something of our jailers. Here they are. Colonel W., our superintendent, could be a gentleman if he wished. With a mind cultured and at once deep and penetrating, he appears to have brutalized himself by contact with those with whom he has associated. I have watched the man closely in both phases — in one, running about the ground like an enraged tiger, whilst his subordinates clear to the right and left, fearful of their tyrannical master. Finally venting his spleen upon some unfortunate one, he subsides into quiet, and his official dignity now feels half ashamed of the disturbance he has succeeded in creating about him!

I have heard him use language that modest ears would hardly dare to listen to — not merely commonplace oaths, but curses both loud and deep, and horrible to hear. A fit disciple of Tom Paine and Voltaire! for W. is an Atheist.

Atheism is his hobby. His arguments are good in the defence of his "creed;" but, reasoner, and a deep one though he is, I do not believe that he has faith in it. Conversing on this subject one day he said, "There is my Bible," laying his hand on a volume of Voltaire!

"And, Colonel W.," I replied, "like Voltaire, on your death-bed you will cry out in your agony upon God to save you."

He pondered for a moment, then said, "Well, I might. Your Bible says, that 'those who believe in Me, even in the eleventh hour, shall be saved.'"

Again, the Colonel can be as suave and polite, as affable and courteous, as any who have moved in the best society — as

* Brooklyn, Long Island, State of New York.

gentle and as tender. It is only, Madame Rumor whispers, that he is cruel when under the influence of morphia or opium. In his movements he is quick and energetic—a man of medium stature. His is a peculiar eye—keen and gray; at times cold and perfectly expressionless, at others full of shrewdness and keenness. Dressed in black coat and gray trousers and vest, his large head covered with a broad-brimmed black slouched hat, you have W. P. Wood, the Vidocq, or, better still, perhaps the Jonathan Wild of America.

Mr. Wilson, the Colonel's right-hand man, the under-superintendent, from what little I saw of him, appeared to be a gentleman, straight-forward in his dealings, and a man of very few words. He dresses plainly, and wears a slouched felt hat. Every one wears felt hats now. "It is only foreigners and Southerners who carry canes and wear tall hats," said a friend of mine to me one day when in conversation with him.

Next to the Colonel, W. is the busiest man in the prison. He it is who has charge of the prisoners, and who rules supreme in the Colonel's absence. Every morning at eight o'clock he comes round and calls the muster-roll of the prisoners in their rooms, and hands them their letters, which, however, are invariably opened and read before they leave the office below.

Colonel Colby, the military commandant, who has charge of this post, I saw but little of; but we all liked him, for he was ever courteous and polite, and had always a good word for us.

Fortunately for myself, I was not under the tender guardianship of the "officers of the Keyes," so of them I can say but little, save that they attended to their business with punctilious strictness.

Another individual in this modern Bastile is a decided toady to Colonel Wood. He rejoices in the name of Tom Stackpole, and has charge of the beds and bedding, and he attempts to imitate him in his every action. In his accomplishment of swearing he is even a greater proficient than the Colonel. In his walk he outdoes him. If there is a man that he hates and fears more than all others it is certainly Colonel W———. Indeed, I think, like Jonathan Wild, the Colonel can trust his menials, because he knows a portion of their life which would not do to publish to the world.

During the late election in the United States, Tom made himself conspicuous by pulling down from the pole upon which it was hoisted the American flag, and tearing it, because it bore upon its folds the names of McClellan and Pendleton. For this hardy act he was promoted to the position that he now occupies.

The female servants of the prison, with the exception of "Aunt Lizzie," were the worst and most degraded beings I ever had the misfortune of seeing. The Five Points of New York, or the lowest dens of infamy, could not produce a worse crowd. Yet this scum were hired to wait upon the ladies who were here held — for Heaven knows what; but prisoners nevertheless.

But "Aunt Lizzie," as she was called by every one here, stood on her dignity. No one insulted her; always laughing and good-natured, Aunt Lizzie prided herself upon belonging formerly to the Snowden family. "My name, sah, am Aunt Lizzie Snowden, sah, and I'm berry proud of it, sah." Straightforward and ever scrupulous, in her Colonel W——— had one faithful attendant. She was not to be bribed nor cajoled. None could see her smiling face and feel gloomy : a good word she had for everybody. She it was who mended our linen and washed our clothes. Aunt Lizzie was certainly a good feature in this prison, and many besides myself will, I am sure, remember her with feelings of gratitude.

Mr. L——— is another gentleman who rejoices in belonging to the corps that is commanded by Colonel W———. He is the

"Jerry Sneak" of this institution. His nose is everywhere, and his eyes are upon every thing. If a visitor comes to see a friend confined here, Mr. L—— stands near at hand, noting down in his memory the conversation, whilst apparently engaged in trimming his nails, or fixing his eyes on dreamland, as he notes down their words. If in the court when the prisoners are walking about, he is always looking on and smiling, or has some soft word of "endearment" to say to new-comers, to bring against them when their time comes. I was particularly the object of his hatred, and our hate was mutual.

I grievously offended him. One day a gentleman called to see me. Our interview was interesting — one purely upon personal matters. Upon entering, I seated myself close to the gentleman. Mr. L—— took a chair, and, placing his legs between us, stretched himself complacently at full length, and prepared, as was his custom, to listen.

Of course, our hope of a conversation was, to all appearances, at an end. For some moments I stood it calmly, but at last I could stand it no longer. "There are," I said, very quietly, "in this prison spies; bearers of stories, ever ready for any thing mean and contemptible, but the meanest and most contemptible of them all is — I beg your pardon, sir," turning suddenly to him, "is yourself, Mr. L——."

"I can't help it," said that individual, looking piteously at me. But the shot had taken effect: Mr. L—— removed his chair to the fire, and our conversation was uninterrupted.

Of the *cuisine* of Fort Delaware there is not much to be said in praise. Two meals are served out to us daily, consisting of one piece of peculiarly constructed bread, and one ditto of indescribable salt, yellowish-colored pork, or meat that has had it nutriment entirely boiled out of it in the making of soup for the garrison, previous to its being apportioned out to the prisoners.

Occasionally a mixture, designated by our persecutors as

soup, and containing an ample sufficiency of maggots, is doled out to us in tin pots. It is an indescribable *olla prodrida* of soups of every kind, and in its appearance reminds one irresistibly of the sty and the trough. Coffee and tea are luxuries never seen in the shed where we receive our rations. Only those who are fortunate enough to have money are ever enabled to procure these articles from the sutler; who, although selling a very good kind, does not forget to charge a very exorbitant price for his considerate (!) kindness.

These meals thus served out to us are called, respectively, breakfast and dinner — misnomers for such luxuries in the outside world, however poor they may be. What would our English friends, who are, I believe, by no means averse to good cheer, think, if they could try it for a few weeks, of "the nutritious food, the unparalleled good treatment of the prisoners held here, of which the Federals boast so loudly?"

These pleasant meals are served to us at nine in the morning and three in the afternoon. The cook-house, as it is named, from whence this food is served out to us by its grinning demons, is a large room, in length about one hundred feet, by sixty in width, filled partially with long and very narrow tables, constructed of pine boards. Upon two generally, though sometimes there were more, are placed at regular intervals our pieces of bread (by courtesy) and our ditto of meat. About half-past eight some subordinate of the cook-house shouts out the command to "fall in, 28 !" or "31 !" and whichever portion of the officers' barracks may be first mentioned, the inmates immediately respond by coming forth from their separate divisions, and falling in, by twos or threes, march up to the entrance of the cook-house.

Here we are generally kept waiting for several minutes until the door is thrown open, when we enter and file in single column down the table, taking our allotted rations as we pass on, until the end of the table is reached, when on again, face to the right about! retracing our steps out of the room, when we are once more fain to return to our dens, or eat in the open air. The latter alternative, however, is not very often chosen, as it is winter, and we are but scantily clothed.

Each division, during the cold weather, is provided with a stove for the purpose of heating, in a measure, places that would have otherwise been untenantable. Over this some one or more of us are generally pretty much occupied in cooking nondescript dishes, some plate composed of odds and ends, and which I find from experience are not altogether unsavory after once conquering the repugnance felt upon being brought into contact with such very unaccustomed food. Coffee-pots, tea-pots, and oftentimes mugs and dippers, are piled upon every conceivable spot or space large enough to admit of such packing; and in cold weather to approach anywhere near the stove is a thing utterly impossible, owing to the numbers surrounding it.

Political prisoners have the privilege of procuring their meals from the kitchen, provided they can make some arrangement with the heads of that department, and have the money necessary to back them in such arrangements. After I had been imprisoned for two weeks, I managed to have "an interview" with the presiding dignitary of this steaming sanctum, which resulted favorably; and henceforth, instead of living, as I had for the past fourteen days, upon bread and water (for I never ate the pork), I dined regularly upon meat, potatoes, and coffee for breakfast, dinner, and supper, having for my comrade and messmate Major R——, quartermaster on General Ramseur's staff.

Several messes of this description were thus formed, many of them having from six to eight members. By feeing the "cook-master," we managed to get several extras occasionally, so that, altogether, we contrived to get along better than we should had we been without money or without friends.

For a consideration, some one of the lower class of men confined here enacts the duties of cook, and sets and clears off the dishes (tinware) from the table (in our case a cheese-box on legs), and announces the meals when ready for us. We might have fared better, but Rumor whispers that the sutler and presiding officials at the fort are leagued together, and that the order prohibiting luxuries being forwarded here by friends was made as much for the benefit of themselves as for the irritation that it occasioned us, as it is utterly impossible to procure any thing unless through the shark of a sutler, who charges exorbitantly for his politeness.

Chapter XXVI

I have already spoken of poor Miss McDonough. She was taken prisoner last summer, upon the charge of having murdered a Federal officer. At the time of this alleged murder, Miss McDonough was nowhere in the vicinity, and it was only in hopes that her brother would be advised of her arrest, and surrender himself in her stead, that this shameful seizure was made.

James McDonough was a Lieutenant in Mosby's command, somewhere in the Valley of the Shenandoah, and Captain B. was shot by him (not murdered) when, during a skirmish, he refused to surrender himself prisoner. It was for this justifiable act of war she was made to suffer. Miss McDonough was compelled to remain in a room * perfectly stifling with noisome smells. Add to this the fact, that she was continually fretting for fear that her brother would deliver himself up for her. Can it then be wondered at that she should have died there, far away from her friends and those she loved?

* The same in which Belle Boyd was held so long.

During my sojourn in the Carroll Prison, I one evening called upon Mrs. ——, a lady prisoner from Galveston, Texas, who tended Miss McDonough with motherly care during her illness. Poor Mollie was then in a state of semi-insensibility, and was barely conscious of what was going on about her, when W——, the superintendent of the prison, burst into the room, shouting out at the top of his voice, "Hooray! Jem McDonough's caught, and will swing, by ——! before the week is out."

Miss McDonough slowly raised herself in the bed until nearly upright, stared wildly about her for an instant, and, uttering a piercing shriek, fell insensible upon the floor.

I sprang forward, but Mrs. —— was beside her before me; and I, turning full upon the author of this outrage, remarked excitedly, "By ——! Colonel W——, if I ever catch you in Virginia when I get a command, you shall swing for this, sir!"

Another instance of Yankee brutality and vindictiveness was related to me by the young gentleman himself, Mr. R. Coyner, a private in the old 7th Virginia regiment of cavalry. At the time of his capture he was on furlough at Moorfields, Virginia. On the 12th of October, 1863, he was taken prisoner by a force of Federal infantry, under Captain Jarbon, and conveyed to Petersburg, Western Virginia, when he was handed over to Colonel Mulligan, who not only paroled him, but treated him with kindness and attention. Here he remained until the 24th of October, when he was sent, under a strong guard, to New Creek Station, on the Baltimore and Ohio Railroad, where he arrived late at night on the 25th. Here his sufferings began. He was thrown into a large, damp cellar, where were huddled together about seventy Yankee deserters, murderers, and bounty-jumpers, where he was kept until the 26th, subsisting upon hard biscuits and cold water, which were served to them twice during the day. On the 26th he was taken from thence and carried to Baltimore. Upon his arrival he was placed in Campbell's slave-pen, then under the charge of the infamous Colonel Fish, who was afterwards sentenced to the Albany Penitentiary for various crimes. Early on the morning of the 27th, Mr. Coyner was again ordered out of his place of confinement, and conducted, still under guard, to Fort McHenry, which he reached about eleven A.M., of the same day, and was immediately placed in what is known as the 'Solitary Cell."

Here the company was as select as that at New Creek Station, comprising as it did murderers and thieves, and other wretches of the deepest dye. In this solitary cell, where he was doomed to pass a weary interval of time, no windows admitted the light of day, no lamp was permitted at night. The apartment, or rather den, was cold and noisome; its walls thick with mildew, the floor covered with filth of every kind, and literally swarming with insects; none of the prisoners held here being ever allowed to leave the place for any purpose whatever.

Here young Coyner, upon entering, found two other Confederate soldiers with ball and chain attached to their legs; the cause assigned for this treatment by the Yankee authorities being simply that they were *Confederates*. Young Coyner himself had not remained here more than an hour when the sergeant entered, and with the assistance of his men placed a 42-pound ball and chain upon his left ankle, adding that if he attempted to take it off, he would shoot him. He remained here, and in this condition, for three months and a half, and his sufferings, as he related them to me, were certainly horrible in the extreme.

The first night that he passed in this "hell upon earth," as he termed it, could never be obliterated from his memory. A mock court-martial was held, before which he was arraigned upon the charge of being a rebel and guerrilla; the remainder of those in the den looking on, laughing spectators of the scene.

Of course, the result of this court-martial may be inferred : he was found guilty, and the court pronounced the following sentence upon him, viz., "To be tossed in a blanket *until life-less.*" This was immediately carried into effect, the Federal guards looking on, amused spectators of the scene, taking no heed of his piteous appeals to them for mercy or protection, but on the contrary inciting his persecutors by words and gestures to carry the sentence into effect.

Handed over to them, he was tossed thirteen times, each time falling heavily upon his head or sides; when, finally, more dead than alive, he was permitted to crawl off amidst the jeers and laughter of his tormentors, who were highly elated at the manner in which they had eventually succeeded in eliciting groans from their unfortunate martyr.

Thoroughly sick, and feeling like one more dead than alive, poor Coyner, bruised and sore, endeavored to court sleep, and to thus, in a measure, drive off the fearful thoughts that were at times nearly driving him mad. He eventually fell into an uneasy slumber, and may have slept for an hour, when he was awakened by fire being applied to his feet by the "judge advocate" of this mock court, who gloried in the name of Kelly, and who exultantly boasted of having murdered his captain for greenbacks.

This fresh torture of young Coyner was considered the very acme of pleasure and amusement by his tormentors, some of whom held him, whilst others applied the burning paper to his feet, the fire being supplied to them for this purpose by the sentries. He showed me the scars caused by the severe burns that he had received — scars that he will take with him to the grave.

It was in vain that he appealed for mercy. At last, wearied out, they permitted him to go free for the time being. "By these miserable brutes," said young Coyner, "I was not permitted to speak in defence of my country, nor yet assert my rights. If I remonstrated with them, I was knocked down and kicked by my brutal persecutors, oftener beaten.

"This kind of treatment I endured for a period of three months and a half, when I was ordered out of this horrible place by the Provost-Marshal, whom I found to be kind and compassionate, and who in my case was but obeying his superiors. He placed me in a very nice and comfortable room which the Confederate officers held, and removed from my ankle the ball and chain that had so long been my companions in my misery.

"Here I remained until the 12th of May, when I was removed to Fort Delaware to serve out a sentence of court-martial, viz., 'Hard labor for the war' — that had been passed upon me by my tyrannical captors."

It is worthy of remark that, out of those nine officers who composed one of the most atrocious military commissions that was ever assembled, and before whom he was arraigned, all, with the exception of one of its members, have already met a violent death. Eight were killed before the 20th of June by Southern bullets, and the remaining one lies already at the point of death, struck down by consumption's fatal shaft, which is slowly but surely working out his fate.

"Here I am for the present," he said, in concluding his narrative; "how long I am to remain I know not; but I am willing to suffer any and every thing for my country and her cause."

Previous to my incarceration in Fort Delaware, and whilst I was yet a prisoner in the Carroll, I received a letter from my mother, in which she mentioned that she was about to forward to me a trunk filled with winter clothing and some few little articles necessary for my comfort, but before it came I was sent to the fort. Here the *régime* was much stricter, and prohibited the prisoners from receiving any thing whatsoever in the shape of food, and it was only by special permit that

even clothing was allowed to be sent here, the different
expresses refusing to accept parcels unless they had pasted
upon the outside the passport of the fort. Desirous of keeping
myself warm at least, I wrote to the Assistant Adjutant-
General of the post, George W. Ahl, the following letter :—

Jan. 4th, 1865.

"Officers' Barracks,

"Fort Delaware.

"Capt. GEO. W. AHL,

"SIR :—Will you permit the undersigned to receive
two blankets, and a box that has already been forwarded to him from his mother's residence, Brooklyn,
Long Island?

"And I am, Sir,

"Respectfully,

"S. WILDE HARDINGE."

This I forwarded to him by mail, although my friends scouted
the idea of my ever receiving an answer to it; and their conjec-
tures were correct, for Captain Ahl did not deign to notice it.
Whether it was owing to the weight of his official duties, or
to his supreme contempt for rebels, I was never able to
ascertain.

Finally, however, one day, as I sat thinking upon my dreary
imprisonment, of you my wife, and home associations, affected
decidedly with the "blues," Mr. J., whose misfortune it was
to have been a Democrat and the editor of a Baltimore
journal, said, "Well Mr. H., have you received a reply to
the letter you wrote the other day?"

"No, sir," I responded, gloomily.

"Well, try the General : he ranks several grades above an
adjutant, and is, therefore, not so important as the lesser bird."

"By Jove !" I replied, "the idea is a good one;" and forthwith I wrote.

Certes, the General was far more polite to his prisoners than his adjutant; for the next day I received by mail the following order : —

———, Paste on the outside of the Box.

—Any thing not mentioned in this Permit will be Confiscated.

Head-quarters,
Fort Delaware,
Jan. 10th, 1865.

Mr.———,
Supt. Old Carroll Prison,
Has permission to send :

(1) One box, now in his possession, provided it contains clothing,

To Sam W. Hardinge,
Political Prisoner,
A Prisoner of War at this Fort.
By command of
Brig.-General A. Schoepf,
G. W. Ahl,
Capt. & A. A. A. Genl.,
P. S. Hemings.

Of course, this was all that was desired; and in a few days I had the extreme pleasure of overhauling the contents of this much-coveted box. And, oh ! you of the outside world, who have never in winter slept without blankets, nor indulged in that very dubious luxury, "the softest plank," for a bed in some modern Bastile — you, I say, can never conceive the joy that I felt swelling up within me as "I laid me down to sleep" that night, wrapping myself up in this warm embrace. You, doubtless, would not envy me the luxury; and yet there were plenty of poor fellows here, without money and without friends, sleeping calmly and peacefully around me, as I have slept, without blankets to cover them, only their martial cloaks — and they are very ragged — for a covering.

Chapter XXVII

Wanted at the Fort.—The Order for Release.—Farewells.—
Free at last.—A cool Reception.—An undignified Costume.
—No Conveyance.—The Walk to Wilmington.—Home
once more.—Conclusion of Mr. Hardinge's Journal.

On the 3rd of February, whilst seated with Major R. and
Adjutant C——, talking of our anticipated exchange, the
sergeant of the barracks came into the division and inquired
for me. I immediately descended from my perch, and presented myself before him, inquiring as I did so the purport
of his visit.

"You're wanted at the Fort—General P—— wants you.
Follow me," was the reply.

Half wondering what it was, and drawing closer about
me my apology for a blanket, for it was a very cold afternoon,
I followed my conductor until I reached the fort, when I was
immediately ushered into the august presence of the commandant, who stared hard at me, without, however, saying
any thing. One of his aides, evidently a secretary, handed me,
after a few moments had elapsed, the following document,
which was to be my safe-conduct by sea and land : —

"Special Orders
  "No. 62.   "Head-quarters,
                           "Fort Delaware, Del.,
                               Feb. 3d, 1865.

"S. Wilde Hardinge (Political Prisoner) is hereby released from confinement at this Post, in compliance with the following telegram from the War Department, dated Feb. 3d, 1865 :—

  " 'Brig.-Genl. A. Schoepf,
    " 'Fort Delaware,

  " 'The Secretary of War directs the release of S. Wilde Hardinge, a Prisoner at Fort Delaware. Acknowledge receipt, and inform me when Mr. Hardinge leaves the island.

    (Sgd.)   " 'James A. Hardee,
                                " 'Col. and Insp.-Genl.'
    (Seal)   " A. Schoepf,
                                  "Brig.-Genl. Comg."

The General then remarked, "Mr. H——, you have now our permission to leave the island. Will you go to-night or to-morrow morning? Do you go to Baltimore or New York City? I presume you will leave for Europe by the *first steamer?*"

To this I made answer, saying. "I will go now. My destination is New York; and I thank God I am free! Rest assured that I shall not trouble the Government by remaining longer than I can help. Good-afternoon, sir;" and, turning, I left the room and walked rapidly back, still accompanied by the sergeant, to the barracks, that soldier remarking, "By ——! you're an awfully lucky chap."

I was not long, I can assure you, in packing up what few things I had; and then came the final adieux and partings. I confess that I felt badly as I took Major R—— by the hand,

and bade him good-by; for he had ever been a good friend and counsellor of mine. I am not ashamed to confess that my eyes were filled with tears, as one after another of my friends gathered around, shaking hands with me, wishing me a "God speed you, Hardinge!" "God bless you, my boy!" "Hope to meet you in Dixie soon," "Write to me," etc. — words that I shall never forget, for they came from the lips of some of the bravest spirits in the Southern Confederacy. It was very fortunate that I had taken the precaution to hide these notes carefully about my person; for, upon re-entering the guard-room previous to leaving the island, my bundle was first thoroughly inspected, then my pockets, the lining of my felt hat, and my boots. But here the soldier employed for that purpose luckily stopped. I was then permitted to step on board of a small steam-tug which lay at the wharf. This in a few moments cast off from her moorings, and we slowly glided away from the Château d'If of America, daintily picking our way through the miniature bergs that impeded our progress to the mainland, which, although only about seven miles distant, we were nearly two hours in reaching.

It was with feelings of unmistakable pleasure that I felt my feet pressing once more *terra firma,* and experienced the gratifying sensation awakening itself within me that I was once more my own master. So, drawing my tattered blanket about me, I stepped into the hotel that stood near the landing, and inquired the distance to Wilmington.

The proprietor of this country place eyed me suspiciously; the dog who had been basking at the fire rose and growled at me; and the frequenters of the place, who were seated round the stove smoking or drinking, by their looks inferred as plainly as tongue could speak, "He is an escaped prisoner." And no wonder, when I describe to you my presentation dress upon the occasion.

A felt hat, remarkable only for its being crownless, adorned my head; a ragged blanket sufficed — only in a measure, however — to keep the cold from my coatless body; a pair of "inexpressibles," horribly dilapidated, encased my lower extremities; a boot on one foot, and the other wrapped up in old rags. Is it a wonder, then, that I was an object of doubtful character?

Seating myself near the fire, I called for a glass of wine, which was handed to me by the bar-tender, who muttered something about a desire that he had of seeing "the color of my money."

To this I replied by drawing out my pocket-book, and offering him a fifty-dollar greenback, desiring him to give me small moneys for it. In an instant the conduct of those present underwent a complete change; the bar-tender was all smirks and bows, and, with an urbanity that was all the more strikingly apparent from his former behavior, desired to know if I wished to have an apartment.

"No, I wish to go to Wilmington. How far is it from here?"

"Sixteen miles," was the reply.

"Is there any conveyance that will take me there to-night?"

There was none.

"Hem! not if I will pay you well for it?"

"I wouldn't let a dog of mine go out this night," was the answer.

"Then I will walk," I said.

"Walk!" was chorused simultaneously, with astonishment depicted on their countenances.

"Yes, walk!" I reiterated, desperately.

"Well, if you get to Wilmington safely, you will do more than I expect you will, in that garb especially;" and the speaker looked at my costume with a sneer.

"Nevertheless, I am going," I said; and, suiting the action to the word, I rose, and, attended to the door of the hotel by the group of astonished villagers, I commenced the journey.

It had been snowing and raining alternately throughout the day, and the roads in this part of the country, never at any time when I saw them remarkable for their goodness, were ankle-deep with mud. I shall never have the recollection of that night obliterated from my memory. Several times I was on the point of lying down on the roadside; but the love of life and the thought that—God willing—I should soon be at home, were strong within me, and I staggered on through the freezing rain and slushy snow.

Twice on the way I inquired at the door of some farm-houses the direction that I was to take, and once the "gude wife" of the quiet homestead where I gained admittance prepared for me with her own white hands a cup of coffee, and pressed me to stay all night at her hospitable place—an invitation in which she was seconded by the rest of the family. Herself and husband were both English, and I shall not forget their kindness to me; and when I at last rose to depart, the husband, wife, and children bade me a kind adieu, the husband accompanying me down the road some distance.

At last, just as the clock was striking ten, I staggered into the dépôt at Wilmington, just in time to catch the train for New York. I had accomplished the distance in four hours, but it was fully a week before I was able to walk or sit even with any degree of comfort.

Early in the morning I arrived in New York, and drove immediately to my brother's place of business. He was perfectly amazed at seeing me, and laughed immoderately at the deplorable figure I cut.

Eventually, having procured a suit of clothes, and enjoyed the luxury of a bath and the inexpressible feeling of delight that one has in finding his body once more in contact with clean linen, I bade adieu to the United States, and started directly for the shores of hospitable and peaceful England.

Chapter XXVIII

Conclusion of Mrs. Hardinge's Narrative.

My memoirs were written, and a portion of them already in the hands of the publishers, when the startling news came which has thrilled all Europe and filled her inhabitants with horror — the assassination of Abraham Lincoln, President of the United States.

It was always the boast of Americans, were they Northern or Southern in their sentiments, that theirs was the only history that could show to the world a clear, untarnished record of successful Republican rule. But their annals can be no longer so regarded; for, in the sudden demise of Mr. Lincoln by the bullet of an insensate fanatic, that peculiar institution of Europe, the school of the assassin, has transferred itself to the shores of America; and that country can no longer uphold her former boast, that crime such as this had never been perpetrated under the Government commenced by George Washington.

Personally I had no animosity against the honorable gentleman who has wielded the sceptre of Northern power for four long years. His has been a trying position. No man probably in the pages of History took his seat under more inauspicious circumstances. The Press of the world warred furious warfare upon him. He was jeered and scoffed at; he was pronounced uncouth, vulgar, low, servile, and abject; disappointed politicians and opposition cliques vied with each other in calling him upon every occasion the "rail-splitter;" and wiseacres of soothsaying proclivities speedily predicted that, with such a man as Abraham Lincoln at the head of the Government, the Union would most assuredly be split, with as much precision and as quickly as Mr. Lincoln had been known to split rails when a backwoodsman in the Western wilds.

Although a member of Congress previous to his elevation to the presidential chair of all the United States not in rebellion, and having for his political opponent in his presidential campaign that great statesman, the late Mr. Douglas, Mr. Lincoln was not a forensic success.

His speeches and arguments, teeming with wit and dry humor, were better calculated to attract the backwoodsman, by whom he was looked upon as a leading man, than the more mature and riper intellects with which he was in after-days brought into contact. I can appreciate and admire fully the character of such men who exemplify the sentence, "out of nothing came something." As such I looked upon Lincoln, when, month after month, and then year after year, of his presidential term rolled by, and I saw how well he governed the Northern Republic, and how firmly he held the reins of the Federal cause, which from time to time toppled upon the verge of a yawning chasm.

Now all is changed. Can any one believe that Mr. Johnson is the man who is to restore the Republic to what it was, save the nation from bankruptcy, and bring peace and goodwill to America? It might not have been impossible with Mr. Lincoln; for that gentleman held out the olive-branch, concealing no deadly weapon beneath it, to General Lee and his little band of heroes. With Mr. Johnson at the head of the Government of the North, who can foresee any thing save anarchy and dissolution? He will fiddle whilst Rome is burning.

Politically I did not like Mr. Lincoln, for in him I saw the destroyer. As long as it served his purpose, Mr. Lincoln boldly advocated the right of *Secession*. I trust that the accusation will not startle my readers; but such was the case; and I will cite one instance—when, as a representative, he openly avowed "that any nation or people, in any portion of the world, had a right to rise up and rebel against the mother government if they wanted to."

When the North, in 1860–61, declared that she would usurp all rights, and have, whether or no the South wished it, and in direct violation of the Constitution, a strictly Northern President, Abraham Lincoln, still true to his former assertion of the right of Secession, accepted the nomination of the Chicago platform, and by this act inserted the wedge in that log called the *Union*. The log was ultimately split, through force of circumstances.

There are those who maintain that in this world women have no right to interfere in the affairs of state, in politics, in plots, and counter-plots. Others there are who, more chivalrous, are willing to admit that women have as much right to act, think, and speak, as men. I do not set myself up as an advocate of the woman's-rights doctrine, but would rather appear in the character of a quiet lady expressing her sentiments, not so much to the public as to her immediate friends. Therefore, I trust that the former class of gentlemen will here forgive what to them may appear presumption; especially as, in the preceding chapters of my book, I have endeavored to avoid politics as much as possible.

But to return to my subject. The North boldly declared that she did not care much if the South did secede; and the South, never doubting the intentions of the North, took her at her word—seceded; and the consequence has been a civil war, whose magnitude has never been surpassed, and whose slain can be counted, not by tens, but by hundreds of thousands. Mr. Lincoln, as the representative of his nation, took the oath of office to uphold the Union "as it was." Then, after a while, "as it was" became "as it is."

"The Constitution as it is," said the notorious "Senator Jim Lane," of Kansas, "is played out; and I am ready to see any man shot down who favors the Union as it was talked of by Mr. Lincoln." And on the evening of the very next day after Mr. Lincoln had favored a conciliatory treatment towards the South, he was shot down!

Englishmen! I appeal to your impartial judgment. I look to you for the discountenancing of the foul charge which Mr. Stanton has thrown upon the shoulders of the Southern leaders, that he might thereby induce the European powers to withdraw their recognition of Southern belligerency. It is not the chivalrous sons of the South who have done this deed. The papers, indeed, make the assassin use the words, *"Sic semper tyrannis!"* But if this be true, then, as a Virginian woman, I say, never was the State motto of Virginia more unworthily abused.

And, in truth, our people have even more to regret in the death of President Lincoln than have the people of the North. When our noble old chieftain, General Lee, heard of the assassination, he covered his face, and refused to listen to the details of the murder; whilst, in the Libby Prison, where were confined a large number of Southern soldiers, the inmates on one of the floors held a meeting, and denounced the murder, passing resolutions that they were soldiers, and could not therefore applaud assassins.

Yet Mr. Secretary Stanton, with a hatred and malignity that is unsurpassed, charges the commission of this deed upon the South. There are those in the Northern States who will yet move heaven and earth to prove that it was the South; and to prove it, money will be spent, bribes given, and, where money and bribes fail, threats will be used. But I appeal to Europe to judge discriminately between North and South. Do not pronounce too hastily your judgment, nor cast upon a brave and chivalrous people the stigma of assassination.

Many have advised me to suppress this volume, urging that its publication will probably cause my life-long banishment. But I cannot—I will not recede. I firmly believe that in this fiery ordeal, in this suffering, misery, and woe, the South is but undergoing a purification by fire and steel that will, in good time, and by His decree, work out its own aim.

THE END

Notes

Page 101, line 1 ff . See the letter to the editor, signed H.F., in the London (Eng.) *Morning Herald* for Friday, Feb. 3, 1865 (6/3). BB's text accurately transcribes the newspaper account save for the following portion omitted from the sentence ending, "her weekly bills," on page 17, line 10 : ". . . the landlord of 'the fashionable hotel,' where she has spent hundreds of pounds in the last six months, refused to allow her to remove her trunk to a boarding house until she had paid the paltry balance of £6."

Page 102, line 11 : The marriage in fact took place over five months earlier. See page 283, last para., above.

Page 102, line 16 : Two identical dispatches, captioned "Belle Boyd in Distress" and copied from the Liverpool *Courier* of Feb. 4, appeared in the New York *Herald*, Feb. 19, 1865 (8/1), and in the New York *Daily News*, Feb. 20 (2/1). Beginning, "Confederate sympathizers, and indeed all who have a love for adventure and courage," they rehearse the misfortunes of this "somewhat notable character," Miss BB. The earlier dispatch was commented upon by one M., in a letter to the editor captioned "The Distress of Belle Boyd," New York *Herald*, Feb. 27, 1865 (2/3). It follows the same tenor as the letter in the *World* (see next below).

Page 102, line 17 : See the letter to the editor by one C. M., captioned "Belle Boyd," New York *World,* Feb. 27, 1865 (5/5-6).

Page 103, lines 30-33 : In its issue for Tuesday, Feb. 7, 1865 (4/5), the London *Morning Herald* carried a letter to the editor from one C. S., referring to the paper's plea on behalf of BB in its Feb. 3 issue, agreeing with the sentiments, but asking where and to whom should financial aid be sent? "Let the omission be rectified at once." The next day an editorial filler advised that BB's address was 102 Jermyn St. In the same issue and column (Wednesday, Feb. 8, 1865) the *Morning Herald* printed this letter :

To Confederate Sympathisers. To the Editor. Sir,—As the medical attendant in England upon Mrs. Hardinge (Belle Boyd), I can fully corroborate the statement of "H. F." in your yesterday's impression. I may add, moreover, that Mr. Hardinge's captivity is the result of a chivalrous endeavour to rescue his wife's sister from the dread of suffering from the brutal licentiousness of the Federal "officers and gentlemen."—I remain your obedient servant,

Battershell'gill, M.D. Lond.
5 Cambridge-place, Regent's Park, Feb. 4

Records at the Royal College of Surgeons of England, at London, disclose that Walter Battershell Gill (1823-1900), a graduate of the University of London, M.D. 1853, and a Fellow of the Royal College of Surgeons since 1860, was primarily occupied as a private teacher of medicine and as coach to candidates for the examinations at the University of London and the Royal College of Physicians and Surgeons.

Pages 104-107 : An accurate transcription of D[ennis] A. Mahony, *The Prisoner of State* (New York, 1863), pp. 268-272.

Page 106, line 9 : Another "prisoner of state," David Sheward, editor of the Fairfield, Ia., *Constitution and Union,* according to Mahony, *The Prisoner of State,* pp. 247-248.

Pages 107-109 : An accurate transcription, albeit with stanzas five and six transposed, of one of the most celebrated of American songs. James Ryder Randall was teaching school in Louisiana when he heard of the rioting and bloodshed—first in the Civil War—which on April 19, 1861, had accompanied the passage of the 6th Mass. Regt. through his native city.

In 1939, the General Assembly of Maryland adopted Randall's poem as the State song, and in 1961, Governor J. Millard Tawes proclaimed the week of January 1-7 as "James Ryder Randall Week," honoring the 122nd anniversary of his birth. An annotated printing may be found in *300 Years: The Poets and Poetry of Maryland,* ed. Loker Raley (New York [1937]), pp. 81-83. The fifth verse inspired the title of Edmund Wilson's *Patriotic Gore: Studies in the Literature of the American Civil War* (New York, 1962).

Page 109, lines 24-25 : Probably the supper room in Evans' Hotel, at Covent Garden. G. A. Sala describes it in his *Twice Round the Clock, or the Hours of the Day and Night in London* (London [1859]), pp. 333-345, noting that the spot "is immortalised in the first chapter of 'The Newcomes,' " by Thackeray (who was one of Sala's closer acquaintances).

Pages 112-113, line 26 inclusive : An accurate transcription of *Border and Bastille* (New York [1863]), pp. 195-197, by George Alfred Lawrence, the English novelist whose *Guy Livingstone; or, Thorough* (1857) and other "muscular" romances were specially admired by military men. Reporting the war for the London *Morning Post,* pro-Confederate in his sympathies, Lawrence nevertheless could not have seen BB, since he was incarcerated in the Old Capitol from late April to June 5, 1863. In a letter of Feb., 1889, to J. Orton Kerbey—who had himself spied for the Union—BB identified the Englishman as Frank Lacy Buxton, of "Buxton Hall." See Kerbey, *On the War Path: A Journey over the Historic Grounds of the Late Civil War* (Chicago, 1890), p. 22. At the time she had identified him likewise to Rev. W. F. Broaddus (see Note to page 200, lines 25-26, below).

Page 115, lines 8-9 : Shakespeare, *The Merchant of Venice,* IV, i, 196-197.

Page 115, lines 27-28 : This Federal cavalry raid of March 1, 1864, though it failed and Dahlgren was killed, evoked widespread outrage in the Confederacy. See Meriwether Stuart, "Colonel Ulric Dahlgren and Richmond's Union Underground, April 1864," *Va. Mag. of Hist. & Biog.,* LXXII, 152-204 (Apr., 1964).

Page 117, line 15 : Oliver Goldsmith's well-known poem, *The Deserted Village* (1770), has for its theme the superiority of agriculture over trade in a nation's economy.

Page 118, fifth para. : The house at 126 E. Burke St., Martinsburg, West Va., is illustrated in the article (frequently erroneous) by R. B. Sullivan, "Cleopatra of the Secession," New York *Daily News,* Oct. 13, 1940 (pp. 60-61). Its razing was noted in the Martinsburg *Journal,* Aug. 23, 1957 (14/3), with illustration, over the heading, "One of Community's Oldest Buildings Is Now in Process of Being Torn Down."

BB's date of birth was probably May 9, 1844. However, vital statistics for Martinsburg are lacking prior to 1865. BB's father later bought a second home (also subsequently razed) at what is now 501 S. Queen St., which became the family residence throughout the war years.

Page 119, lines 29-30 : W. M. Thackeray's historical romance, *The Virginians* (1857-1859), is laid partly in America and allots a minor rôle to Col. George Washington.

Page 120, lines 1-2 : The four-storey octagonal building of this girls' school still stands on the grounds of Mount Saint Agnes College (a Roman Catholic institution for women unconnected with the earlier academy), in the northwest suburbs of Baltimore. The cornerstone for BB's school—presumed to have been a foundation of the German Reformed Church—was laid May 5, 1855, and the building completed a year later. It stood on twenty-one acres of land and represented an investment of thirty thousand dollars. Unsuccessful, the property was sold at auction on December 15, 1860. See B. Latrobe Weston, "The Story of Mount Washington, Maryland," *Maryland Historical Magazine,* XLIII, 36 (March, 1948).

Page 124, line 24 : Benjamin Reed Boyd (1817-Dec. 6, 1863) is buried in Green Hill Cemetery, Martinsburg. A small photograph of him—poorly reproduced from an unknown original, and owned by Miss Amelia C. McKown of Bunker Hill, West Va.—shows him seated, clad in formal black, with a white shirt front. He had dark hair, mustache, and beard.

The Boyd family plot, on the rear slope of the central rise at Green Hill, holds the following members of BB's family (dates, where provided, are those of the interment permit) : BB's grandmother, Ruth Glenn, aged 62 yrs., 1 mo., Feb. 26, 1866; BB's father, B. R. Boyd, aged 47; BB's mother, Mrs. M. Boyd, May 4, 1880; and five siblings—Benjamin Reed Boyd, aged 1 yr., 1 mo., Apr. 14, 1846; Anna Reed Boyd, aged 3 yrs., 1 mo., Dec. 13, 1849; Fannie Glenn Boyd, aged 1 yr., 2 mos., Dec. 30, 1849; Annie Stewart Boyd, aged 7 mos., Sept. 15, 1854; Nina Boyd, aged 2 yrs. 2 mos., Sept. 20, 1865. Green Hill Cemetery records, under supervision of H. A. Hammann & Sons, Martinsburg, West Va.

Page 125, para. two : Speaking of the number of prominent Virginians who joined this command, James I. Robertson, Jr., says, "So also did the father of the Confederacy's best-known female spy, Belle Boyd." See his *The Stonewall Brigade* (Baton

Rouge [La., 1963]), p. 19. B. R. Boyd was assigned to the Rockbridge Artillery therein.

Page 127, lines 1-2 : Francis Bacon, *Essays: Of Love* (1597),

Page 128, line 27 : BB's bodyservant and favorite slave was Eliza Corsey, later Mrs. Sam Hopewell. Upon her burial in Mount Hope Cemetery, Martinsburg, the headline to her obit in the Martinsburg *Evening Journal,* Dec. 26, 1916 (6/3), reminded readers that she "Was Property of Belle Boyd." The text specified that BB, "the famous Confederate spy, was her last mistress." Descendants "believe that she was at least 101 years old, and possibly older." In Death Register #4, Berkeley County Court, Martinsburg, her age is given as eighty-eight.

Page 134, lines 2-3 : A reflection of this incident—which may be said to signalize BB's advance into the limelight—is found in the entry for Wed., July 24, 1861, in the diary of fifty-eight-year-old Mrs. Lettitia Blakemore, of "Riverside," two miles north of Front Royal : "Miss Boyd came on the cars from Strausburg [*sic*], took breakfast, She was the Lady who shot at a Yankee, and was imprisoned in her fathers house, in Martinsburg." Manuscript in possession of Mrs. Harrison Richards, Riverton, Va.

Page 136, line 12 : BB presumably has reference to Sir James "the Black" Douglas (*c.* 1286-1330), warlike Scots chieftain in the days of Robert Bruce. Several of BB's paternal ancestors claimed Scots descent.

Page 137 n. : At the first battle of Bull Run—First Manassas, to the Confederates—July 21, 1861, the first major engagement of the war, the Southern forces under Gens. Beauregard and Johnston routed the Union army under Gen. Irvin McDowell. Elements of the brigade of Gen. Barnard E. Bee, of South Carolina, who was killed during the battle, broke initially, and it was he who uttered the well-known words. For a discussion see Robertson, *The Stonewall Brigade,* pp. 38-39 and n., and Lenoir Chambers, *Stonewall Jackson* (2 v., New York, 1959), II, 471-472.

Page 138, line 2 : These were BB's maternal aunt, Frances Elizabeth (Glenn) Stewart, and her husband, James Erskine Stewart, lawyer, State legislator, and sometime editor of the Martinsburg *Gazette.* They had taken over and were operating the Strickler House hotel, at the corner of High and E. Main Streets, Front Royal. Now demolished, the site of the hostelry is occupied by a men's clothing store.

Page 138, lines 11-12 : The Italian landscapist, Salvator Rosa (1615-1673), and the Scots poet, Thomas Campbell (1777-1844), were much admired in ante-bellum America. The latter's narrative poem, *Gertrude of Wyoming* (1809), features an Indian raid on the Pennsylvania settlement of Wyoming in 1778.

Page 139, lines 14-15 : On June 23, 1862, at Washington, a Front Royal resident sympathetic to the Union, William E. Seimers, informed Allan Pinkerton, Gen. McClellan's chief detective, that he "has repeatedly heard rebel soldiers say that they had seen Belle Boyd in the rebel camps at Manassas at different times last fall and winter, riding with rebel officers. * * * That when informant left Front Royal on the 16th inst. Belle Boyd was still there; that informant considers her more efficient in carrying news to the rebels of our operations than *any three men* in the valley : that she is generally *regarded as a spy by the secessionists in Front Royal,* and highly thought of by them for her capabilities as such." See Maj. E. J. Allen [cover name for Pinkerton] to Secy. Stanton, Washington, D.C., June 25, 1862, in the Turner-Baker Papers, #3751, Record Group 94, Adjutant General's Office, The National Archives.

Page 139, lines 21-22 : Louis A. Sigaud, *Belle Boyd* . . . (Richmond, Va. [1944]), p. 25, says BB's favorite mount was named "Fleeter," so well trained he would kneel at command.

Page 141, line 25 : Lt. Col. Turner Ashby, of Fauquier Co., Va.—after "Jeb" Stuart probably the most peerless of the cavalry paladins in the Virginia alcove of the Confederate pantheon. He had occupied Martinsburg in early Dec., 1861. On Dec. 14, he was admitted there to Equality Lodge #136, A.F. & A.M., of which BB's father, Benjamin, was a Brother.

Page 141, line 27 (and p. 142, line 9) : "Henry" is presumably a misprint for Turner Ashby (one of whose cousins, Col. Henry Ashby, C.S.A., BB may have met at Knoxville, Tenn.). At this juncture his 7th Va. Regt. of cavalry came under Gen. Jackson's division.

Page 142, line 8 : James Crichton (1560–c. 1585), Scots poet and swordsman, to whom the epithet was applied by John Johnston in his *Heroes Scoti* (1603). James M. Barrie's fantasy, *The Admirable Crichton* (1902), is based on the adventurer's career.

Page 142, line 23 (and p. 143, lines 10-11) : A younger brother to the renowned cavalryman, Capt. Richard Ashby, C.S.A. (1831-1861), was buried in Indian Mound Cemetery near Romney, West Va. BB's account of his death, July 3, is garbled. Reinterred, his body and that of his brother Turner lie today in the same grave in Stonewall Jackson Cemetery, Winchester, Va.

Page 143, lines 19-20 : Doubtless an allusion to James Gardiner (1688-1745), colonel of dragoons, who underwent a Pauline conversion from high living to piety. See the *Dictionary of National Biography* (London), VII, 855-856.

Page 143, lines 24-25 : Last lines, "The Song of the Camp," in *The Poet's Journal* (Boston, 1863), by the Pennsylvania travel writer and diplomat, Bayard Taylor. The poem was republished separately in an elegant edition at London, 1895.

Page 143, lines 29 ff. : This rather celebrated episode featuring Bettie Duvall, of Washington, D.C., occurred about June 28, 1861, at Gen. Bonham's headquarters at Fairfax Court House, Va. His letter recounting the affair to Gen. Beauregard is given in Hamilton Basso, *Beauregard: The Great Creole* (New York and London, 1933), pp. 124-126.

"At this time volunteer girl spies from northern Virginia were bursting into Beauregard's lines at every turn, bearing news that the Yankees were coming. They were received with consideration and applause, although their information was generally vague and available in Washington newspapers." T. Harry Williams, *P. G. T. Beauregard: Napoleon in Gray* (Baton Rouge, La. [1954]), pp. 75-76.

Page 145, lines 16-17 : Kernstown (*sic*), Frederick County, four miles south of Winchester, where on March 23, 1862, Union forces under Gen. Nathan Kimball defeated the Confederates under Gen. Jackson.

Page 146, lines 6-8 : BB's cousin, Alice Stewart. "Grand-mamma" was BB's maternal grandmother, Ruth Burns Glenn (*sic*), second wife of Capt. James Glenn (*c.* 1764-1832), revolutionary veteran, of "Glenn Burnie," Jefferson Co., (West) Va.

Page 146, lines 18-19 : On June 18, 1862, at Washington, a Pinkerton informant, Eugene Blockley of Front Royal, divulged than on June 8 he had encountered BB at the (Union) Provost Marshal's office there, and that she had accused him of having informed the Federals of having seen her at Winchester. ". . . she then turned to the Provost Marshal (Capt. Bates) and denounced *southern* Union men." Informant doesn't know what BB was doing at the Provost Marshal's office, but affirms "that she gets around considerably, is very shrewd, *and is probably acting as a spy.* That she is an open, earnest and undisguised secessionist, and talks secession on all practicable occasions." E. J. Allen [Pinkerton] to Stanton, Washington, D.C., June 25, 1862, in the Turner-Baker Papers, #3751, Record Group 94, The National Archives.

Page 149, line 23 : What has since been dubbed "the Belle Boyd cottage," in the Strickler House yard at Front Royal, is illustrated in Laura V. Hale's pamphlet, *Belle Boyd* . . . ([Front Royal, Va., 1954]). The residence still stands immediately to rear of, and partly attached to, the commercial establishment erected on the site of the hotel.

Page 150, third para. : This officer is identified by Louis A. Sigaud, *Belle Boyd* . . ., pp. 60-61, as Capt. (later Brig. Gen.) Daniel J. Keily, an aide to Gen. Shields. Wounded at the battle of Port Republic, Va., June 9, 1862, he was carried to "Oakley," the Front Royal home of young Thomas A. Ashby, and visited there by BB, presumably for unsuspected information-gathering. "Oakley" is illustrated in Laura V. Hale, *Belle Boyd* . . . (1954).

Page 151, line 4 : An example of the type of cipher BB probably employed, the "double key" or Vigenère method, is provided by Sigaud, *Belle Boyd* . . ., pp. 228-230.

Pages 151, para. two-152, line 32 : BB. says she undertook a thirty-mile round trip by horseback at night from Front Royal to the home of Mr. M. in four hours. The date being *c.* May 18, this statement is acceptable, since for the period *c.* May 17-21, 1862, Ashby was based, with elements of his command, on the outskirts of Strasburg, just a dozen miles west of Front Royal, harassing Gen. Banks' forces there. See Thomas A. Ashby, M.D., *Life of Turner Ashby* (New York, 1914), pp. 164-165, and Douglas S. Freeman, *Lee's Lieutenants: A Study in Command* (3 v., New York, 1942-1944), I, 371-372.

Page 152, lines 12-13 : At this date, *c.* May 18, 1862, the already legendary Ashby, who would be promoted to Brig. Gen. on May 27, had three weeks to live. He was slain in combat about two miles south of Harrisonburg, Va., on June 6.

Page 153, para. one : A wartime sketch of the Union camp at Front Royal, and a likeness of Col. Kenly, are in *Battles and Leaders of the Civil War . . .*, intro. Roy F. Nichols (4 v., New York and London [1956]), II, 287-288. For representative news coverage of the engagement see *Mirror of War: The Washington "Star" Reports the Civil War,* eds. John W. Stepp and I. William Hill (Englewood Cliffs, N. J. [1961]), pp. 122-124.

Page 156, lines 22-23 : Published at Baltimore, the *Maryland News Sheet* ran from Sept. 19, 1861, through Aug. 14, 1862. A nearly complete file is in the Maryland Room, Enoch Pratt Free Library, Baltimore.

Page 161, second para. : Views of Front Royal and the railroad cut, and a likeness of Gen. Shields, are in *Harper's Picture History of the Great Rebellion. . .,* eds. Alfred H. Guernsey and Henry M. Alden (2 v., New York, 1866), I, 345-346. For a more panoramic view, featuring a sketch by Edwin Forbes of the Federal troops entering the town, see *The Soldier in Our Civil War: A Pictorial History of the Conflict . . .,* eds. Paul F. Mottelay and T. Campbell-Copeland (2 v., New York, 1890), I, 324. For admirable present-day photographs of the area, with an excerpt from Gen. Taylor's memoirs mentioning BB (cf. next below), see John W. Wayland, *Stonewall Jackson's Way . . .* (Staunton, Va., 1940), pp. 124-125. For a clear map of the region see Lenoir Chambers, *Stonewall Jackson, op. cit.,* I, 524, and for an able analysis of Confederate strategy in the 1862 campaign, see Millard K. Bushong, "Jackson in the Shenandoah," *West Virginia History,* XXVII, 85-96 (Jan., 1966), with mention of BB on p. 92.

Pages 161-162 : This episode—the most dramatic in BB's text, and the single feat for which she is best remembered—has received impressive confirmation from three of the most closely involved Confederate officers. See Henry Kyd Douglas, *I Rode with Stonewall* (Chapel Hill, N.C. [1940]), pp. 51-52; Richard Taylor, *Destruction and Reconstruction...*, ed. Richard B. Harwell (New York and elsewhere, 1955), pp. 53-54; and Gen. Ewell's brigade records, in Benson J. Lossing, *The Pictorial Field Book of the Civil War...* (3v., Hartford, Conn. [1866-1868]), II, 391 n. Lossing states :

When the writer was at Nashville, early in May, 1866, he was permitted by General Ewell, then residing there, to peruse and make extracts from the manuscript records of his brigade, kept by his young adjutant. In it was the statement, that when Ewell's force was near Front Royal, a young woman was seen running toward them. She had 'made a circuit to avoid the Yankees,' and she sent word to General Jackson, by officers who went to meet her, 'to push on—only one regiment in the town, and that might be completely surprised; if we pressed on we might get the whole.' This 'young lady' was afterward the notorious rebel spy, Belle Boyd, 'who was to my eye,' recorded the adjutant, 'pleasant and lady-like in appearance, and certainly had neither "freckled face, red hair and large mouth," as the *New York Herald* said she had. She seemed embarrassed by the novelty of her position, and very anxious that we should push on.'

Page 163, lines 9-10 : Probably not hay but wheat should ripple here. Gen. Harry T. Hays (*sic*) did not assume command of Gen. Taylor's Louisiana brigade until July 27, 1862, whereas the filibuster, C. R. Wheat, leading his "Tiger" Battalion of the brigade, was in the forefront of the advance (along with Col. Bradley T. Johnson and his Marylanders). See Charles L. Dufour, *Gentle Tiger: The Gallant Life of Roberdeau Wheat* (Baton Rouge [La., 1957]), pp. 173, which also cites BB.

Page 164, lines 12-13 : In an otherwise worthless article by Nan H. Ewing, "Noted Belle Boyd Later Became a Toledo Wife," Toledo, O., *Blade,* March 1, 1944 (Peach Sect., 1/4-6), is an anon. artist's evocation of BB's return to Front Royal through Federal picket lines. She is mounted (!) and, in addition to her flowing garment, sports a poke bonnet and parasol.

Page 164, lines 24-25 : Capt. G. F. Sheetz (*sic*) was widely mourned. For a sketch see Rev. James B. Avirett, *The Memoirs of General Turner Ashby and His Compeers* (Baltimore, Md., 1867), pp. 372-382.

Page 166, paras. four-six : BB recalled this episode with relish in an interview she granted the Toledo, O., *Daily Blade,* Feb. 22, 1886 (3/4). She added : "Long before this, early in the war, I met Theodore Davis, special artist for *Harper's,* and Paul Nicholson, of the *World,* at my own home at Martinsburg." Davis first went into the field for *Harper's Weekly* in March, 1861, according to Robert Taft, *Artists and Illustrators of the Old West, 1850–1900* (New York and London, 1953), p. 70.

Page 167, Jackson's letter : The most reprinted and commented upon single passage in BB's book, it is given by Lenoir Chambers, *Stonewall Jackson,* I, 524–525 and n., with the statement, "No original copy of this letter has been found."

Page 170, lines 15-17 : For a good likeness, see frontispiece to Fred H. Harrington, *Fighting Politician: Major General N. P. Banks* (Philadelphia, Pa., 1948). In *ibid.* pp. 70-71, occurs passing mention of the Front Royal defeat and "that cheerful maiden," BB.

Page 172, line 10 : A paraphrase from Richard B. Sheridan's comedy, *The Rivals* (1775), V, iii, 280.

Page 172, lines 15-16 : He was in fact C. W. D. Smitley, chief scout, Co. B, 2nd (West) Va. Inf. See Frank Reader, *History of* the Fifth West Virginia Cavalry, formerly the Second Virginia Infantry. . . (New Brighton, Pa., 1890), p. 257 et seq., for the whole story.

Page 172, line 16 : Harrisonburg (sic), county seat of Rockingham Co., Va., twenty-three miles northeast of Staunton.

Page 172, lines 26-27 : In her network, if it may be called such, BB employed both male and female slaves; young white girls; and at least one youth, 16-year-old Zephaniah Silver of Martinsburg, a member of Jim Sencindiver's company (on whom see Sigaud, *Belle Boyd*. . ., p. 27).

In this connection is worth recording an informant's report to Allan Pinkerton at his Washington, D.C., office as of June 23, 1862 : John M. Littlefield of Front Royal affirmed "That Betsy White and Belle Boyd, both residents of Front Royal, obtained from Gen. Jackson an order for the arrest of informant, [Eugene] Blockley and other Union men." See E. J. Allen [Pinkerton] to Secy. Stanton, Washington, D.C., June 25, 1862, Turner-Baker Papers, #3751, Record Group 94, The National Archives.

Page 173, second para. : On the contrary, Smitley not only survived the war but lived to marry and produce ten children. See Reader, *History of the Fifth West Virginia Cavalry...*, p. 250.

Page 173, lines 7-8 : A "similar fate" might have befallen BB had she been apprehended during an episode of July 26, 1862. The New York *Tribune* for July 31 (1/6) carried this dispatch from Warrenton, Va., as of Tues., July 29, 1862 :

> The celebrated Rebel "Belle Boyd" was here on Saturday, in company with a Rebel captain belonging to the Black Horse Cavalry, who was here wounded and on his parole, and has since resigned. She offered to take letters to Richmond for three dollars apiece.

Page 176, lines 9-20 : Detective A. Cridge. Extant are copies of Asst. Secy. of War C. P. Wolcott's orders (on behalf of the Secy. of War) to Cridge, dated Washington City, July 18, 1862, to arrest at Front Royal both BB and William Dana, and to the local Army commander to lend assistance; and two identical copies of Gen. Julius White's telegram to Wolcott, dated Winchester, Va., July 29, 5 P.M., querying Cridge's credentials. Turner-Baker Papers, #863, Record Group 94, Army-Navy Branch, The National Archives. The informant, Blockley (see Note to page 146, lines 18-19, above), had already labelled Dana as a line-crosser and spy, and asserted he lived on the north bank of the Shenandoah River, at its forks, between Front Royal and the village of Middletown.

Page 176, line 22: "Each government possessed a secret service, to be sure, but neither one called it *the* Secret Service or used any extension of that title; for in both cases this service had no national organization and little national character." Edwin C. Fishel, "The Mythology of Civil War Intelligence," *Civil War History*, X, 345 (Dec., 1964).

Page 177, Stanton's letter : The text is substantially the same as that of the manuscript cited in the Note to page 176, lines 9-20, above (with the significant omission of William Dana's name). From Washington, July 30, 1862, Asst. Secy. of War Wolcott instructed Gen. White at Winchester to "direct Cridge to come immediately to Washington and bring with him Belle Boyd in close custody, committing her on arrival to the Old Capitol Prison." See *War of the Rebellion. . .Official Records. . . ,* Series Two, IV, 310.

Page 178, lines 30-31. For a photograph of the War Department, at Pennsylvania Ave. and 17th St., Washington, as it appeared at the time, see Roy Meredith, *Mr. Lincoln's Camera Man: Mathew B. Brady* (New York, 1946), p. [13]. Stanton's office was on the third floor. The best biography is Benjamin P.

Thomas and Harold M. Hyman, *Stanton: The Life and Times of Lincoln's Secretary of War* (New York, 1962), which does not mention BB.

Page 180, line 24 : Edgar Allan Poe first published "The Raven" in the *Evening Mirror* at New York City, Jan. 29, 1845. It appeared in book form there in November, same year, as *The Raven and Other Poems.*

Page 181, para. two : On July 30, Lucy Buck of Martinsburg confided to her diary : "Belle Boyd was taken prisoner and sent off in a carriage with an escort of fifty [*sic*] cavalrymen today. I hope she has succeeded in making herself proficiently [sufficiently] notorious now. They say they are going to put her within our lines and keep her there." Buck, *Diary. . .1861–1865* ([Baltimore, Md.], 1940), p. 95.

Page 188, line 30 : Presumably Lafayette C. Baker, on whom see Jacob Mogelever's biography, *Death to Traitors. . .* (Garden City, N.Y., 1960). In his *History of the United States Secret Service* (Philadelphia, 1867), pp. 53–54, Baker claims he was interrogated by BB near Gen. Beauregard's headquarters at Manassas Junction in mid-July, 1861, whilst on his first secret mission into Confederate lines. (One of the book's illustrations is captioned, "Receiving Religious Tracts from Belle Boyd in the Rebel Stockade at Manassas Junction.") The date conflicts with that given by BB for her sojourn in the area (p. 139 of her text).

Page 189, last para. : The Old Capitol Prison, fronting on First St. (Southeast), Washington, had been erected in 1817 to accommodate the Congress. Its later addition, Carroll Prison, adjoined it at A St. For a good illustration see the reprint edition of [Alexander] *Gardner's Photographic Sketch Book of the Civil War,* intro E [verett] F. Bleiler (New York [1959]), plate #90. "It was in a room on the second floor of this part of the prison that the well-known Belle Boyd was confined; and the list of the names of the occupants written on the walls vied in length and respectability with the registers of our largest and best hotels," says John A. Marshall, *American Bastile* [*sic*]. *A History of the Illegal Arrests and Imprisonment of American Citizens during the Late Civil War,* Fourth Edition (Philadelphia, 1870), p. 327. Marshall here refers to BB's second incarceration, on which see Note to p. 231, below.

Page 191, lines 11-13: For a likeness of Wood, who became the first Chief of the Secret Service in the Treasury Department, see James J. Williamson, *Prison Life in the Old Capitol. . .* (West Orange, N.J., 1911), p. 33.

Page 191, lines 25-26 : This, BB's first incarceration in the Old Capitol, extended from July 31 through Aug. 29, 1862.

Page 192, line 11: John B. Floyd, a native of southwest Virginia and later Governor, had been Secretary of War under President Buchanan from March 4, 1857, until his resignation on Dec. 29, 1860. *Boyd's Washington and Georgetown Directory* for 1858, and again for 1860, lists the Secretary's residence as situated at 345 I St., north.

Page 193, lines 21-22 : A text of this oath is provided by Williamson, *Prison Life in the Old Capitol, op. cit.,* pp. 23–24 n.

Page 193, last para. : It was not until the following month that BB at last approached Stanton, via the following letter (in the Turner-Baker Papers, #863, The National Archives) :

Old Capitol Prison
Washington, DC
Aug 8th /62

Hon. E. M. Stanton,
    Mr. Secratary [*sic*].
    I am given to understand that I was arrested at your

instance, and that I am incarcerated here under your orders. The newspapers, whose falsehood and infamous abuse—(I think the *Government* should at least protect me from while a prisoner) amongst other things charge me of being a "Rebel Spy" and "Mail Carrier"—Where do they get their information? I shall esteem it a favor if you will furnish me with a copy of the charges against me, & also inform me what I a young lady of nineteen ought to expect in the future? What do you wish me to do? You surely do not wish to murder me by keeping me in prison, & then Mr. Secratary my dear Pa my natural Protector is denied access to me. Surely it cannot have been with your sanction. Do you wish to punish a young lady for opinions sake by denying her, the sympathy for a moment of her own Father I beg you will give me a reply to this Mr. Secratary & also give orders if my Pa still is in the city to be permitted to see me.

> I am Sir
> Yours Respty
> Miss Belle Boyd
> Virginia

Page 195, verse : "To Lucasta, on Going to the Wars," stanza 4. Composed in prison in 1648 by the English courtier, Richard Lovelace.

Page 197, line 16 : From William Cowper's verse ruminations, *The Task* (1785), Book I, line 749.

Page 198, line 5 : I *Kings,* xxii, 34-38.

Page 200, line 24 : Rose O'Neal Greenhow (*c.*1816-1864) was held in a room "situated in the back building of the prison, on the north-west side, the only view being that of the prison-yard," on Jan. 18, 1862, and remained there until May 31, when she was included in a prisoner exchange to Richmond. See her *My*

Imprisonment...(London, 1863), pp. 213, 202, and 314, respectively. On May 25 "a prisoner captured at Front Royal, Virginia," delighted her with news of the Confederate victory there (*ibid.*, p. 311), but no evidence has come forth to show that she and BB ever met.

Page 200, lines 25-26: Two among them were the Rev. William F. Broaddus and newspaperman G. H. C. Rowe, the reminiscences of both of whom offer admiring confirmation of this phase of BB's career. See Lucille Griffith, ed., "Fredericksburg's Political Hostages : The Old Capitol Journal of George Henry Clay Rowe," *Va. Mag. of Hist. & Biog.*, LXXII, 409–412, 419–420 (Oct., 1964).

Page 201, line 10 : Perhaps one Dr. Camp, described as a "little Frenchman" by G. H. C. Rowe, *op. cit.*, p. 419.

Page 201, last line : On Aug. 7, 1862, Asst. Secy. of War P. H. Watson queried the Military Governor of the District of Columbia, Gen. Wadsworth, concerning an article about BB in the *Evening Star* of the fourth, instant. Its appearance would seem to indicate that the Secretary's order to keep her in close custody had been violated. Ascertain if this was so ! See *War of the Rebellion*...*Official Records*.... Series Two, IV, 349.

Page 202, line 25 : Some five years after BB's demise some doubts as to the true identity of the deceased lingered in Kilbourn, Wisc. "In order to settle the question of identity Major Guy Pierce instituted a correspondence with parties in the south. He received one letter in reply from the noted confederate cavalry leader, Colonel John S. Mosby, who now holds a position in the government service at Washington. Colonel Mosby's reply was not flattering to the subject. He denied any acquaintance with such a person and pronounced her 'performance during the civil war to be as fictitious as those of Romulus and Remus.' Colonel Mosby, however, sent Major Pierce's letter to one of his old command in Virginia, whose reply is given verbatim.

'Leesburg, Va., March 24th, 1906

'Major Guy C. Pierce—Dear Sir :

'Colonel John S. Mosby, my old commander and personal friend, has sent me your letter to him of March 18th. The colonel does not take much interest in Belle Boyd, but I had a very pleasant acquaintance with her. She was very erratic, but life went very hard with her, and I hope that in the bitterness of her experience she made some atonement for the things which we all condemn in her. I would be pleased to know that her remains were respectfully interred and that her memory is honored. Whatever else may be said of her, she was always loyal to the south, I think. . . . She was a large, heavy-set woman, a decided blonde, and if alive now would be sixty-two or sixty-three years of age. Some of her relatives still live at Martinsburg, W. Va., I think. I am sure that some live in Winchester, Va., but I think it likely that they all ignore her.

'Yours respectfully,

'Jno. H. Alexander'

From anon., "Belle Boyd—A Grave between the Lines," Madison, Wisc., *Democrat,* Apr. 28, 1906 (p.7).

Page 203, lines 30-31 : Among these was one Lt. McVay, to whom it was generally understood that BB had become engaged by the time of her departure. All mourned her leaving. "With many it was more than mere regard. There was more than one McVay who aspired to the enviable position which the handsome, dashing, and gentlemanly Confederate Lieutenant succeeded in acquiring." Mahony, *The Prisoner of State, op. cit.,* pp. 278–279. Their *billets doux* were transmitted via the same marble as had seen other service (BB's text, pp. 25–26).

Page 204, para. one. Not all Union sentries behaved so grossly. At least one, Andrew Arrington of the 11th New York Cav., was presented by BB with her silver watch, in its hunting case, for his kindnesses. Arrington later donated the timepiece to the Grand Army Club of Baltimore, for exhibition in its relic room at 305 N. Greene St., there. See "Belle Boyd's Watch," Baltimore, Md., *American,* Jan. 27, 1910 (14/3-4).

Page 205, fifth para. : On Sun., Aug. 25, 1862, Wood, a self-confessed agnostic, jovially roared out this pronouncement. For a text almost identical with BB's see Mahony, *The Prisoner of State* (1863), pp. 257–258.

Page 207, lines 21-22 : Robert Ould remained Asst. Secy. of War in the Confederate Government until July, 1862, when the office of Commissioner for the Exchange of Prisoners was formally established. For a biographical sketch, including a photograph of Aiken's Landing on the James, within Federal lines, see Edward F. Heite, "Judge Robert Ould," *Virginia Cavalcade,* XIV, 10–19 (Spring, 1965).

Page 207, lines 29-30 : Under the caption, "Arrival of Exchanged Prisoners," the Richmond, Va., *Daily Dispatch* for Wed. morning, Sept. 3, 1862 (1/7), noted that some two hundred had reached the city the day before. Among the officers was the recently captured Maj. Norman R. Fitzhugh, Asst. Adj. Gen. of Stuart's cavalry Division. "Miss Belle Boyd, of Winchester, who has become celebrated for the fear in which the Yankees held her, was also among those who arrived."

Page 208, second para. : The Ballard House hotel is illustrated in Stanley Kimmel, *Mr. Davis's Richmond* (New York [1958]), p. 166. The boardinghouse was that of the wife of Confederate Senator Louis T. Wigfall, of Texas. Gen. Johnston was here recuperating from a severe wound received while commanding the Southern forces at the battle of Seven Pines (Fair Oaks) the preceding May 31–June 1, 1862. See Gilbert E. Govan and James W. Livingood, *A Different Valor: The Story of Gen. Joseph E. Johnston, C.S.A.* (Indianapolis and New York [1956]), pp. 161–162.

Page 208, line 22 : A chatelaine is an ornamental hook, clasp, or pin worn at the waist, with a chain attached for holding keys or baubles. At the Confederate Museum, Front Royal, is a similar piece of costume jewelry—a bronze Maltese Cross medal, by C. G. Braxmar Co., N.Y.C.—donated as a BB memento by her great grandson, William Boyd McCabe.

Page 208, line 31 : At the battle of Antietam, Sept. 17, 1862, near Sharpsburg, Md.—the bloodiest single day of the war— Union forces under Gen. McClellan gained a technical victory over the Confederates under Gen. Lee. For a book-length study see James V. Murfin, *The Gleam of Bayonets*...(New York, 1965).

"The Army of Northern Virginia was then marched to the vicinity of Martinsburg, where it remained in repose for several days, then retired to the vicinity of Winchester." It "rested along the lines between the Potomac and Winchester till late in October." James Longstreet, *From Manassas to Appomattox: Memoirs of the Civil War in America,* ed. James I. Robertson, Jr. (Bloomington [Ind., 1960]), pp. 265, 290, respectively.

Page 209, lines 17-19: "In the two months after Sharpsburg his headquarters changed eleven times, although within a small area in the lower Valley. His longest stay was three weeks (September 27–October 18 [1862]) near Bunker Hill, north of Winchester, chiefly in tents on the lawn of the Boyd home." Lenoir Chambers, *Stonewall Jackson,* II, 242. (This was the property of John E. Boyd, father of Gen. Elisha Boyd, of "Boydville," Martinsburg— no kin to BB's father Ben Boyd.) "From the high south bank of the Opequon, which he had occupied on September 21, Jackson moved close to Martinsburg on the 24th to escape filth and vermin before going to the Bunker Hill camp on the 27th. On October 18 he moved forward to Martinsburg to tear up the Baltimore and Ohio Railroad track. . . . He moved back on October 22 to Bunker Hill . . ." (*ibid.,* II, 249–250).

In 1962, the city of Martinsburg issued a commemorative gilt coin captioned, "Belle Boyd and the Colonnade Bridge." On the obverse is BB's left profile, showing her prominent nose. On the reverse is a representation of the bridge, which had been burned by some of Jackson's troops in an earlier foray, June 23, 1861.

Page 210, line 5 : "I have heard of many generous deeds... done by Belle Boyd. Once, when riding out to review some troops near Winchester, she met a soldier, a mere boy, trudging along painfully on his bare feet. She took off her own shoes and made him put them on; they were fine cloth gaiters laced at the side, and trimmed with patent leather. Some one remonstrated; the shoes would not last the boy long enough to pay for her sacrifice. 'Oh,' she said, 'if it rests his poor young feet only a little while, I am repaid. He is not old enough to be away from his mother.' " Margaret Bowden Nash ("Mrs. Nellie Grey"), as quoted by Myrta L. Avary, ed., *A Virginia Girl in the Civil War* . . .(New York, 1903), p. 58.

Page 210, para. two : "When she came to us," declared cousin Sue Boyd of BB's visit to Knoxville, Tenn., in late Dec., 1862, "she showed us a handsome 'Riding Habit'—new; made of the grey Confederate cloth and trimmed in black braid, with the rank of 'Capt.' on the collar." (Quoted in Sigaud, *Belle Boyd. . . , op. cit.,* pp. 106–107.) An identical accolade had been accorded Antonia Ford by Gen. Stuart : the gesture was one of gallantry to a pretty woman, according to Burke Davis, *JEB Stuart: The Last Cavalier* (New York, 1957), p. 71.

Page 210, lines 8-9 : Spencer Compton Cavendish, Marquis of Hartington (*sic*), later 8th Duke of Devonshire and from 1863 Under Secretary for War, landed at New York City on Aug. 24, 1862, on a holiday tour of the Civil War scene. He met President Lincoln, then, crossing the lines without official sanction, had an interview with Jefferson Davis. In late Dec., 1862, or early in the new year he met Jackson and Lee at their respective head-quarters just south of Fredericksburg. Here he was accompanied by Francis C. Lawley, special correspondent for the London *Times,* and by a Col. Leslie, Member of the House of Commons (probably Charles P. Leslie, colonel of the Monaghan Militia, in Ireland). See the *Dictionary of National Biography,* Twentieth Century, Supplement I (1901–1911), p. 324; Chambers, *Stonewall Jackson,* II, 337–338; and Douglas S. Freeman, *R. E. Lee: A Biography* (4v., New York, 1934–1935), II, 485. Jackson's aide, J. P. Smith, observed of Hartington : "He shared my blankets and rode my horses. He saw a fine review of our corps and visited the young ladies of the Rappahannock with great satisfaction. . . ." Southern Historical Society *Papers,* n.s. V, 41 (Sept., 1920).

Page 210, lines 13-14 : Following Lee's invasion of Maryland, the South Carolina brigade under cavalryman Wade Hampton rejoined the main Confederate forces in camp at Opequon Creek, near Martinsburg, on Sept. 22, 1862, and remained there till the latter part of October. See Manly W. Wellman, *Giant in Gray: A Biography of Wade Hampton of South Carolina* (New York and London, 1949), pp. 94 and 101. Cf. also Kyd Douglas, *I Rode with Stonewall, op. cit.,* pp. 186–187.

Page 211 : Jackson's second letter to BB. Its heading should read, "Army of Northern Virginia," and the date should have been late Nov., 1862. As Sigaud points out (*Belle Boyd. . . ,* pp. 113–114), Jackson and his Second Corps removed in late November from the Winchester area to Fredericksburg. One of the halts was at Madison Court House, only fifteen miles from Culpeper Court House, where Lee was maintaining temporary Army headquarters.

Page 212, para. three : The Knoxville, Tenn., *Daily Register* for Sat., Feb. 14, 1863 (1/1), had this to say of BB's appearance (from the file in the Cincinnati Historical Society, Eden Park, O.) :

BELLE BOYD

This fair and fearless Virginia heroine, whose daring defense of her father's house when Charlestown [*sic*], Va., was first invaded by the Yankees, and whose invaluable services in conveying information to our lines in spite of the espionage of the craven foe, have won for her from the Northern press the title of the most courageous and dangerous of rebel female spies, is now sojourning in this city at the residence of her cousin, Samuel B. Boyd, Esq. She was serenaded last night by the Florida Brass Band, and on being loudly called for by the crowd, appeared at the window, and made the following laconic and graceful response :

"Gentlemen, like General Johnston, I can fight, but cannot make speeches. You have my heartfelt thanks for your compliment."

Johnston, who had arrived at Chattanooga in early Dec., 1862, to assume command of the area lying between the Blue Ridge and the Mississippi, conveyed in public a formal attitude bordering on superciliousness, but among intimates was thought charming. See Govan and Livingood, *A Different Valor, op. cit.,* pp. 30–31, 339.

In its issue for Tues., Feb. 17, 1863 (2/1) the *Daily Register* headed its "Personal" column with this para. : "Our city, just now, is full of distinguished personages. Gen. Jo. Johnston, Gen. Price, (Old Pap,) Belle Boyd, and many other heroes and heroines." From the file in the University of Tennessee Library, Knoxville.

Pages 213 bottom–214 top : Mortally wounded May 2, 1863, Jackson died of pneumonia on Sunday, May 10. His body lay in state at the Executive Mansion on May 11, in the Capitol on May 12, and in the Mansion during the early morning of May 13. Col. Samuel (*sic*) Bassett French was aide to Gov. John Letcher His biographical memoranda on various Virginians, in manuscript at the Virginia State Library, Richmond, contain nothing on BB.

Page 214, fifth para. : "His enemy defeated, he rested." *The* epitaph is not, however, upon Nelson's tomb in the crypt of Saint Paul's Cathedral, London, but had been inscribed on one of the tiers of the funeral car that bore his remains to the cathedral. This vehicle is described in the London *Naval Chronicle,* XV, 233 (1806), and in John Fairburn's pamphlet, *Fairburn's Edition of the Funeral of Admiral Lord Nelson* (London, 1806), pp. 102–103, and illustrated in the frontispiece and title page, respectively, of each volume.

Page 215, line 19 : On Friday, June 5, 1863, the Harrisonburg, Va., *Rockingham Register* (2/1) announced : "Miss Belle Boyd, the Confederate heroine, and the victim of Yankee persecutions, has been in Harrisonburg for a few days past. She is stopping at the American [hotel], and is probably en route for her home in Martinsburg." From the file of the paper, Madison Memorial Library, Madison College, Harrisonburg.

On June 9 Lucy R. Buck of Martinsburg recorded in her diary : "Tis said Belle Boyd is in town tonight. What next? My biscuits were pronounced faultless tonight." Buck, *Diary, op. cit.,* p. 161.

Page 215, last para. : At the battle of Winchester, Va., June 13–15, 1863, the Confederates under Gen. R. S. Ewell defeated the Federals under Gen. R. H. Milroy.

Pages 218-219 : In his analysis of the Confederate invasion of Pennsylvania (June–July, 1863) Wilbur S. Nye provides a description of Bunker Hill and sketch maps of that hamlet and of Martinsburg. See his *Here Come the Rebels!* (Baton Rouge [La., 1965]), pp. 125–136.

Of BB's hospital activities the Georgia plantation mistress, Mrs. Jefferson Thomas, heard the following anecdote, which she recorded in her diary for Sept. 17, 1864. Her informant, "Buddy," was probably her older brother, Turner Clanton, Jr., who in 1864 had risen to the rank of lieutenant colonel in Page's brigade of Dabney's command :

> I remember hearing Buddy speaking of her attentions to our wounded soldiers, nursing them assiduously, binding their wounds and dressing them carefully, tenderly smoothing the hair from fevered brows, and said he laughing "she would quickly rise from the Bank upon which she had been sitting and brush the Camp insects, from her dress." Upon one occasion he was thrown in contact with her without knowing with whom he was conversing. Some remark she made caused him to inquire with a tone of surprise, "Are you Miss Belle Boyd?" "Yes" she replied. During the conversation she remarked "I never go unarmed" and drawing a Pistol from her Belt she commenced handling it, giving me as he remarked "a feeling of intense relief when she replaced it in her Belt" so unaccustomed had he been to ladies handling another weapon than "Womens weapon, the toungue [sic]" that he was afraid she would accidentally pull the trigger.

Ella Gertrude (Clanton) Thomas Diary : 1849–1889, vol. July 1861–Sept. 1864, pp. 158–159. Manuscript Dept., Duke University Library.

Page 219, lines 14-16 : At some period BB was also occupied smuggling that much-desired item, quinine, across the lines. In the 1870s a Southern-born hostess entertaining the Bishop of Albany at dinner at a town in New York State invited BB and her husband, Col. Hammond, and heard of the episode. See letter by her daughter, one A.C.C., in Washington, D.C., *Evening Star,* May 14, 1943 (A/8). L. A. Sigaud has identified the letter writer as Mrs. John S. Cotton, born Ada Chapple; the hosts as Dr. and Mrs. Haun; the place as Little Falls, N.Y.; and the bishop as the Episcopalian clergyman, William Croswell Doane.

See Sigaud, "More about Belle Boyd," *Lincoln Herald,* LXIV (Winter, 1962), 177.

Page 222, lines 17-18 : This, BB's second incarceration in the Old Capitol-Carroll complex, extended from Aug. 28 to Dec. 1, 1863. Her commitment paper to the Superintendent there, dated Hqs., Provost Marshal's Office, Washington, Aug. 28, 1863, signed by Provost Marshal Henry B. Todd, is reproduced from the original in The National Archives by James D. Horan for his chapter, "The Siren of the Shenandoah," *Desperate Women* (New York [1952]), ff. p. 162. Following her petition for release the Secretary of War, Nov. 25, 1863, directed "that Belle Boyd be sent South through our lines·" See "Orders and Endorsements Sent by the Secretary of War, XI–XII (Dec· 17, 1861–Dec. 14, 1863)," XII, 437. Army–Navy Branch, The National Archives.

Georgia-born Duff Green (1791–1875), editor of the *United States Telegraph* at Washington, had been a member of President Andrew Jackson's "kitchen cabinet."

Page 223, line 4 : Antonia J. Ford (1838-1871), after release from the Old Capitol, married Maj. Joseph C. Willard, U.S.A., founder of the Washington hotel. Novelist John Esten Cooke depicts her as "Violet Grafton" in his Civil War romance, *Surry of Eagle's Nest* (1866). See Cooke's *Wearing of the Gray. . . ,* ed. Philip van Doren Stern (Bloomington, Ind. [1959]), pp. 208–209 and n., and Ben H. Miller, "Antonia Ford, Confederate Spy," Baltimore, Md., *Sunday Sun Magazine,* Jan. 3, 1932 (pp. 13, 15), with likeness.

Page 230, second para. : At this point BB got off a note to Lincoln (now in Brown University Library) the flippancy of which may explain her failure to mention it :

"Carroll Prison"
Washington DC
Sept. 17th 1863

To His Excellency
The President of the U S,
   Mr. Lincoln—
   Tis for the purpose of begging that you will honor me
with a call that I write you,
Yours very Respectfully
Belle Boyd

Page 230, line 26 : Annie E. Jones (1820-   ), of Cambridge, Mass., was committed to the Old Capitol on Sept. 7, 1863, and released on Nov. 7, 1863. Eventually sent to the woman's prison at Fitchburg, Mass., she affirmed in a statement dated March 14, 1864, that she had been a camp follower with Union forces and had several times crossed Federal lines into Confederate-held territory in northern Virginia. Special File #19, Records of the Office of The Adjutant General, Record Group 94, Army-Navy Branch, The National Archives. Her career has been summarized by Mary E. Massey, *Bonnet Brigades* (New York, 1966), pp. 73-76.

Page 231, lines 24-25 : Quoting from this para. of BB's text, Charles O. Paullin, "History of the Site of the Congressional and Folger Libraries," Columbia Historical Society *Records,* XXXVII-XXXVIII (1937), 187, identifies this individual as William T. Smithson, whose place of business was at 544 Seventh St.

Under War Dept. General Order #371, Nov. 18, 1863, Secretary Stanton had sentenced Smithson to confinement in the Albany, N.Y., penitentiary. It was charged that, under the pseudonym of "Charles R. Cables," the defendant "did, at or near Washington, forward, by a vessel on the Potomac River the said letter[s] above set forth, enclosed in an envelope addressed in cypher—with the intent that the said letter[s] should be delivered to a person in the service of the rebel government, and an enemy of the United States." As a separate (7 pp., 12mo.) the trial transcript came on the auction market in Jan., 1967.

Page 236, lines 1-3 : A Washington dispatch of Tues., Dec. 1, published in the New York *Daily Tribune* for Wed., Dec. 2, 1863 (1/6), declared : "BELLE BOYD. Capt. James B. Mix of Gen. Martindale's staff left this afternoon for City Point with the notorious Belle Boyd, who is to be delivered to the Rebel authorities in that place."

Page 237, para three : Fresh from the Dept. of the Gulf and his New Orleans notoriety, Gen. Butler had assumed command of the Dept. of Virginia and North Carolina, with headquarters at Fort Monroe, about Nov. 11, 1863. See Lenoir Chambers, "Notes on Occupied Norfolk, 1862-1865," *Va. Mag. of Hist. & Biog.,* LXXIII 133-134 (Apr. 1965). His meeting with BB is noted by Hans L. Trefousse, *Ben Butler: The South Called Him BEAST!* (New York [1957]), p. 145.

Page 238, lines 28-29 : Julia L. and Anne C. Lomax, sisters to Gen. Lindsay L. Lomax. The military correspondence from Gen. Butler's headquarters, Dec. 6 and Dec. 8, 1863, ordering them returned to Baltimore, is printed in their mother Elizabeth L. Lomax's *Leaves from an Old Washington Diary, 1854-1863,* ed. Lindsay L. Wood ([New York], 1943), pp. 226-227. Butler's Provost Marshal, Capt. John Cassell (*sic*), was much taken with one of the girls.

Page 238, line 29 : Euphemia Mary Goldsborough (1836-1896), daughter of Martin and Anne (Hayward) Goldsborough, of Talbot County and Baltimore, Md. A courier for the Confederacy, she also tended Southern wounded after the battles of Antietam and Gettysburg. Her diary, portable writing desk with concealed compartment, and other memorabilia are owned by her granddaughter, Mrs. Stuart W. Crim, of Summit Point, West Va.

Referring to the Fort Monroe episode, Miss Goldsborough entered in her diary for Dec. 4, 1863 : "I forgot to say that horrid woman, Bell Boyd, was sent up on the same truce boat with me, but enough of her."

Pages 239-240 : Lest readers boggle at the booty found stowed aboard BB, see G. A. Sala's anecdote about a pretty "Secesh" arrested along the New York-Washington espionage route whose person was toting a cargo at least the equal of BB's. Sala, *Things I Have Seen and People I Have Known* (2 v., London, Paris, and Melbourne, 1894), I, 261-262.

Page 241, verses : From Vincenzo Monti, "Doppo la Battaglia di Marengo" (1799), lines 1-4. See his *Opere*, in *La Letteratura Italiana: Storia e Testi*, eds. R. Mattioli, P. Pancrazi, and A. Schiaffini (75 v., Milan and Naples, n.d.), LIV, 791.

Page 243, last para. : The Richmond, Va., *Daily Dispatch* for Friday morning, Dec. 4, 1863 (1/4), announced that the flag-of-truce boat had arrived the previous afternoon. Its only identified passenger was BB.

Page 245, lines 1-2 : See the Anglican Communion's *The Book of Common Prayer . . .*, American Revision (New York, 1928), from the services for burial of the dead, at graveside.

Page 245, lines 23-24 : Percy B. Shelley, "Mont Blanc—Lines Written in the Vale of Chamouni" (1816), Canto III.

Page 246, lines 20-21 : These letters must be presumed lost. However, the following epistle (now at the Huntington Library) to Lincoln's friend, and BB's fellow western Virginian, Ward Hill Lamon—currently Marshal of the District of Columbia—from a hostelry at 801–809 E. Main St., Richmond, speaks for itself. Views of the hotel may be had in Stanley Kimmel, *Mr. Davis's Richmond* (New York [1958]), pp. 14-15.

Spotswood Hotel
Richmond Va
Dec 18th /63

Col Ward H Lamon,
  Dear Sir,

    To you I feel I have the right to apply (under the existing circumstances) I feel you will do all in your power to aid me. *You know* full well all regarding my arrest, imprisonment, & release. Since I have been sent South, my Father has died. Tis for the purpose of begging you will use your influence with Mr. *Lincoln* & Mr. Stanton, that I write. I have written to both of them regarding my case. I wish a Parole to be allowed to return to my Mother & remain there. You knew my Father, my Mother, & you know me. For god's sake use your influence (for I know you have it) with Mr. Lincoln, for me to return to ma. I know she is nearly broken hearted. Relieve my grief. My father dead. My Mother, nearly wild with grief & I an *exile*. Oh, God! 'tis too hard. I pray you will listen to my entreaties. Anser [*sic*] soon.

Respectfully Yours
Belle Boyd

For a likeness of Lamon see Roy Meredith, *Mr. Lincoln's Camera Man . . ., op. cit.,* p. 74, and Meredith, *Mr. Lincoln's Contemporaries: An Album of Portraits by Mathew B. Brady* (New York, 1951) p. 143. This latter volume also contains, on pages 182-183, familiar photographs of BB and Pauline Cushman.

Page 247, para. two : Mrs. Semmes was the former Anne E. Spencer, of Cincinnati, O. Her husband, who would be promoted to Rear Admr., C.S.N., on Feb. 10, 1865, was at the moment commanding his commerce raider, *Alabama,* in Far Eastern waters. With three of their children, Mrs. Semmes had arrived in Richmond from Cincinnati, via Baltimore, only by the time of Stoneman's raid against that capital (Apr. 29–May 8, 1863), according to W. Adolphe Roberts, *Semmes of the Alabama* (Indianapolis and New York [1938]), p. 223. If this is accurate, then the time discrepancy—the date of BB's text being Dec.–Feb., 1863–1864—awaits explanation.

Page 247, paras. four-five : For typical foreign dispatches by Secretary of State Judah P. Benjamin for March, 1864, see James D. Richardson, comp., *Messages and Papers of the Confederacy, including the Diplomatic Correspondence, 1861–1865* (2 v., Nashville [Tenn.], 1905), II, 630 ff. There is no mention of BB.

Page 248, lines 7-9 : The master of this three-masted steamer, Capt. "Henry," employed a cover name to conceal his identity as George H. Bier. Sigaud (*Belle Boyd . . .,* p. 153) has confirmed that Bier was a former lieutenant in the United States Navy who, after leaving that service, served as a Major on Jackson's staff for the period Sept., 1862–Jan., 1863.

Page 250, lines 2-3 : In his own account of their voyage E. A. Pollard has no reference to BB, save obliquely. Referring to their vessel's capture by the *Connecticut* (May 10, 1864), he declares : "But for that peculiar nuisance of blockade-runners —women passengers—the Greyhound might have been burnt, and the last duty performed in the face of the rapacious enemy." See Pollard, *The Third Year of the War* (New York, 1865), p. 326. For his likeness see the engraving facing p. 323.

Page 255, para. one : BB's receipt, made out to William J. Bromwell, Disbursing Clerk of the Dept. of State, C.S.A., dated Richmond, March 28, 1864, to the amount of "five hundred— *Dollars* in gold, on a/c of my expenses, as bearer of despatches, for the Dept. of State," is reproduced by L. A. Sigaud in the article cited in Bibliography (p. 415, below).

Page 262, lines 11-12: Pollard's indignant correspondence with the British Minister to Washington concerning the capture of the *Greyhound* is printed in the Boston, Mass., *Daily Courier,* June 3, 1864 (1/1-2). He included it in his pamphlet, *Observations in the North: Eight Months in Prison and on Parole* (Richmond, 1865) and in his *The Third Year of the War, op. cit.,* pp. 331-339, 371-373.

Page 264: Shakespeare, *The Merchant of Venice,* V, i, 55-57.

Page 264, line 22 : The male lead in Bulwer-Lytton's drama, *The Lady of Lyons* (1838). In their obits on BB the theatrical papers, *New York Clipper* and the *Dramatic Mirror,* both noted that she had made her English début at the Theatre Royal, Manchester, as "Pauline" in this play. (A playbill, and the June 1, 1866, issue of the Manchester *Observer,* in the Central Library of the Manchester Public Libraries, pinpoints the date.) BB's coach, the Long Island-born Walter Montgomery—whose real name was Richard Tomlinson—customarily starred in the same drama as "Claude Melnotte" (*Dictionary of National Biography,* XIII, 771-772).

Page 266, last lines : An intended misquotation from Lord Byron, *Don Juan,* Canto III (1821), stanza 41.

Page 270, lines 22-23 : Earlier popular in London, *Bel-Demonio,* starring Mlle Felicita Vestvali, had premièred at Niblo's on May 16, 1864, and ran until July 2. Our trio probably saw it on opening night or the next, May 17. See George C. D. Odell, *Annals of the New York Stage* (15 v., New York, 1927-1949), VII, 562-563. For a rare stage photograph, taken in 1863, of the "Magnificent Vestvali" see Lloyd Ostendorf, "Faces Lincoln Knew . . .," *Lincoln Herald,* LXIV, 194-195 (Winter, 1962).

Page 271, line 8 : "SHODDY . . . *a.* Of a person : Pretentious by virtue of ill-gotten wealth, etc., but inferior in moral worth, character, and breeding—first used of those who made fortunes in army contracts during the Civil War by supplying inferior goods known as 'shoddy.' " *A Dictionary of Americanisms on Historical Principles,* ed. Mitford M. Mathews (Chicago [1956]), p. 1,524.

Page 274, line 4 : John S. Keyes (1821-1910), a native of Concord, Mass. He served as U. S. Marshal, Massachusetts District, for 1863-1866, and became judge of the East Cambridge District Court in 1874. This personage, said E. A. Pollard, "was a little Yankee with gimlet eyes, and who, with the fondness of his nation [*i.e.,* the North] for official insignia, had adorned himself with a long tail coat, scrupulously blue, and garnished with immense metal buttons marked U. S." Pollard, *The Third Year of the War, op. cit.,* p. 340. About 1866 Keyes himself wrote of the episode :

> The steamer laden with cotton captured running out of Charleston [*sic*] was sent to Boston, and on her arrival [May 19, 1864] a boyish young middy reported at my office, her arrival. Taking George Keyes, a Deputy, and some friends with me who happened to be at the office, I proceeded on board.
> There I found the most delapidated [*sic*] cabin in which were a middle aged and a rather young lady with a black servant and a rather truculent looking Southerner as passengers. To the ladies I was introduced by the young Naval man [Hardinge] who had brought home the prize, they passing under the names of Lewis, and to the man as Mr. Pollard.
> I had been warned by a telegram from Newport, where

they stopped for coal, of who they were and after a little talk I poked over the steamer. Beside the cotton there was a blooded stallion on board in a sort of pen made by cotton bales, and a game cock. This last I found had been the cause of the condition of the cabin, as every mirror on board had been used up in his fights with the reflection of himself, for the amusement of the ladies.* * *

Quoted from Keyes' unpublished, multi-vol. autobiography, in possession of his grandson, Raymond Emerson, of Concord, Mass.

Page 275, line 29 : Richard Bickerton Pemell Lyons, 1st Earl Lyons, was appointed British Minister to the United States in Dec., 1858, and remained in Washington until Feb., 1865, when ill health forced his recall. See the *Dictionary of National Biography,* XII, 358-359.

Page 277, line 11 : Doubtless the telegram acknowledged in a letter to Welles by Keyes from the Marshal's Office, Massachusetts District, Boston [Monday], May 30, 1864. Keyes' epistle reads in part : "I received your telegram of the 28th inst. and pursuant thereto committed E. A. Pollard to Fort Warren. * * * Miss Boyd and servants have this day gone to Canada by the through train."

Page 277, lines 20-21 : The article, "Belle Boyd a Prisoner," Washington, D.C. *Daily National Republican,* May 25, 1864 (2/4), declared that a letter had been this day received by the Secy. of the Navy, forwarded by U.S. Marshal Keyes at BB's request. She says she was permitted to leave the South for a foreign land in order to recover her health, much abused by imprisonment. She was the "Mrs. Davis" (*sic*) captured aboard the *Greyhound,* and hopes to get to Canada and remain until "this cruel war is over," in order to be close to her mother, who resides in that vicinity. "She says she assumed the name of

Davis 'in order to escape newspaper notoriety.' This declaration is *positive evidence of insanity,* upon which Belle's earnest plea to be released from imprisonment will undoubtedly receive favorable consideration."

Marshal Keyes' own comments (from his MS autobiography, *op. cit.*) run as follows :

> Pollard was released on his parole, and Belle and servants remained at the hotel on their word not to escape. Harding [*sic*] went to Washington to report to the Department and after some days Mr Secretary Welles sent me an order to put Pollard in Ft Warren and see Belle etc. safe to Canada.
>
> I was much relieved by this, for her ladyship, when she got over her sea trip, started out shopping and my office was soon filled with startling reports of her presence in the stores, and her gold coins with which she paid for her purchases etc. etc. She was proving a troublesome customer as she was overrun by curiosity seekers and had no discretion herself.
>
> I took the party in a sleeping car for Montreal, put them safely in their berths, told the conductor who they were and got his promise to see them safely through and caught the down train at Rutland, Vt. and came back home to breakfast, glad to be so well rid of her.

Page 281, para. three : One such journal was quoted as follows, by the Washington, D.C., *Daily National Republican* for Tues., June 21, 1864 (2/4):

> BELLE BOYD.—The famous Virginian lady, Miss Belle Boyd, who has done such good service to the Confederate cause, passed down the river to Montreal, on the steamer Banshee, on Sunday morning. The lady carried a small but sufficiently persuasive revolver pistol in her skirt belt, a precaution not altogether uncalled for, for on this neu-

tral boat, plying only in neutral waters, she was dogged by two Federal spies, whose business it is to watch her. Miss Boyd has resolution enough to defend herself from any attempted foul play by these gentry.—*Kingston* (Canada) *News* (Secesh).

Pages 285-287 : An accurate transcription of the article entitled, "Confederate Wedding," London *Morning Post*, Friday, Aug. 26, 1864 (3/2). Following "on many occasions"—at end of first para., p. 286—both book versions omit some fifteen newspaper lines relating to Hardinge's wartime exploits. On Sept. 22, 1864, BB wrote Jefferson Davis from her Brunswick Hotel address, enclosing an English-newspaper account of the wedding. "Though I loved him," BB observed of Hardinge, "I asked the advice of Mr. Hotze & other Confederates here before I took the step, fearing that my Country [*i.e.,* the Confederacy] would judge me wrong." See *Lincoln Herald* citation in Bibliography, p. 416, below.

Page 286, para. two : Of the wedding guests named, three— Fearn, O'Sullivan, and Williams—rate entries in the *Dictionary of American Biography*. On Hotze, who founded *The Index* as a Confederate organ at London, see Charles L. Dufour, *Nine Men in Gray* (Garden City, N.Y., 1963), pp. 267-297. For background see Paul P. du Bellet, *The Diplomacy of the Confederate Cabinet of Richmond and Its Agents Abroad . . .,* ed. William S. Hoole (Tuscaloosa, Ala., 1963).

On the day of the wedding the secretary of the United States Legation at London greeted the news as follows : "It seems that the rebel strumpet Belle Boyd was married at St. James' church, Piccadilly, to-day to some poor idiot. He is said to be a deserter from our Navy by the name of Hardinge." See Benjamin Moran, *Journal . . . 1857-1865,* eds. S. A. Wallace and F. E. Gillespie (2 v., Chicago, 1948), II, 1,317.

Page 296, line 14 : Provost Marshal and commandant of Forest Hall was one Capt. Kilpatrick. See "Affairs in Georgetown," Washington, D.C., *Evening Star,* Dec. 14, 1864 (2/6).

Pages 296-304 : Starting with "Forest Hall, or, as it is . . .," this section constituted Chap. X (pp. 137-157), vol. II, of the London edition of BB's memoirs.

Page 302, line 1 : Headlining the "Capture of Harding [*sic*], the Husband of the Notorious Belle Boyd," on Friday last at Martinsburg, and his present arrival in the District, the Washington, D.C., *Evening Star* for Tues., Dec. 6, 1864 (2/1), reported in part : "Harding asserts that his wife is still in Europe and is writing a history of her life and adventures, and that he is engaged in writing a novel, the title of which is 'The Wreck'." Military authorities believe, however, that BB is lurking in the Martinsburg area and that her husband's tale of having gone there in order to conduct his sister-in-law, Manie [Mary] Boyd, back North to educate her is false.

Harding brags of his wealth, but when searched only $14 was found upon him. He is a medium sized man, with dark hair, dark hazel eyes and thin, smooth face. He dresses tastefully in broadcloth, wears a "tall beaver," and carries a cane. He cannot be called handsome, but his actions indicate that he thinks a great deal of himself, and he appears to have the gift of "gab" in abundance, and while being conveyed to the Old Capitol he conversed freely with the officer having him in charge, and boasted of his wealth and education.

A brief notice also appeared in the Washington, D.C., *Daily Morning Chronicle,* Dec. 7, 1864 (2/3).

Pages 310-318 : Starting with *"December 21st,"* this section constituted Chap. XII (pp. 172-189), vol. II, of the London edition of BB's memoirs.

Page 311, line 11 : Presumably George William MacArthur Reynolds, the London editor and sensation novelist, whose bibliography is extensive and elusive. The two series of his *Mysteries of London,* each in four volumes, appeared during 1846-1855. See the *Dictionary of National Biography,* XLVIII, 43-45.

Page 311, line 21 : BB's mother died at the home of her son-in-law, O. W. Rowland, near Charles Town, West Va., on May 3, 1880, "aged about 54 years." (Death is said to have been from stomach cancer.) Of her burial at Martinsburg the local paper observed : "Among others accompanying the remains was the celebrated Belle Boyd, daughter of the deceased. It was her first visit for years to the scenes of her childhood and of the daring exploits of her girlhood during the war. The circumstances of her visit were extremely sad." See Martinsburg, West Va., *Independent,* May 8, 1880 (5/3), and Charles Town, West Va., *Spirit of Jefferson,* May 11, 1880 (2/4).

Pages 319-320 : On Dec. 28, 1864, Mrs. S. A. W. Harding (*sic*) addressed the Government in a letter that has been abstracted as follows : "Says that 'Belle Boyd,' now her son's wife, is 'enciente' [*sic*] and needs her husbands presence in Europe and asks his discharge from prison as she believes there is nothing to justify his detention." On Jan. 7, 1865, this plea was referred to the jurisdiction of Gen. Sheridan. See "Letters Received," Miscellaneous Branch, #40 (Supplement 1), Adjutant General's Office, p. 392, document #1550 H : Army-Navy Branch, The National Archives.

Page 321, line 23 : Before the war a stagecoach stop, Montgomery Hall became a leading hotel that accommodated many members of the Confederate Congress when Montgomery was the capital. The central section of the building still stands. A good photograph may be found in Peter A. Brannon, *The Organization of the Confederate Post Office Department at Montgomery* . . . (Montgomery, Ala., 1960), p. 46.

Pages 327-330 : Starting with "The places where the prisoners . . ." this section constituted Chap. XIV (pp. 210-218), vol. II, of the London edition of BB's memoirs.

Page 334, last line : The Episcopal minister, Ovid A. Kinsolving, of the Virginia clerical family. For a likeness, in a biography of one of his sons, see Arthur B. Kinsolving, *Texas George: The Life of George Herbert Kinsolving, Bishop of Texas, 1892-1928* (Milwaukee and London, 1932), facing p. 4. On his Fort Delaware incarceration see Isaac W. K. Handy, D.D., *United States Bonds, or, Duress by Federal Authority* . . . (Baltimore, Md., 1874), pp. 548 ff.

Page 335, line 7-page 338, line 26, inclusive : Hardinge's journal is here misplaced through someone's inadvertence. The passages describe the Old Capitol prison at Washington, not Fort Delaware.

Page 336, line 24 : Colby did not return this compliment. In his "The 'Old Capitol' Prison," referring to BB's second incarceration there, in *The Annals of the War* . . . *Originally Published in the Philadelphia Weekly Times* (Philadelphia, 1879), pp. 507-508, Colby dismissed her and her husband as opportunistic "light weights." Mrs. Baxley, said he, was a far abler spy than BB.

Page 353, last line : As to Hardinge's ultimate fate, U. S. Marshal Keyes declared in his autobiography that Hardinge was lost at sea in the *Star of the East,* en-route to Cuba with a band of filibusters. Presumably the cryptic reference refers to the so-called Ten Years' War, 1868-1878, the Cuban insurrection against Spain.

Page 354, lines 4-5 : Lincoln was fatally shot by the actor, John Wilkes Booth, at Ford's Theater, Washington, D.C., on the evening of April 14, 1865. Secy. of State Seward, ill abed in his home, was stabbed by a fellow conspirator.

Page 356, lines 8-10 : An accurate paraphrase of a speech by Lincoln in the House of Representatives, Jan. 12, 1848. Given at length in *A Treasury of Lincoln Quotations,* comp. Fred Kerner (Garden City, N. Y., 1965), p. 247.

Page 357, line 5 : After "became 'as it is,' " the following passages from vol. II, 462-463, of the London edition of BB's memoirs were silently deleted by the American publisher—

> Finally, when Richmond fell and Lee surrendered, unwilling to be what Andy Johnson, "Beast" Butler, or "Jim" Lane of Kansas wanted him to be, a tyrant, he [Lincoln] openly avowed his intention of effecting, if possible, a speedy union of North and South on the most conciliatory terms.
>
> This was sufficient. He was from henceforth a doomed man; the sands of his life were numbered; and he slept, little dreaming of his danger, of the sword hanging above his head.
>
> Not only was Lincoln doomed, but so also were all those most in favor of conciliatory measures towards the South and her traders.

A few months before his death in 1868, at Philadelphia, the former Northern detective chief, L. C. Baker, left a cipher message alleging that Secy. of War Stanton had been the ultimate instigator of Lincoln's assassination. See Robert H. Fowler, "Was Stanton behind Lincoln's Murder?" *Civil War Times,* III (Aug.-Sept., 1961), 5-23.

Page 357, line 7 : James Henry Lane, soldier and politician, was primarily an agitator. On July 11, 1866, he committed suicide. Despite the implications of this quotation, he was a staunch supporter of Lincoln. See Wendell H. Stephenson, "The Political Career of James H. Lane," Kansas State Hist. Soc. *Publications,* III (1930), 98, 164-165. For a less analytical treatment see Kendall E. Bailes, *Rider on the Wind: Jim Lane and Kansas* (Shawnee Mission, Kan., 1962).

Appendix

A century ago people were using terms such as "spy," "secret service," etc., loosely if not confusedly by the standards of today. As a result, certain exclusions and inclusions of titles in the Catalog that follows became mandatory. Let us consider the exclusions first.

For example, Edward A. Pollard's *Letters of the Southern Spy, in Washington and Elsewhere* ([Baltimore, 1861]) was discovered to be merely a volume of political essays, another of the prolific descendants of Giovanni Marana's popular romance, *L'Esploratore Turco* (Paris, 1684), englished as *Letters Writ by the Turkish Spy*.[1] Lt. William Pittenger's *Daring and Suffering: A History of the Great Railroad Adventure* (Philadelphia, 1864), which was several times reissued with the word "spy" spicing up its title page, is concerned with sabotage, not espionage. James D. Bulloch's bulky *The Secret Service of the Confederate States in Europe* . . . (2 v., London, 1883) has almost nothing to do with that, but everything to do with its subtitle : *How the Confederate Cruisers Were Equipped*. Here is diplomatic history, not espionage ! And, lastly, the mail carriers. Often lumped with

---

[1] Probably the earliest American offspring of Marana was Peter Markoe's anonymous romance, *The Algerine Spy in Pennsylvania* . . . (Philadelphia, 1787). For a survey restricted to U.S. belles-lettres see Curtis Carroll Davis. "Speak to Me Softly : The Permanent Fascinations of the Spy Story," *Columbia University Forum*, IV, 26–30 (Spring, 1961).

spies by their contemporaries,[2] these men—whose missions were definitely covert,[3] and who formally reported back on the state of affairs in Union territory—were in essence couriers or dispatch bearers, not spies.

So much for exclusions.

Promptly to be placed among the inclusions to the Catalog would be any title concerned with "secret service." During the Civil War this phrase meant just what it said,[4] and had not shrivelled into today's offshoot of the Treasury Department concerned with counterfeiting and protection of the President. Conversely, "espionage" was not only rarely employed but almost never defined as it is today. A hundred years ago it meant "surveillance," or "close observation." Its mate, "counter-espionage," was an unknown term. So, too, was "Military Intelligence." The word "intelligence," however, retained its centuries-old connotation of "information." The phrase "double agent"—a spy working coëvally for opposite sides only one of which is aware of this—had yet to be coined. One reads instead of a "double spy," or "playing double."[5]

Detectives had better be deemed synonymous with spies,[6] even though most of their activity involved operations which

[2] "Rebel spies, mail-carriers, and emissaries, have been carefully protected by this order ever since I have been a member," reported Felix Stidger to his superiors (see Catalog, #21, sub-appendix p. 19). At least one mail carrier was placed under ball and chain on charges of being a Union spy. See *Absalom Grimes: Confederate Mail Runner*, ed. M[ilo] M. Quaife (New Haven, Conn., 1926), p. 86.

[3] "In brief, the working distinction between the two forms of secrecy is that a clandestine operation is hidden but not disguised and a covert operation is disguised but not hidden." Christopher Felix (pseud.), *A Short Course in the Secret War* (New York, 1963), p. 28.

[4] As a cavalryman under Gen. Stineman, J. O. Kerbey even referred to his plain-clothes missions into Confederate territory for the purpose of disseminating false information as "this mounted secret service" (#17, p. 510).

[5] See Rose Greenhow's reference to "that double spy, Applegate . . ." (#2, p. 96). Philip Henson several times acted "the double spy" for Maj. Gen. Grenville M. Dodge (#16, p. 35).

[6] To select only one example, the terms were employed interchangably during the trial at Indianapolis in Dec., 1864, of members of the Order of the Sons of Liberty (#21, p 163).

today would be performed by the Federal Bureau of Investigation or the Criminal Investigation units of the Army's Military Police. Upon occasion "detective" even tiptoed within the connotation of another term equated with "spy." This was "scout."[7] To the Confederate forces the word "scout" plus the word "spy" added up to a Janus coinage. When a Butternut trooper engaged in espionage, affirms Douglas S. Freeman in *Lee's Lieutenants* . . .(I, 374 and n. 35), he was considered a scout. When a Southern civilian did the same thing, he was a spy. To the Federal forces this usage was similarly understood. And both sides often used the terms interchangeably.[8] For both sides, moreover, the activity was a substantive, with a connotation now lost : "reconnaissance." For this prevalent usage see the title of item #10 in the Catalog.

So much for inclusions.

The Catalog that follows has been compiled from entries found in the Union Catalog at the Library of Congress, the New York Public Library, the Enoch Pratt Free Library, and several smaller repositories. While it does not pretend to definitiveness, it offers a moderately comprehensive coverage of its subject. Not all of the editions cited have been personally examined. For rare titles a repository is given. Authors' names appear as they stand on the title page of their first edition. Their birth

[7] Equating the two, William Callender felt that he possessed "those qualifications, in no mean degree, which are required in a scout and detective" (#13, p. 22). This view was atypical. L. C. Baker, for example, was constrained to stress the distinction between scout and detective (#10, pp. 34–35).

[8] "You must be a scout, then,'' a Rebel said to Lorain Ruggles. "Yes, I am a spy; where do you belong?" (#9, p. 62). J. O. Kerbey knew that if he failed to transmit certain data to Washington, "it would prove pretty conclusively that as a Spy, or scout, I was not reliable . . ." (#17, pp. 233–234).

In 1911 a Northern commentator declared that by far the larger number of individuals dubbed spies would, by a military man, be labelled scouts A scout served under a chief in an organized group within Union lines, carrying dispatches, seeking tactical information, and in general performing *some* of a spy's work—hence the confusion. George H. Casamajor, "The Federal Secret Service," in *The Photographic History of the Civil War* (New York and London, 1957 [reprint]), VIII, 284.

and death years have been ascertained from internal evidence and from their entries in the Library of Congress card catalog.

Of the twenty-four individuals listed, six have found a place in *The Dictionary of American Biography* (1929–1936). For the North these are Baker, Miss Cushman, Pinkerton, and Richardson. For the South : BB, and Stringfellow. Three of the individuals listed are carried in *The Oxford Companion to American History,* comp. Thomas H. Johnson (New York, 1966). For the North these are Miss Cushman and Pinkerton. For the South : BB. Four of the texts have been cited in *A Dictionary of Americanisms on Historical Principles,* ed. Mitford M. Mathews (2 v., Chicago, 1951). For the North these are Baker, Pike, and Richardson. For the South : BB.

CATALOG

Item No.	First Pub.	Author	Title	Allegiance
1	1863	[John Fitch]	*Annals of the Army of the Cumberland . . . By an Officer* (Philadelphia : J. B. Lippincott & Co.). Pp. 671. Illustrated.	North
1-A			Sixth edition (Philadelphia, 1864).[9]	
1-B			Another edition : *Police Record of the Spies, Smugglers and Rebel Emissaries in Tennesssee. Being Selections from the "Annals of the Army of the Cumberland". . .*(Philadelphia, 1863).	

[9] The Fourth edition was the first to which the author subscribed his name on the title page. He had previously withheld it, he said, because authorship was not his trade; but since the work had attracted unanticipated attention, it was now being attributed to others (#1–A, p. 5).

2 1863 Mrs. [Rose *My Imprisonment and the* South
      O'Neal]   *First Year of Abolition Rule*
      Greenhow *at Washington* (London :
      (*c.* 1816–1864) Richard Bentley). Pp. 352.
              Portrait frontispiece.

3 1864 S. Emma E. *The Female Spy of the* North
      Edmonds *Union Army...*(Boston : De-
      (1841–1898) Wolfe, Fiske & Co.). Pp. 384.
              Frontispiece.

3–A   *Nurse and Spy in the Union*
             Army... (Hartford, Conn. :
             W. S. Williams & Co.; Phila-
             delphia : Jones Bros. & Co.,
             1865).

3–B   *Kranken-und Spionendienst*
             fur die Unions-armee . . .
             (Hartford : W. S. Williams
             & Co.; Philadelphia and Cin-
             cinnati : Jones Bros. & Co.,
             1865).

3–C   *Unsexed: or, The Female*
             Soldier... (Philadelphia :
             Philadelphia Publishing Co.
             [*c.* 1866]).

4   [for Pauline *An Inside View of the* North
      Cushman] *Army Police. The Thrilling*
      (1833–1894) *Adventures of Pauline Cush-*
             man, the Distinguished Ameri-
             can Actress, and Famous
             Federal Spy of the Depart-
             ment of the Cumberland

(Cincinnati : Rickey & Carroll). Pp. 50 (pamphlet). Portrait.

Copy : Western Reserve Historical Society Library.

4–A

Another edition : *The Romance of the Great Rebellion; the Mysteries of the Secret Service: a Genuine and Faithful Narrative of the Thrilling Adventures... of Miss Major Pauline Cushman, the Famous Federal Scout and Spy, in the Department of the Cumberland* (New York : Wynkoop & Hallenbeck). Pp. 60 (pamphlet). Portrait frontispiece.

Copy : Western Reserve H. S. Library.

5   1865 Corporal [James] Pike (1834–*c.* 1876)

The Scout and Ranger: North *Being the Personal Adventures of Corporal Pike of the Fourth Ohio Cavalry... Fully Illustrating the Secret Service* (Cincinnati and New York : J. R. Hawley & Co.). Pp. vi. 394. Illustrated.

5–A

Carl L. Cannon (ed.), *Scout and Ranger: Being the Personal Adventures of James Pike of the Texas Rangers in 1859–60,* Narratives of the

Trans - Mississippi Frontier (Princeton, N. J., 1932).
Reprints the Texas phase, or about one-third of the original text.

6	Albert D. Richardson (1833–1869)	*The Secret Service, The Field, the Dungeon, and the Escape* (Hartford, Conn. : American Publishing Co.; Philadelphia, Pa., and Cincinnati, O. : Jones Bros. & Co. : Chicago, Ill. : R. C. Treat). Pp. 17–512.[10] Illustrated.	North

6–A

Der Geheime Dienst, das Feldlager, Gëfangnitz und die Flucht... (Hartford, Conn. : American Publishing Co., 1865).
Copy : Harvard University Library.

6–B

Another edition : short-title of #6 (Washington, D.C. : The National Tribune, 1897).

7	1865 Belle Boyd [Hardinge] (1844–1900)	*Belle Boyd, in Camp and Prison. With an Introduction by a Friend of the South* (London : Saunders, Otley, & Co., two vols.). Pp. 291, 280.	South

7–A

Belle Boyd in Camp and Prison. Written by Herself,

[10] Only Section I, "The Secret Service" (pp. 17–124). falls within present concern.

intro. George Augusta [*sic*] Sala (New York : Blelock & Co., 1865). p. 5–464.

7 B–C   Reprinted : *ibid.* (1866; 1867).

8   F[erdinand] L. Sarmiento   *Life of Pauline Cushman,* North *the Celebrated Union Spy and Scout...* (Philadelphia : J. E. Potter). Pp. 374. Illustrated.

8–A   Another edition (New York : United States Book Co. [n.d.]).

8–B   Another edition (Philadelphia : Keystone Publishing Co., 1890).

9   1866 E[dward] C. Downs   *Four Years a Scout and* North *Spy. "General Bunker," One of Lieut. General Grant's Most Daring and Successful Scouts...* (Zanesville, Ohio : Hugh Dunne). Pp. xii, 404. Illustrated.
Career of Lorain Ruggles (1823–   ).

9–A   *The Great American Scout and Spy...,* Third Edition, revised (New York : Olmsted & Welwood, 1868).

9–B			Reprinted (New York : Olmsted & Co., 1870).	
9–C			*Perils of Scout-Life...* (New York : M. L. Byrn, 1873).	
9–D			Reprinted : *ibid.* (1875).	
10	1867	General L[afayette] C. Baker (1826–1868)	*History of the United States Secret Service* (Philadelphia : L. C. Baker). Pp. 704. Illustrated.	North
10–A			Another edition (Philadelphia : King & Baird, 1868).	
10–B			Another edition (Philadelphia : Parmelee, 1869).	
10 C–H			Abridgements : *The United States Secret Service in the Late War...* (Philadelphia : J. E. Potter & Co. [1899]). Same title (Hartford, Conn. : Park Publishing Co., 1889). Same title (Rochester, N.Y. : H. B. Graves [*c.* 1889]). *Spies. Traitors and Conspirators of the Late Civil War...* (Philadelphia : J. E. Potter & Co., 1894). *Daring Exploits of Scouts and Spies...* (Chicago : Thompson & Thomas [1894]). *Secret Service...* (Washington, D. C. : The National Tribune, 1898).	

11		S[olomon] Woolworth (1819–*post* 1905)	*The Mississippi Scout; or,* *A Detail of What the Writer* *Saw, in a Scout, inside the* *Rebel Lines around Vicks-* *burg, in 1863* (Chicago : [for the author]). Pp. 16 (pamph- let).	North
11–A			Another edition : *Experi-* *ences in the Civil War* (New- ark, N.J. : [for the author] 1903). Pp. 3–80 (soft-bound). Frontispiece.	
12	1876	Loreta Janeta Velazquez (1842–)	*The Woman in Battle...*, ed. C. J. Worthington (Hart- ford : T. Belknap). Pp. 606. Illustrated.	South
13	1881	William Callender (1838–)	*Thrilling Adventures of...*, *a Union Spy from Des* *Moines* [ed. J. M. Dixon] (Des Moines : Mills & Co., Print- ers). Pp. 116. Copy : Des Moines, Ia., Public Library.	North
14	*c.*1882	Rev. Frank Stringfellow (1840–1913)	*Scout Life.* Pamphlet. Copy : R. Shepard Brown, Cherry Hill, N. J.[11]	South

[11] "He also published his lectures in a small pamphlet called 'Scout Life'—which I have found invaluable in writing this book—and turned over the money from the sales to the church fund." R. Shepard Brown, *Stringfellow of the Fourth* (New York [1960]), p. 292. "I have a copy of the original pamphlet by the Scout himself, and a copy of Mr. Peavey's reprint. Since the two are identical, I'll be happy to let you have Mr. Peavey's reprint, but I shouldn't like to let the original out of my hands." R. Shepard Brown, Philadelphia, Pa., Feb. 10, 1964, to Curtis Carroll Davis.

14–A James D. Peavey (comp. and ed.), *Confederate Scout: Virginia's Frank Stringfellow.* ([Onancock, Va. : Eastern Shore Publishing Co., 1956]). Pp. 62 (pamphlet).

15 1883 Allan Pinkerton (1819–1884) *The Spy of the Rebellion; Being a True History of the Spy System of the United States Army during the Late Rebellion...* (New York : G. W. Dillingham Co.). Pp. xxxii, 607. Illustrated. North

15–A Reprinted : *ibid.* (1895).

15–B Another edition (New York : G. W. Carleton & Co., 1883), with additional backmatter entitled, "The Hardships and Privations of a Detective's Life" (pp. 609–688).

15 C–D Reprinted : *ibid.* (1884; 1886).

15–E Another edition (Chicago : A. G. Nettleton & Co., 1883).

15–F Another edition (Toronto : Rose Publishing Co., 1884).

15–G Another edition (Hartford, Conn. : M. A. Winter & Hatch, 1885).

16   1887   George S.   *Philip Henson, the South-* North
            Johns   *ern Union Spy. The Hitherto*
                           Unwritten Record of a Hero
                           of the War of the Rebellion
                           (St. Louis : Nixon-Jones Print-
                           ing Co.). Pp. 97 (pamphlet).
                           Frontispiece.
                           Henson's dates : 1827–.

17   1889   Major   *The Boy Spy: A Substant-* North
            J[oseph] O.   *ially True Record of Secret*
            Kerbey   *Service during the War of the*
            (18 –1913)   *Rebellion. . . . The Only Prac-*
                           tical History of War Tele-
                           graphers in the Field. . . (Chi-
                           cago, Philadelphia, and San
                           Francisco : American Mutual
                           Library Assn.). Pp. vii, 557.
                           Illustrated.

17–A   Another edition (Chicago,
                           New York, and elsewhere :
                           Belford, Clarke & Co., 1889).

17–B   Another edition (Chicago :
                           M. A. Donohue & Co. [1890]).

18   1892   Capt. Thomas   *A Confederate Spy. A* South
            N. Conrad   *Story of the Civil War.* Peer-
            (1837–1905)   less Series #63. Issued
                           Monthly. September, 1892
                           (New York : J. S. Ogilvie). Pp.
                           142. One illustration.

18–A   Reprinted [ed. Mrs. Glenna
                           D. Anthony] (Lynchburg,

Va.: Artcraft Printing Co.,
1961). Three illustrations.

Copy: Jones Memorial
Library, Lynchburg, Va.

18–B   Another edition: *The
Rebel Scout, A Thrilling
History of Scouting Life in
the Southern Army* (Washington, D.C.: National Publishing Co., 1904).

19   1903   George   *Spencer Kellogg Brown:* North
            Gardner   *His Life in Kansas and His
            Smith (ed.)   Death As a Spy, 1842–1863,
                          As Disclosed in His Diary*
                          (New York: D. Appleton &
                          Co.). Pp. x, 380. Illustrated.

20   1903   David   *Heroes and Spies of the* South
            Humphreys   *Civil War* (New York and
            (1832–19)   Washington: Neale Publish-
                          ing Co.). Pp. 223. Frontis-
                          piece.

21   1903   Felix G.   *Treason History of the* North
            Stidger   *Order of Sons of Liberty...
            (1836–19)   Knights of the Golden Circle
                          ... 1864* ([Chicago: for the
                          author], 1903). Pp. 246, 30
                          (sub-appendix). Illustrated.

22   1908   Rev. J. T.   *A Spy in the Service of the* South
            Mann   *Confederacy: How It Feels
            (1843–19)   To Be Hung by the Neck and
                          Die* (Pensacola, Fla., Sunday

			Journal, 1908). Pp. 15 (pamphlet off-print). Copy : Library of Congress.	
23	1911	Bvt. Major H[enry] B[ascom] Smith (1841–1916)	*Between the Lines: Secret Service Stories Told Fifty Years After* (New York : Booz Brothers). Pp. 343. Illustrated.	North
24	1929	Capt. Louis A. Newcome (*c.* 1845– 19)	*Lincoln's Boy Spy* (New York and London : G. P. Putnam's Sons). Pp. vi, 197. Frontispiece.	North
25	1961	[Sgt. Henry J. Acker] (18 –)	*Gulf Spy: Sgt Henry J. Acker, 23rd Wisconsin Vol. Inf.* [ed. James R. H. Spears] (Tall Timbers, Md. : Headquarters Press). Pp. 24 (pamphlet).[12]	North

---

[12] James R. H. Spears, in a letter dated Indianapolis, Ind., Jan. 6, 1964, repeats the statements of belief in its authenticity provided in his anonymous Introduction, #25, p. 3). "The story was published with very little editing. Commas, periods, and some paragraphing were the only changes made. Nothing was omitted. *** I personally wish Sgt. Henry Acker had written at greater length. If the story *is* a fabrication, he made a great mistake in his post-war choice of professions."

Bibliography

MANUSCRIPTS

Chicago, Ill.
BB, document signed by. Richmond, Mar. 28, 1864. Receipt for travelling expenses (in gold) from Confederate States of America. Printed in Louis A. Sigaud, "More about Belle Boyd," *Lincoln Herald* (Harrogate, Tenn.), LXIV, 174-181 (Winter, 1962).
Purchased by the Abraham Lincoln Book Shop on behalf of an unidentified client.

Front Royal, Va.
BB, two poems by. One beginning, "When forced to part from those we love . . ." (Front Royal, July 28, 1861). The other entitled, "To Caddie Dear" (Front Royal, Aug. 14, 1861). Both published in Laura V. Hale's illus. pamphlet, *Belle Boyd: Southern Spy of the Shenandoah* ([Front Royal, Va., 1954]).
In Kathleen Boone autograph album, Warren Rifles Confederate Museum.

Martinsburg, West Va.
Affidavit, signed by Alex. Parks, Jr., W.M., for Equality Lodge #44, A. F. & A. M., Martinsburg, Jan. 22, 1876. Certifying to the identity and whereabouts of "the real Belle Boyd. . . ."
Collection of Mrs. G. Roderick Cheeseman, of "Boydville."

415

New York City

BB, autograph letter by. Kilbourn, Wisc., June 10 [1900], to Isabelle and Byrd Hammond. Partially printed in Sigaud (citation under Chicago, Ill., above).

Collection of David Hunter.

Providence, R. I.

BB, autograph letter signed by. Washington, Sept. 17, 1863, to the President of the U.S. [Abraham Lincoln].

John Hay Collection, Brown University Library.

San Marino, Calif.

BB, autograph letters signed by. Richmond, Va., Dec. 18, [18]63; Washington, March 2, [18]68; and Washington, April 7 [1868]—all to Ward Hill Lamon.

Henry E. Huntington Library and Art Gallery.

Upper Montclair, N. J.

BB, autograph letter signed by. Evansville, Wisc., May 21, 1900, to Isabelle Hammond. Partially printed in Sigaud (citation under Chicago, Ill., above).

Collection of Robert K. Black.

Washington, D. C.

BB, autograph letter signed by. Old Capitol Prison, Washington, D.C., Aug. 8, [18]62, to Hon. E. M. Stanton.

Washington Duffee, Brigade Surgeon, Hqs., I Army Corps, Va., July 30, 1862, autograph letter signed, to Secretary Stanton.

Turner-Baker Papers, #863, Record Group 94, Army-Navy Branch, The National Archives.

BB, autograph letter signed by. London, Sept. 22, [18]64, to Hon. Jefferson Davis. Printed in Louis A. Sigaud, "William Boyd Compton : Belle Boyd's Cousin," *Lincoln Herald,* LXVII, 22-33 (Spring 1965).

Record Group 109, (microfilm copy M-347, roll #35), Army-Navy Branch, The National Archives.

BB, autograph letter signed by. London, Dec. 26, 1864, to Douglass Wallach.

Collection of Crosby N. Boyd.

BB, autograph letter signed by. London, Jan. 24, 1865, to Honble. Abraham Lincoln, President of the U. S. America. Printed in Louis A. Sigaud, "When Belle Boyd Wrote Lincoln," *Lincoln Herald,* L, 15-22 (Feb., 1948).

Lincoln Papers, Library of Congress.

PUBLISHED PRIMARY SOURCES (SELECTED)

Ashby, Thomas A., M.D., *The Valley Campaigns* . . . (New York, 1914).

Avary, Mrs. Myrta Lockett (ed.), *A Virginia Girl in the Civil War, 1861-1865: Being a Record of the Actual Experiences of the Wife of a Confederate Officer* (New York, 1903).

Boyd, Belle. (For editions of her Civil War reminiscences see Appendix, pp. 407-408, above.)

"Miss Belle Boyd, 'The Rebel Spy,' " Richmond, Va., *Southern Illustrated News,* Oct. 11, 1862 (5/2-3). With likeness by T. D. Cowell.

> Reprinted : H. W. R. Jackson, *The Southern Women of the Second American Revolution* . . .(Atlanta, Ga., 1863), pp. 8-9
> *The Confederate Reader,* ed. Richard B. Harwell (New York [1957]), pp. 138-140

Buck, Lucy Rebecca, *Diary . . . 1861-1865* ([ed. Mrs. George D. Rowe, Baltimore, Md.] 1940). Mimeograph reproduction of Ms in possession of Dr. William P. Buck, Birmingham, Ala.

> Copies : Library of Congress, Washington, D.C.
> Randolph-Macon Woman's College Library, Lynchburg, Va.
> Samuels Library, Front Royal, Va.
> University of Virginia Library, Charlottesville
> Virginia Historical Society, Richmond

Conrad, Capt. Thomas N., *A Confederate Spy: A Story of the Civil War* (New York and London, 1915).

Doster, William E., *Lincoln, and Episodes of the Civil War* (New York and London, 1915).

Galwey, Thomas Francis, *The Valiant Hours,* ed. Col. W. S. Nye (Harrisburg, Pa. [1961]).

Gilmor, Col. Harry, *Four Years in the Saddle* (New York, 1866).

Kerbey, Maj. J[oseph] O., *The Boy Spy: A Substantially True Record of Secret Service during the War of the Rebellion...* (Chicago, Philadelphia, and San Francisco, 1889).

Newspaper Dispatches

1862   May 31   New York *Herald* (1/6).

New York *Times* (8/2).

Philadelphia *North American*. . . (2/4).

June 12   New York *Daily Tribune* (3/4–5).

July 19   Philadelphia *Inquirer* (4/3).

Reprinted as "A Company of Fair Rebels," *Frank Leslie's Illustrated Newspaper* (N.Y.C.), XIV, 318 (Aug. 9, 1862).

Reprinted, *Southern Illustrated News* (see above).

Aug. 4   Washington, D.C., *Evening Star* (3/6).

Reprinted as "Arrest of Belle Boyd, the Female Rebel Spy," Frederick, Md., *Examiner,* Aug. 6, 1862 (2/7).

Latter in Civil War reprint series, *Valley News Echo* (Hagerstown, Md.: Potomac Edison Co.), Aug. 1962 (1/3–2/6).

1863   Feb. 14   Knoxville, Tenn., *Daily Register* (1/1).

1864 May 25 Washington, D.C., *Daily National Republican* (1/7).

    Aug. 24 London (Eng.), *The Index: A Weekly Journal...*, IV, 542.

    Aug. 26 London (Eng.), *Morning Herald* (4/5).
London (Eng.), *Morning Post* (3/2).
London (Eng.), *Shipping and Mercantile Gazette* (8/4).
    Reprinted in New York *World*, Sept. 8, 1864 (2/6).
Paris (France), *Moniteur Universelle.* Unlocated.

1886 Feb. 22 Toledo, O., *Daily Blade* (3/4).

1889 Feb. 11 New York *World* (3/6).

    Feb. 12 Baltimore, Md., *Sun* (4/6).

    Feb. 15 Petersburg, Va., *Daily Index-Appeal* (4/2).

1894 Apr. 19 Baltimore, Md., *American* (8/3).

Smith, Capt. James P., C.S.A., "With Stonewall Jackson in the Army of Northern Virginia," Southern Historical Society *Papers,* n.s. V, 21 (Aug., 1920).

Stevenson, James H., *"Boots and Saddles": A History of the First Volunteer Cavalry of the War. Known As the First New York (Lincoln) Cavalry...* (Harrisburg, Pa., 1879).

Strother, D. H., *A Virginia Yankee in the Civil War: The Diaries of David Hunter Strother,* ed. Cecil H. Eby (Chapel Hill, N.C. [1961]).

Wayland, John W., *Virginia Valley Records.* . . (Strasburg, Va., 1930).

Williamson, James J., *Prison Life in the Old Capitol, and Reminiscences of the Civil War* (West Orange, N. J., 1911).

PUBLISHED SECONDARY SOURCES (SELECTED)

Andrews, J. Cutler, *The North Reports the Civil War* ([Pittsburg, Pa., 1955]).

"Belle Boyd," Washington, D.C., *Evening Star,* May 8, 1943 (A-8). Editorial.

Blakely, Stephens L., "Belle Boyd, a Fantasy Based on Logic," *Christopher Gist Historical Society Papers* (Covington, Ky., 1952-1953), pp. 80-91.

Boatner, Mark M., III, *The Civil War Dictionary* (New York [1959]).

" 'Boydville' and Belle Boyd," Martinsburg, West Va., *Journal,* June 23, 1965 (6/1-2). Editorial. Reiterating that BB was no kin to Gen. Elisha Boyd, of the War of 1812, who built the town's finest mansion.

Canan, Col. Howard V., U.S.A. (Ret.), "Confederate Military Intelligence," *Maryland Historical Magazine,* LIX, 34-51 (March, 1964).

Carse, Robert, *Blockade: The Civil War at Sea* (New York and Toronto [1958]).

Cochran, Hamilton, *Blockade Runners of the Confederacy* (Indianapolis and New York [1958]).

Cole, H. E., "Belle Boyd, Rebel Spy," *Wisconsin Magazine,* II, 32, 42-43 (May, 1924). With photograph of boulder marking BB's grave (cf. Everman and Stluka, below).

Conservation and Development, Virginia Dept. of, *State Historical Markers of Virginia,* Sixth Edition (Richmond, 1948).

Creager, Marvin H., "Perils of Belle Boyd; or, The Lady Spy!" Milwaukee, Wisc., *Journal,* Sunday, March 20, 1949 (Sect. V). Illustrated.

Crombie, Alice H., *A Tour Guide of the Civil War* (Chicago, 1965).

Cunningham, Frank, *Knight of the Confederacy: General Turner Ashby* (San Antonio, Tex., 1960).

[Dabney, Virginius], "Belle Boyd—Thanked by 'Stonewall' Jackson," Richmond, Va., *Times-Dispatch,* June 2, 1952 (p. 12). Editorial.

Dannett, Sylvia G. L., and Katharine M. Jones, *Our Women of the Sixties* (Washington, D.C., 1963). Pamphlet.

Davis, Burke, *They Called Him Stonewall: A Life of Lt. General T. J. Jackson, C. S. A.* (New York [1954]).

———, *Our Incredible Civil War* (New York [1960]).

Davis, Curtis Carroll, "Companions of Crisis : The Spy Memoir As a Social Document," *Civil War History,* X, 385-400 (Dec., 1964).

———, "The Civil War's Most Over-Rated Spy," *West Virginia History,* XXVII, 1-9 (Oct., 1965). Attempts an analysis of the legendry that has arisen 'round BB's name.

Death Notices

Baltimore, Md.	*American,* June 12, 1900 (2/2). In detail.
	Sun, June 13, 1900 (6/8). In detail.
Boston, Mass.	*Evening Transcript,* June 12, 1900 (p. 7).
Dayton, O.	*Daily Journal,* June 12, 1900 (1/7).
Kilbourn, Wisc.	*Mirror-Gazette,* June 16 (5/3), June 23 (5/2), 1900. In detail.
Lynchburg, Va.	*News,* June 12 (5/4), June 14 (3/1), 1900. From Baltimore *Sun.*
Milwaukee, Wisc.	*Journal,* June 12, 1900 (2/2). From Kilbourn *Mirror-Gazette.*
Nashville, Tenn.	*American,* June 12, 1900 (2/6).
New Orleans, La.	*Daily Picayune,* June 12, 1900 (4/7).
New York City	*Dramatic Mirror,* June 23, 1900 (19/2).

	New York Clipper, June 23, 1900 (372/2).
	Times, June 13, 1900 (6/7). In detail.
Philadelphia, Pa.	*Evening Telegraph,* June 12, 1900 (4/1). In detail.
Richmond, Va.	*Dispatch,* June 12, 1900 (3/2).
Roanoke, Va.	*Times,* June 12, 1900 (5/3).
San Francisco	*Chronicle,* June 12, 1900 (2/5). In detail (partly from *New York Times*).
Springfield, Mass.	*Republican,* June 14, 1900 (6/3).
Toledo, O.	*Blade,* June 14, 1900 (6/2).
Utica, N. Y.	*Daily Press,* June 12, 1900 (1/7).
	Observer, June 12, 1900 (1/4).
Washington, D.C.	*Evening Star,* June 14, 1900 (15/3). In detail (from *New York Times*).
Winchester, Va.	*Evening Star,* June 13, 1900 (1/4). In detail.

Eaton, Clement, *A History of the Southern Confederacy* (New York, 1954).

[Everman, Willis A.], "At the Grave of Belle Boyd," *Confederate Veteran,* XXVII, 353 (Sept., 1919). A Greenville, Miss., resident explains how he came to erect the boulder in Spring Grove Cemetery, Kilbourn, Wisc.

Hale, Laura Virginia, "Belle Boyd Dress Displayed," Strasburg, Va., *Northern Virginia Daily,* Nov. 18, 1963 (p. 3). Illustrated.

Hamilton, Charles, *Collecting Autographs and Manuscripts* (Norman, [Okla., 1961]).

Hamlin, Percy G., *"Old Bald Head" (General R. S. Ewell): The Portrait of a Soldier* (Strasburg, Va., 1940).

Hay, Thomas Robson, "Boyd, Belle," in *Notable American Women, 1607-1950: A Biographical Dictionary,* ed. Edward T. James (3 v., Cambridge, Mass., to appear).

Henderson, G[eorge] F. R., *Stonewall Jackson and the American Civil War,* intro. Gen. Walter Bedell Smith, U.S.A. (London and elsewhere [1961]).

Herbstruth, Grant M., "Benedict DeBar and the Grand Opera House in St. Louis, Missouri, from 1855-1879," unpub. doctoral dissertation, Dept. of Speech, University of Iowa (Iowa City, 1954). See pp. 215, 723.

"Hundreds To Re-enact Battle of Front Royal," Washington, D.C., *Post and Times-Herald*, May 18, 1962 (A-3).

Kane, Harnett, *Spies for the Blue and Gray* (New York, 1954).

Leech, Margaret, *Reveille in Washington, 1860-1865* (New York and London [1941]).

Likenesses (additional to those in present volume)

American Heritage Picture History of the Civil War, The, ed. Richard M. Ketchum et al. (New York, 1960).

Embattled Confederates: An Illustrated History of Southerners at War, ed. and comp. Hirst D. Milhollen and Bell I. Wiley (New York, Evanston, and London [1964]).

Greenway, Rev. Cornelius (Brooklyn, N.Y.), owner. Cabinet photograph, BB in Confederate stage costume, signed "Belle Boyd, the Rebel Spy."

Horan, James D., *Mathew Brady: Historian with a Camera* (New York [1955]).

Meredith, Roy, *Mr. Lincoln's Camera Man: Mathew B. Brady* (New York, 1946).

Photographic History of the Civil War, The, ed. Francis T. Miller (10 v., New York, 1911-1912), VIII, 291. Reprinted, New York and London [1957].

Sigaud, Louis A., *Belle Boyd: Confederate Spy* (Richmond, Va. [1944]). See also below.

Starnes, Lucy G., "Girl Spy of the Valley," *Virginia Cavalcade,* X, 35-40 (Spring, 1961).

Swartz, Mrs. Mary Hunter (Berkeley Springs, West Va.), owner. Framed newspaper (?) portrait, head and shoulders, measuring $3\frac{3}{4}''$ x $4\frac{3}{4}''$ over-all. Pasted on back of frame in ink in BB's hand is: "Kind regards to Dr. Jackson [*flourish*] Miss Belle Boyd Front Royal Virginia [*vertically, on right-hand side:*] Martinsburg Virginia."

de Lue, Willard, "Story of Belle Boyd, Confederate Girl Spy," Boston, Mass., *Daily Globe*, June 6, 1952 (8/1-4). This article by a regional columnist typifies the continuing reaction to BB's renown in various parts of the country. Cf. Tucker, below.

Massey, Mary Elizabeth, *Bonnet Brigades* (New York, 1966).

Nicolson, Roland Q., "Most Daring Exploits of Belle Boyd . . . Occurred in and Near Front Royal," Strasburg, Va., *Northern Virginia Daily*, Nov. 27, 1940 (Sect. 8, p. 57). Features an adverse analysis of BB's memoirs by the Virginia State Writer's Project, W.P.A.

Poore, Ben. Perley, "Government Secret Service," *Chataquan*, VII, 210-213 (Jan., 1887).

Preston, Wheeler, *American Biographies* (New York and London [1940]).

Roland, Charles P., *The Confederacy* ([Chicago, Ill., 1960]).

Shetler, Charles, comp., *West Virginia Civil War Literature: An Annotated Bibliography* (Morgantown, West Va., 1963).

Sigaud, Louis A., *Belle Boyd: Confederate Spy* (Richmond, Va. [1944]). The only book-length study, this family-approved biography scants BB's post-war career in general and ignores certain episodes entirely.

Simkins, Francis B., and James W. Patton, *The Women of the Confederacy* (Richmond and New York [1936]).

Simmons, Henry E., comp., *A Concise Encyclopedia of the Civil War* (New York and London [1965]).

"Spy, A, Bell Boyd, Joins the Heroines," *New York Times Magazine*, June 16, 1929 (pp. 11, 20). Illustrated. Typical of various articles stimulated by the (abortive) plans of the U.D.C. to remove BB's remains from Wisconsin to Virginia. Cf. also the Milwaukee, Wisc., *Journal*, Dec. 18, 1928 (p. 11), and Watson, below.

Starr, Louis M., *Bohemian Brigade: Civil War Newsmen in Action* (New York, 1954).

Stluka, Ed., "Confederate Heroine Honored Today in Wisconsin Village," Richmond, Va., *Times-Dispatch*, May 30, 1952 (p. 5). Illustrates boulder marking BB's grave. See also Stluka's

"North-South Day To Be Launched Here on June 1," Wisconsin Dells, Wisc., *Events,* May 31, 1956 (p. 1).

Straus, Ralph, *Sala: The Portrait of an Eminent Victorian* (London [1942]).

Tolbert, Frank X., "Wreckers Destroy Belle Boyd's Home," Dallas, Tex., *Morning News,* Jan. 1, 1964 (Sect. 1, cols. 1-2).

Tucker, George H., "Belle's Toll Was Grandpa," Norfolk, Va., *Virginian-Pilot,* May 8, 1965 (p. 17).

Vandiver, Frank E., *Mighty Stonewall* (New York, Toronto, and London [1957]).

Watson, Elmo S., "Belle Boyd Goes Home," Tappahannock, Va., *Rappahannock Times,* March 11, 1929. Illustrated.

Winks, Robin W., *Canada and the United States: The Civil War Years* (Baltimore, Md. [1960]).

Wood, Leonora W., *Belle Boyd: Famous Spy of the Confederate States Army* (Keyser, West Va., 1940). Pamphlet.

Yocum, Jack H., "A History of Theatre in Houston, 1836-1954," unpub. doctoral dissertation, Dept. of Speech, University of Wisconsin (2 v., Madison, 1954). See I, 200-201.

REACTIONS TO "BELLE BOYD IN CAMP AND PRISON . . ."

CREATIVE

Boucicault, Dion, *Belle Lamar.* Booth's Theater, New York City. Première, Aug. 19, 1874. Drama.

Bruce, Philip Alexander, *Brave Deeds of Confederate Soldiers* (Philadelphia [1916]). Juvenile.

Chambers, Robert W., *Secret Service Operator 13* (New York and London, 1934). Historical romance.

Denison, Charles W., "The Spy of the Shenandoah," *Potter's American Monthly Illustrated Magazine* . . . (Philadelphia), XIII, 285-290 (Oct., 1879). Tale.

Harte, (Francis) Bret, "Mary McGillip : A Southern Novel. After Belle Boyd. With an Introduction by G.A.S-LA," in *Condensed Novels. And Other Papers* (New York, 1867). Vol. I, in

The Writings of Bret Harte, Riverside Edition (20 v., Boston and New York [1906-1914]). Satire.

Heaster, Georgia, "Belle Boyd Takes a Message," *West Virginia Review,* XXI, 18-19 (Sept., 1944). Fictionized essay.

Kane, Harnett, *The Smiling Rebel* (Garden City, N.Y., 1955). Historical romance.

Sickels, Eleanor, *In Calico and Crinoline: True Stories of American Women, 1608-1865* (New York, 1951). First pub., 1935. Juvenile.

Turner, Lewis McK., *Belle Boyd, the Rebel Spy* (Baltimore, Md., 1928). Pamphlet. Verse.

EXCERPTS

Archer, Charles F. W., *Our Soldiers: War Reminscences by "Carleton"* . . . *Collected* . . . *for the Boston Journal* (Boston, 1893).

Botkin, B.A., ed., *A Civil War Treasury of Tales, Legends and Folklore* (New York [1960]).

Confederate, A, ed., *The Grayjackets: And How They Lived, Fought and Died for Dixie* (Richmond, Atlanta, and elsewhere [1867]).

Jones, Katharine M., *Heroines of Dixie: Confederate Women Tell Their Story of the War* (Indianapolis and New York [1955]).

——— "———, comp. and ed. *Ladies of Richmond, Confederate Capital* (Indianapolis and New York [1962]).

REVIEWS

| 1865 | Feb. 25 | London (Eng.), *Illustrated London News,* No. 1,303 (p. 179). By G. A. Sala (unsigned). |
| | June 10 | London (Eng.), *The Athenaeum,* No. 1,963 (p. 778). |

June 17   London (Eng.), *The Spectator,* No. 1,929 (pp. 673–675).

June 22   London (Eng.), *The Index: A Weekly Journal of Politics, Literature, and News,* V, 395.

July 18   New York City, *Daily News* (2/6). Announcement.

July 22   New York City, *World* (3/2). Listing.

July 31   New York City, *Daily News* (3/3).

Aug. 3   New York City, *Evening Post* (1/1–2).

Index

NOTE: This index is keyed to the editorial framework, as well as to the text, of the present volume. Misspellings of proper names in the text have been silently corrected.

For military officers' ranks, North or South, no distinction is made among brevet, provisional, or regular commissions. Ranks of General officers are as given for the period in Ezra Warner, *Generals in Gray* . . . ([Baton Rouge, La., 1959]) and in his *Generals in Blue* . . . ([*ibid.*, 1964]).

Throughout the book the symbol "BB" stands for Mrs. Isabelle (Boyd) Hardinge Hammond High.

"Nasby, Petroleum V." (D. R. Locke), 41

Nash, Maj. Joseph van H., C.S.A., 78

Nash, Mrs. Margaret (Bowden). Quoted on BB, 78–79

Nassau, B.W.I., 215

National Cyc. of Amer. Biog. Entry on BB, 58

Nease, Mrs. Addie of Kilbourn, Wisc., 58

Nelson, Admr. Lord. Epitaph, 42, 214

New Castle, Del., 323–324

New Creek Station, (West) Va., 343–344

Newell, Mr., blockade passenger, 250, 262

Newfoundland, 282

New Orleans, La. 238; BB married at, 22–23

Newport, R.I. *Greyhound* coals at, 393–394

New York City. BB at, 19, 270–271; Hardinge at, 37, 269–271; 288–289, 353

New York Hotel (N.Y.C.), 288

New York Times Mag. Discusses BB, 56

Niagara Falls, Ont., 280–281

Niblo's Theatre (N.Y.C.), 270

Nicholson, Paul, reporter, 371

Norma (Bellini), opera, 408

"North and South . . ." BB recites, 31

"North - South Understanding Day," 63

Norton, A. B., of Dallas, 28

"Oakley" homestead (Ft. Royal, Va.), 68, 368

oath of allegiance, 193–194, 323, 328

Observations in the North . . . (Pollard), 392

Observer (Manchester, Eng.). Cited on BB, 18, 392

Ochiltree, Hon. Thomas Peck. Quoted on BB, 61–62; sponsors BB, 21–22

Office of Strategic Services, 8

Ohio, U.S.S., 278

Old Capitol Prison (Washington, D.C.): BB at 61, 72–77, 101, 104–106, 110–112, 189–208; Hardinge at, 302–320, 335–338

Omphale, 40

Opequon Creek, 380, 382

Osceola, steamer, 324

O'Sullivan, Hon. John Louis. At BB's wedding, 286

Ould, Robert, Commissr. of Exch., C.S.A., 207

P., Gen., U.S.A. At Ft. Del., 349–350

P., Ida, prisoner, 224–225

Paige, Nat., reporter. Quoted on BB, 66–68

Paine, Thomas, 335

Paris (France), 39, 120, 284

Parker, Mr., prisoner, 306

Parks, Alex, Jr., W. M., of Martinsburg, 415

Patterson, Maj. Gen. Robert, U.S.A., 127, 135, 137

Paull, Mrs. at BB's wedding, 286

Pendleton, Congressman (U.S.) George Hunt, 337

Pennsylvania Ave. (Washington, D.C.), 20, 192, 373

People's Theatre (Toledo, O.). BB's début at, 29

"Pet of the Confederacy, the" (nickname for BB), 85, 382

Petersburg, (West) Va., 343